Thomas J Williams

Historical Sketch of the 56th Ohio Volunteer Infantry

during the great Civil War from 1861 to 1866

Thomas J Williams

Historical Sketch of the 56th Ohio Volunteer Infantry
during the great Civil War from 1861 to 1866

ISBN/EAN: 9783337410346

Printed in Europe, USA, Canada, Australia, Japan

Cover: Foto ©ninafisch / pixelio.de

More available books at **www.hansebooks.com**

AN HISTORICAL SKETCH

...OF THE...

56TH OHIO VOLUNTEER INFANTRY

DURING THE GREAT CIVIL WAR
FROM 1861 TO 1866

...BY...
THOS. J. WILLIAMS
FORMER FIRST LIEUTENANT OF THE REGIMENT.

CONTENTS

Chapter I.—	Organization, Etc.	9
Chapter II.—	Fort Donelson, Etc.	13
Chapter III.—	Corinth, Siege of.	18
Chapter IV.—	Helena and Thereabout.	23
Chapter V.—	Milliken's Bend and Port Gibson.	33
Chapter VI.—	Champion's Hill.	41
Chapter VII.—	Siege of Vicksburg, Etc.	54
Chapter VIII.—	The Teche Expedition.	58
Chapter IX.—	The Red River Campaign.	65
Chapter X.—	Snaggy Point on the John Warner.	73
Chapter XI.—	Our Veteran Furlough.	85
Chapter XII.—	Patrol Duty in New Orleans, Etc.	89
Chapter XIII.—	Our Services in New Orleans, Etc.	101
Chapter XIV.—	Our Muster Out, Etc.	111
Chapter XV.—	Biographical Sketches.	134
Roster of the Regiment.		145

"We want the brave old flag to wave,
　From Texas up to Maine,
From Delaware to Golden Gate,
　Around and back again;
Over each blade of grass that grows,
　And every grain of sand,
The Stars and Stripes and Union,
　Thank God, for these we stand."

INTRODUCTION.

(Extract from Official Report of Gen. Alvin P. Hovey, Commander 12th Div., 13th. A. C.)

"It is useless to speak in praise of the 56th Ohio. They have won laurels on many fields, and not only their country will praise, but posterity will be proud to claim kinship. . . . . . They have a history that Col. Raynor, and their children, will be proud to read."

Events, with respect to men engaged in ordinary vocations, are not without interest. When, however, momentous conditions intervene, or arise, to engage men in activities that alarm a continent and astound the civilized world, men stand aghast and propound: "What is to be the end?"

Genial and customary occupations give place to imperious demands, with which most men are unacquainted; then from the field, forge, trade and professions, all avenues of thrift, hope and peace, the cry is heard: "To arms! our civil liberties are assailed!" Men respond with alacrity. They are massed in powerful combination, whose business, henceforth, is war. The deal is blood and iron. Hideous spectacle! with which the soldier gradually becomes familiar; grows intrepid and cheerful as he goes marching on. Men of peace, the bulwark of a nation, all transformed.

Comrades and friends, what a scene! Are you reminded of

regiment. He was behind the gun, having his eye on the sight, sure! You know how that was done.

The scanning of the pages will doubtless revive sorrows and heartaches, pangs and sighs; yet there will be dear memories, reveries and delights. The tenderness linked to the place clothed in green, where lies the dear one, "Killed in action," or "Died in hospital." Let's see! What would life and history be, stripped of their twinnings and suggestions of immortality? Our comrade wrote to commemorate deeds of valor—and of sacrifices rarely paralelled. Comrades and friends will rejoice with me that the work is well done. To the posterity of the one it will be of inestimable value, to the descendants of the others it will be instructive. The young will learn of the intense zeal and loyalty necessary to maintain freedom's flag unfurled at the masthead, and the student of our national characteristics will be encouraged. In fine, all lovers of good government, and lovers of those who fought to make ours such, will chorus· "Praise God from whom all blessings flow."

Apart from all other sterling qualities of the soldier, that of cheerfulness was a distinguished trait of the men of the Fifty-sixth. Most of the comrades have completed the journey of life. To those who are still wending their way over the Bridge of Mirza, let me commend the same cheerfulness, for to him that endures is the victory. To have fought for our country is somewhat. To have fought for it in the Fifty-sixth Ohio, and in the Army of the Tennessee, should be counted a badge of distinction, not to be surpassed by any mark worn, or to be worn, by any soldier in any age and country.

Under the guidance of God, let us continue our efforts in the

cause of humanity, the cause of purity in private and official life, and in the exercise of those duties which promise the only assurance of the final rollcall of: "Well done, thou good and faithful servant," the eternal welcome. Being always mindful that: "Righteousness exalteth a nation; but sin is a reproach to any people."

GEORGE GRINDLEY.

Washington, D. C.,
　December, 1899.

CHAPTER I.

Organization at Camp Morrow, Portsmouth, Ohio.

In the endeavor to write a short history of the regiment, of the dangers and hardships endured and surmounted, in that greatest of all wars, that was waged for the preservation of the Union, I beg your indulgence. I greatly regret its incompleteness in so many particulars. From my position in the ranks of Company C, until the fall of Vicksburg, my view was limited, and the things I saw may have appeared different to others, and the many things that I failed to see may have been far more important than those which came under my observation. The limited diary I kept during our entire service is correct as to time and place and other matters, so far as it extends. I would much prefer that some other member of the regiment of larger opportunities and greater ability had undertaken this work. That there is so much of it of a personal nature is probably a great fault, but there being no record obtainable of orders to the regiment, or to its officers, is the only excuse offered, and firmly believing that every regiment or separate company that had any service of note should have a history in some permanent form of its services, and in hopes that these few facts, unembelished, may find favor with the comrades who still remain, and their families, as a memorial of our active and long service, and the privations encountered by day and night, and as a slight testimonial to our brave and noble comrades who gave up their lives on the deadly battlefield, in prison pens, and from hospital cots of affliction, for this great land, is the history written. We uncover and bow low our heads as being unable to sufficiently honor them.

The Fifty-sixth Ohio was simply one of the numerous organizations which responded to the call of President Lincoln, when the gloomy clouds of treason hung dark and threatening over the

country. It was composed of men from every calling and vocation in life. The regiment did no more than its duty, going where ordered and performing whatever was required of it. The raising of recruits was slow work, as the region of country had been sending a large number of men into the service from the beginning of the war. From this section one full company went into the Twenty-seventh Ohio Volunteer Infantry, one in the Thirtieth Ohio Volunteer Infantry, two into the Thirty-sixth Ohio Volunteer Infantry, one into the Twenty-second Ohio Volunteer Infantry, and four companies into the Second Virginia Cavalry. The Thirty-third Ohio Volunteer Infantry left Camp Morrow for the field a few days before the Fifty-sixth entered it; and the Fifty-third Ohio Volunteer Infantry was being recruited at Jackson at the same time the Fifty-sixth was at Portsmouth. After much solicitation the order was given to organize the regiment, and on the 8th day of October, 1861, the camp was organized. Peter Kinney was appointed Colonel, Wm. H. Raynor, Lieutenant Colonel, and Sampson E. Varner, Major; W. N. King, Surgeon; Henry E. Jones, Adjutant; W. S. Huston, Quartermaster, and Rev. Jonathan E. Thomas, later on, was appointed Chaplain.

THE FIFTY-SIXTH OHIO VOLUNTEER INFANTRY.

The regiment at first contained nearly a thousand men, and was recruited at different times to about 1,200 men, of whom fully one-fourth were killed or died of wounds and disease, and at the final muster out, there were only about 170, the remainder having been mustered out at the expiration of three years.

The original companies of the regiment: Company A, was recruited from the counties of Gallia and Jackson. It was the first company in number, and was composed of an extra good lot of men, both in size and quality.

Company B was recruited in Portsmouth, O., and every member was of German birth or parentage. The officers and some of the men had seen service in the German army in their Fatherland,

and in our early service they entertained us very pleasantly with their fine singing of "Litori, Litori," etc.

Company C was recruited about half and half from Scioto and Jackson counties. All but two were young men from 16 to 25 years of age. They were under strict discipline and well cared for by their Captain.

Company D was recruited at Portsmouth, Ohio. Most of the men were from Scioto county, but they had a fine squad of men from Gallia county, led by Lieutenant Schaefer. The great majority were young, active men and made number one soldiers.

Company E was composed largely of Gallia county men, but it also had a number from Jackson county, and was composed of firstclass men in every particular. Their Captain was of fine education, and capable for any position.

Company F was recruited in Scioto county mostly. Like the foregoing, the men were mostly young and equal to any in the land. Captain Wilhelm of this company received a medal for gallantry at Champion's Hill.

Company G. This company was raised in Scioto county, and like other companies this one had some of the best men in the regiment. Captain Stimmell, of this company, made a hazardous escape from the enemy, after being captured.

Company H. This company was recruited mostly in Scioto county from the farmers and the furnaces, and a body of firstclass soldiers they were.

Company I was recruited in Pike county, and, like the others, the men were of the best class, and were not behind the foremost in any thing that made good soldiers.

Company K was composed of Jackson and Scioto county men, and most of them were the equal of the best, and were never backward in the performance of duty.

Men came in steadily, and were mustered in as they volunteered from time to time. The arms furnished the regiment were the clumsy old Belgium muskets, which, when fired, would almost kick a man over. The time was diligently improved in perfecting the men in the essential duties of a soldier's life. By December

12, 1861, the regiment was filled to the minimum number, and was anxiously awaiting orders to report to the front. On January 23, 1862, the Ohio river was very high, up into the city considerably. Camp Morrow having become a sea of mud, on the 21st the regiment moved up on high ground, near Colonel Kinney's residence. On January 30 there was a heavy fall of snow, and it was very cold. The weather was worse than usual that season, and the change from home comforts to camp life was hard on a large number of the men. An epidemic of measles broke out, and fully one-fourth of the command were afflicted with them, and, with the exposure in camp, many of them were unfit for service thereafter. February 6, 1862, the regiment received orders to be ready to move at an hour's notice, and for the next few days our camp was thronged with our relatives and friends, taking a final farewell with many of our comrades.

On the 10th of February, 1862, the regiment was ordered to report at Paducah, Kentucky. On the 11th we were very busy in packing up and getting all ready to move. The regiment was greatly pleased that, at last, it was to start for the front. And on February 12, 1862, late in the afternoon, the Fifty-sixth Ohio went on board the steamboats Champion No. 3 and Poland, and left Portsmouth at Dusk. The wharf was crowded with relatives and friends to bid us a last goodby.

COLONEL WILLIAM H. RAYNOR
See page 131

Colonel, Brevet Brigadier General, U.S. Vols.

CHAPTER II.

FORT DONELSON, CRUMP'S LANDING AND SHILOH.

There was a very boisterous time the first night out. As a number were trying to drown their grief in the flowing bowl, their conduct was foolish in the extreme, and they kept all awake with their drunken revelry. The regiment was greatly cheered from the north side of the Ohio river, but on the south side it was mostly dark and silent. On the night of the 13th our boat was laid up for some time, having bursted one of her steam pipes.

We reached Paducah, Kentucky, on the 15th, early in the morning, and that afternoon left for Fort Donaldson, Tennessee, a short distance up the Cumberland river, and on the 16th, before day, we tied up just out of range of the guns at the fort. At daylight they saw our boats and opened fire on us, and a number of cannon balls struck quite close to our boats. Here, for the first time, we set foot on the "sacred soil." Soon after day the regiment landed and started for our line of battle, around the fortifications; but before we had become established we were recalled, as the enemy had hoisted the white flag in token of surrender. The regiment again went aboard the boats that had brought us there, and they ran up the river and landed us in the Fort grounds.

There were thirteen thousand prisoners, who surrendered to our forces. They made a large army, and seemed surprised to find we were not all savages, their officers having told them that they would be butchered by our troops, if captured. The regiment went into camp just outside of the rebel works. The dead lay as they fell, most of them shot through the head, as they fought behind breastworks. These were ghastly sights for green troops to see, and the awful spectacle can never be forgotten. Here our time was improved by drill, target practice and guard duty. On the 20th, we had our first dress parade after leaving Ohio. Our rations at this time were very poor, and we thought we were half starved.

If there was anything that Captain Williams was particular about, it was cleanliness. While here one Sunday on inspection one of our men of mature age, and noted for being generally dirty, on this day was more so than usual. The Captain detailed myself as Corporal, and two men, to take him to a pond near camp and strip and scrub him with brooms. After that he was much cleaner. On March 6 a heavy snow fell, and we received orders to move to the Iron Landing, on the Tennessee river. On the 7th we left early. It had turned warmer and the snow was going fast, and the mud was ankle deep. We were loaded pretty heavily, and, as this was our first march for any distance, it was very hard upon us, and the road was lined with overcoats, blankets and other things that we thought we could not live without, but we soon changed our minds on that subject. About noon we passed Peytona Furnace. Some of the troops in advance had set it on fire, and it was burning as we passed by. We camped that night in a wild looking place within about two miles of the river. This was our first night to lay out without shelter of any kind, but we enjoyed our night's rest first rate.

On the 8th we moved up to within half a mile of the Landing. At this point we camped, drilling and performing guard duty until March 13, when we moved to the Landing, and after remaining there for about three hours we went aboard the steamboat Tigress, which steamed across the Tennessee river to Paris Landing, and went into camp in a cornfield near the river. We were called out after midnight by the long roll. The night was pitch dark, and no bottom to the mud.

March 15, 1862, we had a hard and cold rain, and at dark we embarked on the steamship Iowa, bound up the Tennesse river. On the 16th the guerrillas fired into us, but fortunately hit no one, and on the 16th we reached Savannah, Tennessee, about noon. Here we lay on the boat, at the wharf, until late in the afternoon of the 17th, when we steamed up the river. After a run of ten miles we landed at Crump's Landing. On the morning of the 18th we moved out about half a mile and went into camp. This was a very fine place to camp.

March 20th, 1862, the regiment received their first pay, which rejoiced us greatly, as we had been bankrupt for a long time. On the 21st, while on picket, we captured two of the enemy, and I took them to headquarters and turned them over to the proper authorities. March 25th, our brigade was reviewed by General Lew Wallace, to whose division of the Army of the Tennessee we were attached. On this night, at 9:30, E. D. Evans, a comrade of our mess, who had been poorly for some little time, died in our tent, and the next day, at 5:30 p. m., he was buried with the honors of war, Colonel Kinney kindly reading the beautiful burial service of the Episcopal church at the grave.

On March 27th, an order was issued that the men be vaccinated, as the smallpox had appeared in some of the commands. We had little idle time, as we were busy in drill and guard duties every day. On March 31, 1862, our division moved up about five miles to Adamsville, a small place, and went into camp a short distance beyond. This was called Camp Wallace.

Our brigade at this time was composed of the Twentieth, Fifty-sixth, Seventy-sixth and Seventy-eighth Ohio Infantry, and commanded by Colonel Chas. Whittlesy of the Twentieth Ohio, and a part of the Third Division, commanded by General Lew Wallace. The enemy had been very active in our front for several days, and it was rather expected that they would attack our position. From their actions in our front we were put on our guard, and on the mornings of April 5 and 6 Wallace's whole division was in line of battle long before day, looking for the enemy to attack; but the thunder of artillery and the crash of musketry at the break of day, on April 6, 1862, indicated that the battle, bloody and terrible, was on at Pittsburg Landing, and not where we were. Late that afternoon we fell back to Camp No. 2, about halfway back to Crump's Landing. From here the most of our division went on to the battle line. Our regiment and other troops were left to guard Crump's Landing, where we had a large and valuable amount of stores. Our being left to guard this point caused dissatisfaction among many of the officers and men, and some attempted to go to the battlefield on their own motion.

Comrade Henry Kugleman, of Company C, and the writer, avoiding the guards, struck out for the battle ground. We must have gone about two miles in that direction. The woods were full of men falling back. Several officers ordered us to return, but we did not stop until we found our route would take us out in the rear of the enemy, and as our force was rather light to tackle the rebel army, we fell back in good order to our camp, never being missed; but we got drenched by a heavy rain that overtook us. A large number of stragglers from the battlefield drifted to our position, and our officers gathered up and sent back in an organized body eight hundred men to assist their brave comrades. There was a good deal of sickness in the regiment at this place, some sixty of them being sent to the general hospital at Paducah, Kentucky.

On April 16, we were called out at 2 a. m., the enemy making an attack on our outposts. We lay in line under arms until daylight, and early in the morning we moved back to Crump's Landing. On the next day we were ordered to Pittsburg Landing, guarding a large train en route, and reached our division at dark.

The next day we pitched our tents in an oats field. Here we were kept busy, drilling by brigades, regiments and companies for as much as six hours a day. At this time they issued whisky to the men, but did not keep it up long. On April 24, our division was ordered on an expedition to Purdy, Tennessee, about twenty miles distant. We went to within five miles of Purdy. We had hard rain most of the day, and lay out in the woods. We were roused up by heavy firing on our pickets, and formed line and lay on our arms until daybreak. The next morning the division moved early, the Fifty-sixth on the extreme right. We drove the enemy's force to within a mile of Purdy, when we were ordered back on quick time. We had fallen back some little distance, our regiment bringing up the rear, when we heard the tramp of horses coming at a charge. The brush and trees shut off the view of the road completely. The Fifty-sixth halted, formed into line, and prepared to meet whatever was coming. When they came into view, we saw they were all our own men except one that was in the enemy's uniform. Two of our officers were on either side

holding him, as he was making a desperate effort to shoot a major in our uniform. Our sympathies were with the man in blue, and we would have been glad to shoot the man in gray, if allowed to do so. We soon heard that the man in gray was Carpenter, a member of the Fifth Ohio Cavalry, and a native of that part of Tennessee. He was a large, strong man, with a long black beard, and appeared to us like vengeance personified. The man he wanted to kill was a so-called Major Bell, who pretended to be on the Union side, but really was in the service of the enemy, and one of them. It was on his report that this expedition was undertaken. He reported but a small force at Purdy, and that it would be to our interests to take the place. The report was that Carpenter came out of their lines, met our skirmishers, asked them to stop, and send him at once to the officer in command. Carpenter reported that there were from twenty to thirty thousand men in Purdy behind strong fortifications. We heard afterward that Major Bell was executed as a spy by our forces. The regiment was highly praised for their conduct on this hard and dangerous expedition, it being said that tried veterans could not have done better. On this expedition it rained nearly all the time, and the mud was awful. We reached our camp at 5 p. m. of April 25. All of the whisky in camp was issued to those who drank the stuff.

April 28, 1862, our division left camp at noon in the direction of Purdy again, and we bivouaced at 10 p. m., within seven miles of the place. Rain fell all that day and night very hard. We lay around in the woods all day of the 29th, and on the 30th we returned to our camp. Our expeditions to Purdy became a byword in the regiment during our entire service. The hard rains, the mud, and the cold could not be forgotten.

CHAPTER III.

Siege of Corinth and on to Memphis.

May 4, 1862, our division was ordered up toward Corinth, Mississippi, and on this day we had a regular deluge of rain. The regiment was marching through a large body of deadwood timber, and the rain came so hard we had to halt. The thunder and lightning were fearful. We were completely soaked; there was nothing to be had with which to turn such a flood; even our shoes were filled with water. This rain storm was memorable as being the hardest we encountered in our service. That evening we encamped at Pea Ridge, where we remained for a few days. On Sunday, May 11, a beautiful day, the writer then a Corporal in Company C, and two other comrades, were ordered to report to the Captain for special duty. Captain Williams informed us that orders had been received from General Wallace that a detail of a Corporal and two privates be sent to his headquarters for special duty. The Captain stated for our encouragement that he wanted the company and regiment well represented at division headquarters, and that he felt sure we would do so.

In good time we reached General Wallace's tent and reported to him. As we neared headquarters we "caught on" to the special duty we were to perform, as we saw three comrades of our regiment under guard there. General Wallace received us pleasantly, stating that the comrades under arrest were guilty (in violation of orders) of killing a yearling, the property of a family near there. The General ordered us to have them cut a pole, string the beef carcass on it, and to see that the comrades kept up a steady tramp around some large trees near his tent. It was about 10 a. m. when they began their march. The General told the guards to be as comfortable as possible. About 11 o'clock p. m. he came out and ordered that the men dig a hole and bury the beef. That done, we were to turn them over to the commanding officer of the

regiment. No doubt, this was the hardest tramp these comrades had ever taken. I am credibly informed that this episode was published and illustrated in Harper's Weekly a short time after.

May 18, 1862, we were ordered in towards Corinth. We moved up a few miles to a poor little place called Monterey. Here we remained until May 22. There was heavy firing in the direction of Corinth, and on the 22d we moved up and joined McClernand's division, on the extreme right of our line. We were busy building fortifications, and on outpost and in picket duties. The water here was the worst we experienced in all our service. Our forces gradually closed up on the north and east side of Corinth. General Halleck, in his grand startegy, seemed content with a long distance contest. This continued until May 30, 1862, when the enemy, at his leisure, evacuated Corinth. On May 31 the regiment was paid up to April 1.

June 2, 1862, our division was ordered to go to Memphis, Tennessee, which was distant one hundred and ten miles through the enemy's country. June 3 we passed through Purdy, and found the fortifications there as Carpenter, our scout, had reported. On the 4th our route was through a beautiful region. At night we camped in the woods. We marched over pine ridges on the 5th and encamped within six miles of Bolivar. We passed through that place on the 6th, and encamped just beyond in sight of the town. We were delayed on account of wagon trains crossing the Hatchie river. On the 7th a number of the boys obtained passes and visited the town.

June 8 was Sunday, and the ringing church bells took our minds back to our northern homes. On the 9th a train of cars came down from Jackson, Tennessee. We started early on the 10th. Our route was through a fine section of country, and, after a march of 27 miles, we camped within seven miles of Somerville. On the 11th our brigade led the advance. Water was very scarce, and the roads clouds of dust. We passed through Somerville and camped within 25 miles of Memphis, Tennessee. On the 12th we started early. Our knapsacks were hauled, which helped us greatly. That night we camped at Union Depot, not far from Memphis. June 15 one of our men was captured near the picket line.

On the morning of June 17 we were roused up at midnight, and started for Memphis at 3 a. m. We reached there at 10 a. m., and encamped in the Fair Ground. This camp for the next few days was fairly thronged with peddlars of eatables and notions of all kinds. On June 22 the regiment was sent out on the Memphis and Charleston railroad about 25 miles to rebuild a railroad bridge. On going out by the train, at a place near a large plantation, the train stopped awhile. An elderly woman and two young ladies came down to the gate near our car to see the "Yankee" boys. We had several good singers, and they entertained them with some patriotic songs. This made them angry, and they fairly screamed themselves hoarse for Jeff Davis, Beuaregard, etc. A happy thought came to one of the boys, and he jumped off the car shouting: "Come on, boys; let us kiss these girls." The women went at once, and we saw some fast running, to the great amusement of all.

We encamped near the bridge on the plantation of Mr. Davis. He was of Wesh birth, but had located there some years prior to the war. Work on the bridge began at once. On the next day the boys of our mess brought in two of the old planter's bee-hives and a lot of new potatoes, so we fared sumptuously for the next few days. June 25, as Colonel Kinney and a part of Company B were coming out to the regiment they were captured by the enemy under General Forrest, and the train destroyed. Colonel Kinney escaped from them in a few days thereafter. The enemy had moved quite a force of cavalry in the region between us and Memphis. Our communications were cut off, and the Fifty-sixth Ohio was ordered to return to Memphis at once. June 26, at 9 a. m., we started. The enemy's mounted troops followed us closely and appeared on every side, which made our progress slow. At 10 p. m. we halted in some timber for a little rest, but soon moved on again. Shortly after day the enemy seemed to swarm from every side, and it looked very serious for the regiment. At one point they appeared about to charge us. The officers cautioned the men to be cool and wait for orders. In Company C, at this time, we were forced to witness a pitiable or contemptible sight. When Captain Williams was talking to the company, the enemy

hovering on every side in plain sight, a young fellow named Wm. S. Hill brought his musket to an order arms, and broke down and cried like a baby. The Captain took him by the collar, and put him out of the ranks at once. Tommy Morris, our drummer boy, spoke up, saying, "Captain, give me his musket, and let him take my drum." This the Captain did at once. We never saw Hill after this. We supposed he staid with the regiment until we reached Memphis and then deserted. The rebels were afraid of our long range muskets, and the bold front we presented to every side under the skillful handling of Lieutenant Colonel W. H. Raynor.

This short expedition was very hard on the regiment, it being so hot and dusty, with the loss of sleep, many were entirely exhausted when we reached our camp in the city, at 10 a. m., June 27, 1862. On June 30 the regiment was ordered to Fort Pickering, just below the city, and the streets of the city were thronged with people to see us as we marched through. Our new camp at the Fort was covered with weeds and brush as high as our heads, and we were mustered for pay. July 1, 1862, the regiment was ordered into the city to perform guard duty at General Grant's headquarters. Here we had a fine camping ground. We continued at this duty until July 22. On the 20th the regiment marched through the city for display mostly. On July 23 we were ordered to Helena, Ark., by boat. Tents were struck early, and there we lay around all day waiting for a boat. A laughable affair took place in Company C. Comrades will all know that nothing was so tiresome as that kind of waiting. A middle-aged comrade, worn out in waiting, went to a saloon near camp and got stupidly drunk, returning to the company, he lay down where his tent stood, totally oblivious of time and place. Seeing his condition, one of the boys remarked that he was dead, and that he ought to have some kind of a funeral service, so one of our comrades with a talent in that kind of work, and in possession of a good strong voice, took charge. They sang appropriate hymns, and then he proceeded to deliver a eulogy on the departed. The effort could not have been excelled by the ministers whom he imitated. The audience was large and deeply impressed, and th whole matter was

ludicrous in the extreme, and our drunken comrade was rather sore over the episode when he came to himself again.

We remained in our camp all night, and on July 24 we got off early. As the regiment marched down the levee to the boat a funny incident took place. Two members of the regiment who had deserted some time previous, ran right into the regiment and were taken in charge. They were on their way to take passage on a boat up north. One was disguised as a chaplain and the other as a suttler, but our meeting caused a material change in their route.

LIEUT. COLONEL SAMPSON E. VARNER
See page 141

CHAPTER IV.

HELENA AND EXPEDITION THEREFROM.

We embarked on the steamboat Golden Era and reached Helena July 24, 1862, at 5 p. m., landing below the town on General Hindman's plantation. Our camp was on the river bank, and we had a regular bedlam nearly all night. A lot of the officers and men had secured some liquor, and they made the night hideous with their drunken revelry. Where we camped was just inside the levee, and we had plenty of water, as the Mississippi river flowed by our front door. There was not a tree near, and that sandy plain was about as hot a place as could be found in the land on those July and August days. The regiment suffered very much from fevers, congestive chills and bowel trouble, about fifty of our men dying from said diseases contracted at this place, situated in the swamps of the Mississippi valley. July 31 a large fleet passed for points down the river. On August 5 the Fifty-sixth Ohio was transferred to the Second Brigade of the Second Division, commanded by General Carr.

August 25, 1862, Comrade Daniel Phillips of Company C was buried with the honors of war by the company, on a pretty knoll, near the residence of the Confederate General Hindman, who owned a beautiful place here. Comrade Phillips was a firstclass soldier and a fine young man, and we deplored his death greatly. His brother, Lewis Phillips, was discharged here December 6, 1862, from disease contracted in this miasmatic region, as this place in the swamps of the lower Mississippi valley was a radical change from the hills of Ohio.

Our regiment, while here, were for a short time in a brigade with the Fourth Iowa Infantry, and the Thirteenth Illinois Infantry. These regiments were constantly on the lookout to get ahead of each other. One day a member of the Thirteenth Illinois died,

and his comrades went upon a hill nearby and dug a grave to bury their man. The Fourth Iowa also had a man to die, and a lot of them started to dig his grave, but when they saw the Thirteenth Illinois at work digging the grave for their man they returned and waited for them to leave the grave, and then took their man and buried him in the grave the Thirteenth Illinois had prepared.

While here the regiment, or portions of it, were on various expeditions by land and water. On August 28 a detachment, of which Company C was a part, started on a scout down the river. We embarked on the steamboat White Cloud, and started at 6 a. m. That night we anchored near Carson's Landing, Mississippi, there being a rebel camp a half mile back from the landing. The gunboat with us shelled their camp as we went out, and on our arrival we charged them, and they fled at their best speed. Corporal Henry Kugleman, of Company C, took the only prisoner. He was hidden upstairs in a house. We secured quite a lot of stores, etc., here. On the same day, the 29th of August, we had another skirmish at Gladdis Landing. We passed Napoleon, Ark., and anchored a few miles below. On the 30th we reached Eunice, Ark., where we secured a fine wharfboat, and took it in tow and started back for Helena. On the 31st we were fired on by the rebels, of which there were a large number. We opened out on them and they skedaddled; and we reached Helena on September 2 at midnight. This was a hard and dangerous expedition.

On September 5, 1862, a detachment of the regiment, which again included Company C, was ordered on another expedition down the river. We went on the boat Key West, No. 2. The first night out we anchored below Oldtown. On the 6th we reached Napolien, and found that the wharfboat there that we came for was of no account. We then started back. Our boat ran all night, and we reached Helena early on the 7th, after a very tiresome trip.

From September 11th to the 13th a large number of rebel prisoners passed down to be exchanged; also on the 17th more of them passed. On October 6 the Seventy-sixth Ohio Infantry, of our brigade, left up the river. On the 7th the regiment was paid for

two months, and was sent about four miles on outside picket duty, and the writer, with a proper guard, was stationed at the house of Dr. Turner nearby as safeguards, and on that night our fare was far superior to the rest of our comrades. We returned to Helena on the eve of the 8th, and found that our camp had been moved to a new place back of town on the hills. On October 17 a small detachment of the Fifty-sixth was over in Mississippi on picket duty, and two men of Company F were slightly wounded.

On the 18th Colonel Raynor returned from sick leave, and on the Twentieth the writer had to report at the sick call for the first time in a service of one year. One of the worst things about this place and Memphis was the ease with which liquor could be procured by those who desired it, and as a consequence we witnessed some shameful scenes. Some of the officers, and more the shame to them, were worse than the men, but at this late day it will answer no good purpose to report the shameful things witnessed; for then, as now, liquor makes a fool of him who uses it to excess. On the 29th a squad of us on picket duty over in Mississippi secured a lot of fresh meat, and our mess fared finely for a few days. For the next few days the regiment was busy in getting out timber to build cabins in which to winter. November 15, 1862, the regiment was ordered on a scout down the river. We went aboard the steamboat Tecumseh and lay at the wharf all night. On the 16th we started early. Our boat ran on a sandbar in the evening and lay there all night. On the morning of the 17th the Decatur pulled our boat off the sandbar, and we ran down to the mouth of White river and tied up for the night. On the 18th we ran to Montgomery's Landing, and the cavalry we had aboard disembarked, and we proceeded up White river a short distance and tied up. The river was so low our boat could not turn around, and she had to back out, and proceeded to Montgomery's Landing, took on our cavalry and tied up over night. November 20 our boat ran up stream a short distance and anchored on the Mississippi side. On the 21st we started again, ran all day and after night, which was bright with moonlight. After we had all retired to the soft side of the deck we heard

a shout, "Stop the boat; a snag ahead!" It aroused all of us at once, and we could plainly see a great snag, the body of a large tree, sticking up twenty feet or more in the air; but the pilot paid no attention to the warning, but ran the boat right into it. The end of the snag came up through the cabin deck within a foot of my bunk on the floor of the cabin deck. A lot of the boys made a hunt for that pilot, and had they caught him he would have had a short shift, as all felt he tried to sink the boat and drown us. Our boat anchored near here, and we reached Helena at noon. The dangers we encountered on these expeditions were not given a thought at that time.

On November 27, 1862, our division went on an expedition down the Coldwater river in Mississippi. The Fifty-sixth Ohio left camp at break of day, and went aboard the steamboat Nebraska, which ran down the river a short distance and landed us at Delta, Mississippi. This little town had been destroyed by our gunboats. We camped here over night, and on the 28th we started early. The mud was almost impassible. After a march of 22 miles we encamped. On the 29th we were off early, and reached the mouth of the Coldwater river at 4 p. m. The enemy had retired from this position on the approach of our cavalry. The 30th was Sunday, and we lay in camp all day, and the rain fell in torrents, which did not help the traveling in that low, swampy country. On Dec. 1, 1862, at 4:30 p. m., we were ordered to March at once, as our cavalry was hotly engaged some six or eight miles to the front. We crossed the Coldwater on a pontoon bridge, and in quick time moved to the scene of conflict. It was dark when we started, and in pitch darkness we groped our way through mud and water for over six miles. It was so dark that you could not hear well; one of those nights when you have to walk by faith, and not by sight. The enemy again retreated out of reach, and we returned, spending the whole night on that desperate trip.

On December 3 our regiment was sent up the Coldwater about five miles to guard a ferry. Here a small party of us went out for forage. We found a place unvisited by our troops, and we soon

had a good supply. We loaded a cart and drove a little flock of sheep along, and were making an effort to catch all of their chickens. A young lady came out and kindly asked that we leave them a few of the chickens at least. She was so pleasant about it that the boys were called off, and we returned to camp with a good supply. A few days after, Company C was out after forage. At one place some of the boys took about all a poor woman had, in spite of her entreaties. I tried to stop them, but they would not listen, and, feeling it was so outrageous, I reported it to Captain Williams, and he promptly made them restore the goods to the poor woman, and she, in her joy, could not thank us enough for the favor extended. These men were not bad or heartless, but had a sort of feeling or indifference for people in the enemy's land.

On December 5 we all started for Helena again by slow marches. We reached the river on the 7th, and boarded the steamboat Empress, which took us to Helena, and we had a good reason to rejoice at the end of this expedition. On December 16, 1862, a riot broke out in our camp. A lot of men being crazed by liquor at about 11 p. m. overpowered the camp guards, and treated Captain Chenowith shamefully. The Captain was one of the finest men in the regiment, and he would have been fully justified in shooting some of those rioters. These men for a short time ran things with a high hand. Colonel Kinney, about midnight, sent a written order to Captain Williams to take Company C, also to Captain Cook of Company K, and put a stop to these lawless acts, and to arrest the participants. Company C ran right into the main crowd of them. Captain Williams was armed with a heavy wooden poker. There was no argument. "Fall in!" was the command, and if any hesitation was shown or resistance offered, the Captain's poker and the butt ends of our muskets settled matters at once, and inside of twenty minutes all that had not secreted themselves were safely in the guard house; and once more quiet reigned in camp. The next morning, December 17, 1862, as I went out of my cabin I saw Coloney Kinney pass at a rapid walk in the direction of Company D quarters. I stood and watched to see

where he was going, and what was up. He halted before a cabin door and knocked. Some one opened the door, and after talking a moment, the Colonel drew his revolver and fired into the cabin. That shot killed Sergeant Frank Wallace of Company D. Some one had reported that Sergeant Wallace was a leader in the riot of the previous night. For a little while it seemed there might be serious trouble in the regiment over this sad matter; but through the kindly influence of Colonel Raynor, Dr. King and the company officers, as well as the cooler headed men, any serious outbreak was prevented, as they felt that it was more of an accident than anything else. But there was a general feeling of sadness over this unfortunate affair, and it was a sorrowful funeral up on the hills back of Helena that evening at dusk, as we laid in the bivouac of the dead the remains of a gallant comrade, who gave up his life, but not on the battle field. There was a trial of this affair by a military court, the Colonel was exonerated, and some time thereafter he resigned and left the service. Then W. H. Raynor was promoted to Colonel, S. E. Varner to Lieutenant Colonel and Captain C. F. Reiniger to Major. On December 18 the regiment was disgraced on dress parade by a Second Lieutenant and Acting Adjutant being so drunk that he could not perform his duties, and was placed under arrest by Colonel Raynor. He was a sample of some of the men who were promoted in the early part of our service, because they were from a certain locality or had "a pull" with those in authority over such matters. These men were totally incompetent for any position of honor or trust. But this was materially changed later on in our service, and men stood on their merits, regardless of locality.

January 6, 1863, the regiment was ordered outside of our picket line on the north side of town. We started after midnight to try and capture a force of rebels who had, on the morning previous captured a picket post on our line. They belonged to a regiment of new troops and had been in service only a short time, and had not been properly instructed as to the enemy's tricks. The night was cold, and lying in the woods quietly for about five hours was very unpleasant. But the enemy did not show up, as

they were on the lookout for a trap of some kind. January 10, with our division, we were ordered on an expedition up White river in Arkansas. The Fifty-sixth Ohio went on the steamboat Rose Hambleton at noon, and the boat crossed to the Mississippi side and lay there until dark of the 11th, when we left with the fleet down the river. We ran all night and tied up about daylight near White river. On the 12th we ran up White river as far as Pararie's Landing, where we remained over night. On the 13th we ran up the river all day. There was not a house to be seen, it being all swamps.

On the 14th the weather turned real cold, and our state rooms on the Rose Hambleton were the soft side of the deck and very uncomfortable. We passed St. Charles, but found no enemy. Our regiment had two men as sutlers, and while good men in general, they would not expose themselves or their goods where there was the remotest prospect of danger. But they had just reached the regiment with a big stock as we started on this expedition, and they were in a manner compelled to go along. On this night the boys of the regiment made a raid on their stock and cleaned out their whole outfit. After this bad treatment they never staid with us any more.

On January 15 we started late and ran as far as Clarendon, and laid up over night, and on the 16th we reached Duvall's Bluff, but the enemy continued to fall back and kept out of reach. Here, as we tied up our boat on the bank, was a drove of hogs. Colonel Raynor jumped ashore and called to us that we ought to save that pork. Comrade William Crabtree and I singled out a good sized shoat and soon had secured the porker. We only fired one shot, but many others from the various boats had landed, and there was a good deal of shooting around there. General Hovey, our division commander, sent out his body guard to arrest all who were out shooting pigs, etc. They gobbled us up, and took us hog and all before General Hovey. He was busy talking to some people. There we stood with a gun in one hand, and holding the pig's hind leg with the other, when a kindhearted staff officer, seeing our funny condition, came over to us and told us to light

out for our regiment. We fairly flew, and the pig went with us; and we had some nice, fresh meat for a day or two. This was the only time that I was under arrest, and Comrade Crabtree was mortally wounded just four months to a day later.

On this trip we explored the country in every direction, but the enemy failed to make a stand. We started on our return on the 19th. On the 21st we tied up at an island, having broken our wheel. We arrived at Helena on the 22d, and found our cabins had been torn down in our absence, but we soon built a new cabin, as timber was plenty.

February 11, 1863, we were ordered to march with two days' rations. We went aboard the steamboat Moderator, and lay at the wharf all night. On the next day we ran down into the Yazoo Pass and on into Moon Lake. We landed where the Coldwater river ran out of this lake, and encamped in some old plantation buildings, on the Monroe plantation. In this region there was a good deal of cotton, and considerable effort was made to secure it. On February 15 a select number of Company C went on a scout to locate some of it. We went out some distance to a large plantation. Captain Williams was in command, and while he was talking to a white man in charge we investigated and found they had lots of good things to eat, and we were anticipating quite a feast. But one of the boys saw at a distance through the trees a body of cavalry approaching. From their clothes and the distance we could not tell whether they were of the enemy or our own forces. When they saw us they halted and got ready for action. We fell back in the direction of our camp through a large cotton field. In the center of this field was a large cotton gin, which we aimed to reach; but they came down upon us fast and furious. We halted and formed into a hollow square twice as they were about to charge us. One of their scouts got up close enough to see us plainly, and he shouted that they were Union troops of the Sixth Missouri cavalry. They greatly admired our action in forming into square and waiting to be charged, with the odds so largely against us. Moon Lake, where we were, was a

small body of water near the Mississippi river, the levee was cut and the river at high flood ran into the lake, and it was deep enough for our largest boats. Where we were camped was where the Yazoo Pass left the lake. The water from this pass ran into the Coldwater river, and it emptied into the Tallehatchie river, and it into the Yazoo river, which entered the Mississippi above Vicksburg a few miles. A large expedition of our forces, with many gunboats, went down by way of this pass in an endeavor to find a route to the rear of Vicksburg. But on the Tallehatchie the enemy had constructed a strong fort in a dense swamp that could not be reached from our side. On March 21, 1863, Company C was sent to guard the steamboat Curlew, loaded with ammunition, down this waterway. We found the pass very crooked, and we bumped against trees every few yards. On the 22d we passed the steamboat Luella, sunk. On the 23d we met the Hamilton Belle going up stream; nothing but woods to be seen, hardly any houses in sight. On the 25th we passed where the regiment camped last fall, and on the 26th we passed several boats and arrived at our headquarters at noon on the 27th. And after dark the boat we were on took on a lot of cotton and ran down to within a mile of Fort Pemberton, and landed the cotton for our forces to build fortifications with. The night was as dark as pitch and the rain fell in torrents, and dreadful thunder and lightning added to the tumult. The only thing out of the ordinary while here was seeing Colonel Pyle of a Missouri regiment separate two of his men, who were engaged in a fight. The Colonel was 6 feet four or 5, a large and very strong man. He walked up to the fighters, took each of them by the back of the neck, pulled them apart, and then bumped their heads together several times, and then flung them to either side. The Colonel was a minister, and did not believe in that sort of fighting. He was afterwards promoted to Brigadier General, and some of us had the pleasure of hearing him preach in New Orleans, at Christ Church, on Sunday, October 2, 1864.

On April 1, 1863, we started back up the pass, and reached the regiment on the 3d. Our gunboats and steamboats that went

down this pass were badly dismantled in this crooked and narrow stream, and after every effort our forces were compelled to abandon the enterprise.

April 7, 1863, the regiment was ordered back to Helena, where we remained until April 12. While we were stationed in and about Helena our Chaplain, Rev. J. E. Thomas, was detached and placed in charge of a large number of freedmen, who had congregated about Helena, and he continued in this work until his final discharge, on November 5, 1864. In his supervision of these contrabands he was enabled to do a great amount of good for these poor freedmen, who were cast out helpless from slavery to depend upon their own resources. He put them at the work of raising cotton, corn and vegetables for their own use, and for the benefit of the government, and he was highly commended by General Buford, the department commander, for the excellency of his work, as the cotton they raised and sold brought the government a large amount of money.

On July 4, 1863, the rebel Generals, Holmes, Price and Mearmaduke, with a force of 7,646 men, made an attack on Helena. General Prentiss was in command of our forces of 4,000 men, and had as a strong ally the Gunboat Tyler. The enemy, as usual, lacked nothing in bravery. Holmes reported his loss in this battle at 173 killed, 687 wounded and 776 missing. Our loss was less than 250 all told.

LIEUT. C. GILLILAN, CO. A
See page 137

CHAPTER V.

MILLIKEN'S BEND, GRAND GULF, PORT GIBSON AND FOURTEEN MILE CREEK.

On April 12, 1863, we were ordered to join General Grant's army at Milliken's Bend, Louisiana, which was a few miles above Vicksburg. We embarked on the steamboat Alone, and left on the 13th to join the forces then gathering to make the last successful effort to capture Vicksburg, which had become the Gibraltar of the Western Continent. By this time the Fifty-sixth Ohio had been assigned to the Second Brigade of the Twelfth Division, Thirteenth Army Corps.

And, as we have since learned, at St. Louis and other points on the Western rivers, there were rich and influential men engaged in running steamboats on the Mississippi and other rivers, which while doing business for the government, were giving substantial aid and assisting the rebel cause by carrying recruits, contraband mail, and drugs and goods of all kind, and in every way aiding and encouraging the rebellion.

We had not been on this boat long before we found that the officers and crew of the Alone had little, if any, respect, for a Union soldier; and, on April 14, the blackguard barkeeper of this boat grossly insulted Willis Walker, a member of Company C. This comrade was a noted forager, and had the nack of getting what he went for. He promised the barkeeper that he would even up with him before we left the boat. Out on the cabin deck of the boat they had two large boxes, securely locked. One of them contained the table supplies for the boat, and the other the barkeeper's extra stock. After midnight we were roused up and told to come below at once. On going down to the lower deck, we found that Comrade Walker and his partners had the entire contents of the two boxes laid out for a banquet, which we disposed

of quietly and hurriedly. What we failed to consume was consigned to the river, as it was not safe to leave a crumb in sight, though some of the boys could not part with the liquor they had, but kept it well hidden. The loss was discovered at daylight, complaint was made, but our officers failed to find who was guilty.

On the 15th of April we landed at Milliken's Bend, Louisiana. Here the raid was reported to our headquarters, and our Brigade Commander, General Slack, was ordered to investigate the matter. The regiment was formed in line near the levee. In the rear of our line was a body of backwater from the river. As General Slack passed down the line the men who had any liquor left in their canteens would throw them into the backwater behind them, the straps of the canteens floating. Captain of Company — waded in and fished them out about as fast as they fell, and, stringing them on his shoulder, he reached the left of the regiment at the same time as the General did, and while they blessed the rebels and all their friends, they took a bumper to the success of the Union cause, to the great applause of a multitude of comrades of other regiments, who were giving this free show their close attention. This episode gave us a reputation, which later on came near depriving us of our colors. Some foragers of other regiments, when caught in unlawful acts, such as burning houses, etc., gave the Fifty-sixth Ohio credit with their membership; but upon investigation, and being confronted with our officers, we were cleared of the charge. Our stay at Milliken's Bend was short, leaving there April 16. We went into camp at Richmond, Louisiana, the same evening. We moved forward early on the 17th, and passed through some beautiful country. On the 18th and 19th we continued our marching, and on the 20th reached Bayou Pirre and encamped. Our pioneers were building a pontoon bridge, and we lay in camp here drilling considerably and holding dress parades. April 28 we moved on amid torrents of rain, the roads being nearly impassible, and camped two miles from the Mississippi river. This was a regular swamp, not a dry place in sight. The pioneers of our division built here about 2,000 feet of bridging, so we could cross the bottomless places. On April 29 we marched to the river

at Perkins' plantation. At this place there were several steamboats and barges at the landing. Here we left our knapsacks. Each comrade was loaded down with one hundred rounds of cartridges, and then marched aboard a coal barge. Our whole brigade was on one small steamboat and coal barge. We barely had standing room. The boat ran down to Hard Time's Landing, in sight of Grand Gulf, two miles down the river. Grand Gulf was naturally and artificially very strong. Soon after our arrival seven of our gunboats moved down, and a daring and continuous bombardment of the fortifications was kept up for five and a half hours, the flagship Benton leading the fleet. They circled slowly in front, each sending a broadside into the rebel works. General Grant and some of his staff were on a steam tug near our boat, closely watching the work of the gunboats. The enemy sent a few shells in their direction, to keep them at a proper distance. Then the tug retired out of range. This contest gave a fine display of the never failing courage of our brave sailor comrades. It seemed at times as though their boats would steam up to the wharf.. It was apparent to those who witnessed this contest that gunboats, though manned by the bravest men, were not equal to land batteries served by men of valor and skill. Several of the gunboats were damaged, and all of them withdrawn. The failure to silence the rebel batteries relieved us from the dreadful task of landing to storm their rifle pits. This was one of our lucky escapes.

Late in the afternoon we disembarked and marched across a point on a high levee, which brought us out on the river below Grand Gulf. Here we saw a live alligator basking on a log in the swamp. Our regiment led this advance, and as soon as we struck solid ground we filed off and went into camp. Who can ever forget that grand sight, as regiment after regiment passed to camp below. All of the Thirteenth and a part of the Seventeenth Corps passed. The snakes had pre-empted our camp ground, and our rest was not good, as they were disposed to dispute our right to be there. The gunboats, transports and barges ran past the Grand Gulf batteries about midnight under a heavy fire.

On April 30 we boarded a gunboat, which ran down and landed

us at Bruinsburg, Mississippi, six miles below. Here we were served with two days' rations that were to last five days, or until we could get more. At 5 o'clock p. m. we started on the road to Port Gibson, Mississippi, some 12 miles inland. One of the never-to-be-forgotten sights as we climbed the hills, a mile or more back from the river, was the display of pickled pork that had been issued to us and was carried on our bayonets. At 8 p. m. we halted to make coffee and rest a little, but started on soon, there being a constant skirmish in advance. We were on the road all night, and this was the third night for us without much, if any sleep. The most of us took short naps as we marched along. At daybreak we halted in the valley of a small stream for breakfast. Some of the more active or hungry ones had finished their meal, but many had not made a start, when the enemy's artillery boomed on the hill just ahead. "Fall in!" was the order, and up the hill we moved at a double-quick, halting in a deep cut in the road near the top of the hill.

In a few moments we were ordered to a position on the right of the road in an open field. In our front some 600 years was a piece of timber, in which there was a heavy contest going on, and a number of the wounded who could do so were falling back to our position. At the left of the road in the yard of a house was one of our batteries pouring shot and shell into the rebel battery in their front. In a few moments we were ordered forward. We moved right obliquely, which brought us to the road. As we came to the fence the rebel battery knocked it over our heads. Some of our men were hurt by the flying rails.

We crossed the road and moved down into a cane-brake at the left of the road, between our battery and that of the enemy. We made our way through the cane-brake, and formed at a fence on a slight ridge. In a few moments General Hovey and his staff rode down in the road to our right. He asked for the commanding officer of the regiment, Colonel Raynor responding. He was ordered to support the Thirty-fourth Indiana Infantry in a charge on the rebel battery in front. The Thirty-fourth Indiana was in the timber on the right of the road, and the Fifty-sixth Ohio to

the left of the road in a corn field. The Thirty-fourth advanced, but their progress was slow. The Fifty-sixth made a rush to secure a good position on the hillside, and were in advance of the Thirty-fourth. We were in close range and the enemy poured their shot and shell into our midst. I was hit by a grapeshot on the foot, bruising it considerably. As soon as our men fell into line we charged forward. The enemy stood their ground until we were in a few feet of them, when they broke to the rear, and we followed fast after them over the brow of the hill. A rebel officer was about to mount his horse when Captain Williams took Comrade Will Morris' musket and gave him the contents. The enemy was doing their best to escape, but we wanted them dead or alive. In a short time we captured 222 men of the Twenty-third Alabama Infantry and the Virginia Artillery Company, also the flag of one or the other of these organizations. The flag was captured by Corporal David Evans of Company C.

The regiment soon after formed line on a hillside in front, when General Grant and some of his staff rode up. The General shook hands with Colonel Raynor, and thanked the regiment for their gallant conduct, saying that he was proud of the men from his native state. After a short rest, we advanced to the right across a valley and up a high hill, where we lay in line for some time. The enemy now made an effort to cut us off from our forces. As they had a largely superior force, we fell back into the valley, where we found good shelter in the bed of a small stream that crossed the valley. But the rebels moved down as we did, and we had it hot and furious for some time. As we entered the run Sergeant Henry C. Dare of Company C was shot in the knee, by which he lost his leg; Corporal Thomas L. Evans lost an eye by a buckshot, and I was shot through my trousers at the knee, and also on my hip. A rebel officer on a white horse was shot, and his horse trotted into our line, and our Quartermaster kept him for a long time.

Our ammunition being exhausted, we were relieved by the Twenty-second Kentucky Infantry. They came in on the double-quick, their young color bearer 15 or 20 feet in advance. They

presented a fine sight. On retiring we were still under fire. The firing kept up until nearly dark, when the enemy retired to a hill, where they had a large cannon that annoyed us greatly, but our gunners were unable to dislodge it. About sunset an officer rode up to one of our batteries, had a gun loaded, sighted it, and with his glass watched the shot, remarking, "That gun will not trouble us any longer." This ended the battle of Port Gibson, the enemy falling back out of reach.

In this action the Fifty-sixth Ohio had six men killed and thirty wounded and missing. Port Gibson was no great battle, but of sufficient magnitude to test the quality of the men, and we all had good reason to rejoice over the gallant action of the regiment.

On May 2, early, we entered Port Gibson, a real pretty town. The enemy the night before had retired across Bayou Pierre, burning the bridge across that stream.

There has been considerable dispute in the National Tribune by members of Benton's Brigade, of Carr's Division, about the capture of this battery, they claiming that none of our division was near the battery until they had captured it and gone on to further conquests. All of the Fifty-sixth Ohio, who were there, know that there is no truth in their claim; and we may well inquire if they took the battery, "Why did they leave the enemy in possession of their guns with their infantry supports?" The business was to capture guns and prisoners when we could. That was what we were there for. The prisoners and colors taken by the Fifty-sixth Ohio, are all the evidence we need to dispose of their claim. A regiment came up in our rear and fired a volley into us and the rebels we had captured, and it was a common report in the regiment that in that volley they killed Corporal James H. Evans of Company E, one of the best soldiers in the regiment. The total loss of our army in this battle was 130 killed and 718 wounded and missing.

The Thirteenth Corps remained at Port Gibson during May 2, and assisted in the construction of a bridge across the south

branch of Bayou Pierre. May 4, 1863, our division advanced some ten miles north and near the Big Black river, and camped on a bleak hill. Our rations were out, and there was nothing in reach to forage, except the native black beans, which were quite a luxury. But in our extremity two of our mess secured a bee-hive full of honey and bees, and then we had beans, honey and stings; more of the last than we wanted.

On May 6 we moved up to Rocky Springs. This was a much finer camp; and on the 7th we had a grand review of the corps by General Grant. May 12 our division moved early, in the advance, being the only troops near the Big Black river. We came up on the south side of Fourteen Mile creek. The Fifty-sixth Ohio was on the right of our line, and near a road where there was a bridge across the creek. The rebels held the opposite side of the stream, with their sharpshooters so posted as to control the bridge. Company A was ordered to cross the creek above the bridge and drive the rebels away. They soon forced them back to the top of the ridge in our front. Company F was also sent to support Company A, and, soon after, the rest of the Fifty-sixth crossed by the bridge, and the entire division followed. We drove them steadily to within two miles of Edward's Depot, confronting Pemberton's main army. The Fifty-sixth Ohio was given the post of honor, and all of that night we lay on our arms in battle line in a cornfield. The roll of rebel drums in front gave notice of the enemy's presence.

At daylight of the 13th we drove the rebels about half a mile, and then, on quick time, we moved to the southeast until we struck the Raymond road, which we followed all day. The rain fell in pitiless fury. We had streams to wade, and, thoroughly soaked, lay out in the woods all night. On the 14th we passed through Raymond. Here we saw a large number who were wounded in the battle of the 12th, when the Seventeenth Corps routed the enemy.

May 15th we were off early, and reached Clinton, within ten miles of Jackson, Mississippi, at noon. From here our division made a square turn to the west, on the road to Vicksburg. This

road ran near the railroad, and at night we camped near Bolten Station. This ground was the enemy's outpost. They were driven off, and we took possession of their camp fires. The detail for picket duty was heavy, and as night came on there settled down upon the camp that indefinable feeling that can not be described, but can never be forgotten, and many of our comrades stood their last watch on the picket line that night; and the sharp report of musketry here and there caused our rest in camp to be rather broken.

CAPTAIN JOHN YOCHEM
See page 142

CHAPTER VI.

Champion's Hill.

At the commencement of the year 1863 the burden of the war was most sensibly felt throughout the loyal states. It was hard to convince all that the acts of the administration at Washington had always been dictated by the wisest policy. The generals in command, so far, had not proved to be sure leaders to an easy or any other kind of victory, but some had shown themselves altogether incompetent. Others had secured victories by the lavish shedding of blood, and on at least one field a mean and petty jealousy had robbed the country of the precious lives of our brave soldiers.

Swinton, in his excellent book, "The Decisive Battles of the War," in referring to our comrades of the Army of the Tennessee in this battle, uses the following language, on page 480, which goes to show the importance of this battle in the mind of this elegant writer: "And when the doomed Confederate armies, compassed in fatal toils, looked southerly for an outlet of escape, there came rolling across the plains of the Carolinas, beating nearer and nearer, the drums of Champion Hill and Shiloh."

This battle to which we were now approaching sealed the doom of Vicksburg, and it was not only the most complete, but the clearest-cut victory since the war began, and was the culmination of a series of splendid victories that held fully 100,000 men from reinforcing General Lee's army, and thereby making sure the defeat of Gettysburg. And, as has been well said, the high tide of the rebellion was met at Champion's Hill, down in the Mississippi valley, and not up in Maryland or Pennsylvania, and in that stupendous conflict was turned in favor of the preservation of the Union. That it was preserved, and we are today a united

country, that we have so much prosperity, peace and freedom, is due alone to the endurance, gallantry, patriotism and valor of the rank and file of the invincible Union soldiers of the North.

At this time the Twelfth Division of the Thirteenth Army Corps, commanded by General Alvin P. Hovey, was composed of the following troops: The Eleventh, Twenty-fourth, Thirty-fourth, Forty-sixth and Forty-seventh Indiana Infantry, the Twenty-ninth Wisconsin Infantry, Twenty-fourth and Twenty-eighth Iowa Infantry, and the Fifty-sixth Ohio Infantry; also the Second and Sixteenth Ohio Light Artillery, and the First Missouri Light Artillery, Battery A.

The Seventeenth Corps, Logan's division leading, on the evening of the 15th, were in our immediate rear; Osterhau's and Carr's divisions were some three or four miles south, while A. J. Smith's and Blair's divisions were still further to the southwest. These four divisions were north of Raymond, and on two roads that led to Edward's Depot. One of these roads entered the Vicksburg and Jackson road, on the west side of Champion's Hill; the other, further west, entered the same road at Edward's Depot. These four divisions were ordered by General Grant to advance on to the enemy's position, but for some unaccountable reason they failed to do so, or to take any part in the battle.

General Pemberton, having failed to cross Baker's creek to the south, countermarched his army and crossed it near Edward's Depot by a bridge on the main road. His intention was to turn south again, attack our rear and cut us off from our supposed base of supplies at Grand Gulf. But, on the evening of the 15th of May, he received the repeated order of General Johnston to join his army at Clinton, Mississippi, so that with united forces they could give us battle. But at that time, and unknown to both, we had occupied Clinton and passed on beyond; and General Pemberton was ignorant of the fact that General Johnston had been defeated and was retreating north to Canton, Mississippi. Then, when too late, and totally ignorant of the true situation, Pemberton concluded to obey General Johnston's order, and with this

object in view he started, early on the morning of May 16, 1863, east on the road to Jackson, Mississippi. But General Grant, just as early, moved our army west on the same road, which soon resulted in the meeting of the hostile forces. General Pemberton, whether purposely or not, had selected an extra strong position for a defensive battle, on the rugged hill known as Champion's Hill. On its eastern slopes were ravines and gullies, over which grew large trees and underbrush that were almost impenetrable; thus rendering it very difficult to move troops in anything like complete formation, but made it an ideal place for defense. The hill proper is one of the highest in that region, and commanded a fine view of the country to the east, over which our division was advancing.

Champion's house was to the left of the road and quite a distance east of the hill. On the morning of May 16, 1863, Hovey's division moved forward at 6 a. m. Our men were in good spirits, the bloody reception so near being mercifully veiled from sight. We were not long in passing over the short distance from our camp to where the enemy was awaiting our approach. The morning was bright and warm. At one plantation we had a hot time in passing some bee-hives that had been disturbed by our advance. On the slope of Champion's Hill, Hovey's division formed into battle line, and moving forward crossed the field and halted near the timber. There was skirmishing at the edge of the woods all along the line.

The Fifty-sixth Ohio was formed with the right on the road. On our left was the Twenty-eighth Iowa, on our right the Twenty-fourth Iowa, and to their right the Forty-seventh Indiana. The little while we lay in that open field, facing the dark woods, with the whistling bullets coming thick and fast from an unseen foe, was a trying time to all of us. Captain John Cook of Company K now came up to the line. He had been too ill to march with his company, and, as he appeared rather weak to take part in the expected conflict, Captain Williams urged him to retire to the rear, but, with determination, he replied: "I am going in with my boys if it is the last thing I ever do." He went in with his

company, and soon received a mortal wound, of which he died six days later. He was a brave and gallant man, and his death was a great loss to the regiment.

Our skirmishers were soon deployed and moved forward. How intently we watched them as they entered the timber and disappeared from our view, many of them forever. It was but an instant until there came the crash of thousands of muskets. The bullets fell thick and fast all about us. In a few moments, "Forward!" was the order; and the regiment entered the dark woods in the footsteps of our skirmishers. We found they had not advanced far, as the enemy was there in force, and their fire was heavy and hot from the start. Under this fire two brothers, William Bass, Company A, and Byron Bass of Company H, were killed within a moment of each other. The crash of musketry and the boom of artillery were deafening and continual. The memory of those four dreadful hours in that terrible orchestra of death is indelibly fixed in the memory of every comrade who was present, and often in these later years we go back in memory to the din and horrid uproar that seemed to rend and split the air, and neither time nor distance can efface from memory that thrilling battle scene.

We met a stubborn resistance from the very start, and I give the gray clad veterans of the Confederacy due credit for the dauntless spirit that inspired them on this field of death. Every foot of ground forward we had to fight for. We drove them, step by step, in our front to a long cornfield on top of the hill, which was surrounded with timber on all sides.

From here they fell back rapidly to the west side of the field, to where the road from Raymond entered the road we were on. Here from behind a strong rail fence they poured into us a deadly fire. After entering the field a short distance the first of Company C, Henry Richards, fell in death, shot through the brain, and all along the line men were being shot; some killed outright, others wounded more or less seriously. But there was no halt.

"Forward!" was the command. When we were about two-thirds of the way across the field, as we halted to give them a

CORPORAL DAVID EVANS
See page 138

volley, my brother, John H. Williams, was shot through the heart. He was raising his musket to take aim, and as he fell in death he pitched his musket toward the enemy. It fell with the bayonet stuck in the ground, the stock standing up. Captain Williams sprang forward, grasped the musket, and gave the enemy its contents. I saw my brother fall, there being but one man between us in the front rank of the company. I stopped for a moment at his side, hoping he was not seriously hurt, but he never moved. The fatal bullet, like a flash of lightning, had blotted out his life.

There was no stop. One comrade had his arm shot off, and others in the company and many more in the regiment were being hit. But there was no halt; and, closing up our ranks, we pressed on, giving careful attention to every shot fired. We drove them in our front to and beyond the road from Raymond, and it was a sight to see the rebels falling back and casting away their blankets and other impediments as far as we could see on our left.

Our brigade captured the Virginia Battery at the junction of the roads. The enemy fought their guns until most of them were killed or disabled. For a short time there was a lull in the firing in our immediate front, and, by permission of Captain Williams, I returned to my brother's body, as I thought it would be my only chance. I secured his watch and the other trinkets he had, straightened him out and spread his rubber blanket over him. The blanket was folded across his shoulder, and was perforated through the several folds by the ball that took his life.

The enemy's fire began to increase on our left front, and, on my return to the company, Colonel Raynor asked me to go to the commanding officer of the Twenty-eighth Iowa Infantry, and request him to bring his regiment up in line with the Fifty-sixth Ohio. The Twenty-eighth halted in a ravine near the center of the field, but they did not comply with the request. The bullets came thick and fast, and I moved at a double-quick gait in the performance of this duty. On returning to the line, from our position we could see the enemy forming to attack us. The woods in our front were open with a gradual slope toward them, and with their skirmishers well in advance and their forces in two

lines of battle, they charged our force at the fence. As soon as they were in range, those of the regiment who were on their feet opened fire on them. Most of the regiment at this time were lying down behind the fence, and they called from along the line to stop firing, that we were shooting at our own men. But we paid no attention to them, as we knew better. Captain Williams, who was near, said: "Boys, you would better stop, they may be our men." Corporal David Evans said: "Captain, take a look at them." One glance was enough. "Up, boys, and give them hades!" was the command. In a moment the whole regiment was giving them a close and hot fire. Their line overlapped ours as far as could be seen on our left. The open timber in our front gave us a good view of them as they came on. From tree to tree, or any other shelter, sprang their skirmishers until some of them were just across the road from us, and one had dropped behind a rail cut that I could reach with my musket. Their first line under the withering fire we were giving them from our strong position at the fence bore off to our right and left.

On our right the Twenty-fourth Iowa, being in open timber, was driven back after the most desperate fighting. Our right being unprotected, and having no support on our left, our regiment was forced to leave the fence, for which the enemy made a rush. In a moment we were under a most scorching fire from two or three sides, from which our men fell thick and fast.

I witnessed the instant death of two of our gallant young officers, Lieutenant Geo. W. Mauring of Company A and Lieutenant Augustus S. Chute of Company D. In their death the regiment lost two of its most promising officers. Loading and firing, we fell back unwillingly, but at no time did we turn our backs to the foe. At every favorable place we would halt and give them a few rounds. At one point, while we were shooting from the same stump, Richard Davis of Company C fell dead across my feet, shot through the heart. He had just urged me to be more careful, or they would shoot me. One glance satisfied me that he was beyond any earthly help. Before I left this point, a general officer of the enemy and his staff rode up in the road in our front, urging

his men on. I took deliberate aim at him with my Enfield, which never snapped twice on the same load. This, in all probability, was the rebel General Tilghman and staff. The General was killed at this spot.

As we neared the fence on our retreat, the fire was terrific. As I turned to fire, my musket being about at prime, a bullet from the enemy struck the barrel of my musket, the ball exploding. Four small pieces were buried in the back of my hand, and several more in the stock of my Enfield. My musket proved to be in the right place to save me from the fate of my fallen comrades. At this time the screeching shells and the sound of crashing musketry, and the shouts of the contestants, was a sound to hear once in a lifetime, and remember to eternity. One of our boys had his canteen and haversack straps cut off by bullets. Comrade Wm. D. Davis had the top of his cap shot off of his head, and another had the side of his trousers cut off below the knee by pieces of shells that were bursting in our midst. They made a charge for our flag, but Captain Yochem saw the danger and led a counter charge, and they were repulsed. The troops on our right were being forced slowly back, and the enemy was getting in our rear at the fence on the east side.

Near this fence I stopped to help Corporal Thomas S. Jones, who was shot through the leg, to the shelter of some brush. While doing this their advance made a rush for me, halted me, called me hard names, and were nearly close enough to lay hold of me, but I hoped to see them later on, and under better conditions for myself. The comrades who were there can never forget the desperate and deadly work from that on. How we contested for those little ridges; how we clung to every tree, stump and log. If there were any stragglers they were gone to the rear, and it could be seen in the determined face of every comrade the resolve, that if mortal man could hold that battle line, they were the ones to do so. Shells were bursting in our midst, with falling branches from the trees, and flying brush that was being cut down. It was strange that any of us escaped. A piece of shell knocked Captain Williams down. I assisted to take him

to the road nearby. There I saw Generals Grant and McPherson, also Fred Grant, up near the battle line.

Our ammunition was getting low, and we were supplied by staff officers and others bringing it up to the line. A shell struck Corporal David Evans of Company C, and tore a terrible gash in his breast. He was a man of fine physical frame, but from the effects of this wound he died July 14, 1863. He was the comrade that captured the flag at Port Gibson on May 1, 1863.

From this point the enemy failed to drive us, and soon a brigade of General Crocker's division came to our support. As this reinforcement came up to the decimated remnant of our brigade holding that line, the commanding officer requested an officer near me to have those stragglers fall in on the left of his brigade. The officer addressed, with uplifted voice replied: "These are the men who have fought this battle. There are no stragglers here." The gallant officer, as he looked at our powder blackened faces, took off his hat and said: "I beg your pardon. True enough, there are no stragglers on this line."

In a short time we began to drive them back over the same ground, the third time for us to go over it. The enemy toward the last fell back rapidly, fresher troops following them.

General Grant, in his Memoirs, Vol. 1, page 520, says: "Hovey remained on the field where his troops had fought so bravely and bled so freely." He also says: "Hovey captured 300 prisoners under fire, and about 700 in all, exclusive of 500 sick and wounded, whom he paroled." Also, on page 519, he says: "Hovey alone lost more than one-third of his division," and, on the same page, he says: "Hovey was bearing the brunt of the battle." And on page 518 he says: "The battle of Champion's Hill lasted about four hours of hard fighting, preceded by two or three hours of skirmishing, some of which almost rose to the dignity of battle. Every man of Hovey's division and of McPherson's two divisions were engaged during the battle. No other part of my command was engaged at all."

The regiment lost a total of 138 killed, wounded and missing.

JOHN H. WILLIAMS, CO. C
See page 138

It is proper here to give the names of our comrades who, as a part of the young manhood of the United States, fought and died as soldiers never did before, and vindicated the right of liberty to continue to the end of time. That they were the choice spirits of the regiment, all will admit. The killed were: Lieutenant Geo. W. Manring, William Bass, W. R. Allen, John Hoffman, Edward Hollenback, Michael Riftlemacher, Henry Richards, John H. Williams, Richard Davis, Lieutenant Augustus S. Chute, Luke Clifford, Thomas B. Dodds, Turner Eaton, George Rife, Clement D. Hubbard, Martin Downey, M. Freeland, Henry H. McGowan, Wm. F. Porter, Samuel B. Quartz, Byron Bass, Wm. J. Marshall.

The mortally wounded were: A. M. Martindale, David Evans, Wm. Crabtree, Henry H. Lewis, David A. Loveland, John E. Veach, Henry Martin, Archibald George, Wm. Jones, John D. Markell, Geo. W. Rockwell, James Fields, Charles W. Hill, Duncan McKenzie, James D. Boren, Merit Campbell, George Irvine, James Martin and Captain John Cook.

Also the following were wounded more or less severely: Colonel W. H. Raynor, Captain Geor. Wilhelm, wounded and captured, turned on his guard and brought him into our line; Captain W. B. Williams, Lieutenant Martin Owens, Lieutenant J. A. Aleshire, T. Harkison, Martin G. Allen, Chas. Blosser, L. C. Chappell, Jarvis Coply, Elias Johnson, Wm. D. Jones, Wm. T. Saxton, Fred Held, Geo. Emling, Geo. Meisner, Henry Meyer, L. D. Davis, Thos. D. Davis, Thos. S. Jones, Wm. Edwards, S. Dalrymple, E. E. Edwards, Henry Nolte, David Edwards, Joshua Lewis, Thos. J. Williams, Edward Goudy, Daniel Thomas, James Anderson, John Barr, James Odle, Reason Furgeson, Rees Griffith, Daniel Williams, James M. Pease, George W. Cox, Jasper Font, Joel Burnett, F. M. Seth, Wesley Murphy, John Shaw, Jos. Davidson, Lawrence Hahn, James W. Pauley, Martin Powers, Adam Siemon and Joseph Vanfleet, and a number more were captured and missing out of a few over three hundred in ranks.

We went into camp at the right of the Vicksburg road on the enemy's side of the battlefield, powder stained, tired and hungry. That was one day at least that the important matter of dinner was

forgotten, and our supper was a light one. Shortly after dark Lieutenant Roberts, Evan Edwards, A. S. Drennan and Wm. D. Davis of Company C went back with me to give the boys of our company some sort of a burial. We made a torch, and by its light saw some of the awful sights of that desperate battlefield. One, always remembered, was a very large and tall rebel, stiff in death, sitting with his back against a tree; with deadly pallor he seemed to gaze at the horrors before him, and so many lying dead as they fell, friend and foe alike. We soon found our dead comrades. We were without tools of any kind, but a kind hearted comrade, one of the pioneer corps, who was passing, learned our needs and gave us his shovel. With this we soon prepared a grave, and side by side laid our comrades of Company C, their shrouds being their old rubber blankets. The same work was being done by comrades of the other companies; and the remains of comrades who fell there now moulder in the unknown graves of the largest National cemetery in the United States, at Vicksburg.

The dreadful sights on that bloody ground can never be forgotten. Where our brigade charged the enemy's battery at the junction of the roads the dead men and horses were in piles, as they were before our first brigade.

In 1895, in Jackson, Ohio, a stranger, in appearance a grizzled veteran, inquired of me if I had written a sketch of this battle, which he had read in the Standard-Journal, our county paper. I informed him that I had. "Well," said he, "you gave a fair description of the conflict, as I was there, but not on your side, but a member of the battery at the junction of the road that your men charged." For our work in this battle history gives us high honor, so we need not be silent. Hovey's Twelfth Division, Thirteenth Army Corps, out of 4,180 men, lost: Killed 211, wounded 872 and missing 119; total 1,202.

General Grant says he had about 15,000 men engaged. General Pemberton, commanding the enemy, admits he had 18,000 men. Abrams, a Confederate authority, gave him from 23,000 to 26,000 men. "Ohio in the War," says: "The battle of Champion's Hill sealed the doom of Vicksburg." The Count of Paris, in his

History of the Civil War in America, styles Champion's Hill "the hill of death," adding that it (the battle) was the most complete defeat the Confederates had sustained since the commencement of the war.

Harper's History of the Great Rebellion has this to say of Champion's Hill: "When the order came, ordering forward, the left and center, the right under Hovey, had been contending for nearly two hours against superior numbers. Hovey's division of two brigades, nine small regiments, bore the brunt of the whole conflict. Directly in his front was the Confederate General Stevenson's division, composed of four brigades, posted in a strong position on Champion's Hill. He (Hovey) had been repulsed, leaving behind 11 guns captured from the enemy; but his men, undaunted and under cover of a heavy artillery fire, again advanced and carried the closely contested field."

General Hovey in his report speaks in these words: "I can not think of this bloody hill without sadness and pride. Sadness for the great loss of my true and gallant men; pride for the heroic bravery they displayed. It was, after the conflict, literally the hill of death; men, horses, cannon and the debris of an army lay scattered in wild confusion; hundreds of the gallant Twelfth Division were cold in death or writhing in pain, and, with a large number of Crocker's gallant boys, lay dead, dying or wounded, intermingled with our fallen foe. I never saw fighting like this. The loss of my division on this field was nearly one-third of my forces engaged."

General Hovey mentions the troops in these words: "Of the Twenty-ninth Wisconsin, Twenty-fourth and Twenty-eighth Iowa, in what words of praise shall I speak? Not more than six months in the service, their record will compare with the oldest and best tried regiments in the field. All honor is due to their gallant officers and men, and Colonels Gill, Bryan and Connell have my thanks for the skill with which they handled their respective commands and for the fortitude, endurance and bravery displayed by their gallent men. It is useless to speak in praise of the Eleventh, Twenty-fourth, Thirty-fourth, Forty-sixth and Forty-seventh Indi-

ana and Fifty-sixth Ohio. They have won laurels on many fields, and not only their country will praise, but posterity will be proud to claim kinship with the privates in the ranks. They have a history that Colonel Macauley, Colonel Spicely, Colonel Cameron, Colonel Bringhurst, Lieutenant Colonel McLaughlin and Colonel Raynor and their children will be proud to read.", No battle of the Civil War can show a finer display of the valor and staying qualities of the Union volunteer than did Champion's Hill. An hour on that awful field was equal to years of ordinary time. But eight other Ohio regiments lost a larger number of men in any one engagement than did the Fifty-sixth Ohio at Champion's Hill. No battle fought for the preservation of the Union was more important and successful than Champion's Hill. At that time the country, discouraged under the disasters of the previous fall and winter, felt that the very existence of the great republic was in peril. The previous year had been one of mistakes and disasters in the department of war and in the field. The winter had been hard, and extremely so, to the troops in the southwest. At Helena and Milliken's Bend hundreds had died of fevers and other diseases so common in that swampy region. The drums beating the dead march, and the volleys of musketry over the graves of our comrades were too often heard, and in the homes of the North fell with crushing effect upon the hearts of the people. But from this memorable day there seemed no more doubt as to the final success of the Union cause, though the time was long thereafter and the conflicts many and terrible before the end was reached.

The Twelfth Division of the Thirteenth Corps leading, on that eventful May 16, with Logan's and Crocker's divisions of the Seventeenth Corps, met and crushed the Confederate army, one of the most complete and disastrous defeats of the war for the Union; and from this time, until the enemy lay down their arms at Appomattox, the safety of the Union seemed assured.

To understand the importance of this battle, it is necessary to remember that it is a matter of record that the rebel General Pendleton had under his command and ready to support him about 82,000 men at the time our forces crossed the Mississippi river at

Bruinsburg; 60,000 of them were at Grand Gulf, Vicksburg and Jackson, and the rest of his forces at nearby points, all within easy supporting distance; and it is also a fact that General Grant had up to and including Champion's Hill only about 40,000 men.

The records show that General Pemberton had with him in the battle of Champion's Hill eighty regiments of infantry and ten batteries, in all fully 25,000 men. The enemy on their own chosen field were most disastrously defeated by an inferior force. And as a result of that defeat they left behind thirty pieces of artillery, 10,000 stands of small arms, and other war material, over 3,100 dead and wounded and over 3,000 prisoners.

General Grant himself asserts that, leaving out the divisions on the left, that virtually took no part in the battle, we had less than 15,000 actually engaged.

CHAPTER VII.

THE SIEGE OF VICKSBURG AND JACKSON—ON TO NATCHEZ AND NEW ORLEANS.

On May 17 our division moved up to Edward's Depot. The only stand made by General Pemberton's demoralized army was at the crossing of the Big Black river. Here it was found by Osterhaus' and Carr's divisions of the Thirteenth Corps on the 17th strongly posted on both sides of the river. At this point, on the west bank—the main position of the enemy—bluffs extended to the water's edge. On the east bank there is an open bottom a mile wide, surrounded by a stagnant bayou two or three feet in depth and from ten to twenty in width. Behind this bayou the enemy had thrown up rifle-pits. A charge was made by our troops. Not a shot was fired by the gallant assailants until they had crossed the bayou. They then poured in a volley, and, without reloading, swept on with fixed bayonets, and the position was hastily abandoned by the Confederates, leaving in their works eighteen guns, 1,751 prisoners, and large quantities of small arms and stores.

We moved up and reached Black river on the 19th. On the 20th we were sent to Bridgeport, and returned the next day. May 22 we marched up to the line of investment around Vicksburg. We were quartered a short distance in the rear of our trenches, and in close range of musket balls. Shells and round shot were too frequent callers. On May 23 the regiment was in the trenches and had an exceedingly hot time of it. The regiment was on duty every day, on guard in the rifle-pits or digging in the trenches. There was hardly a man who did not have many narrow and wonderful escapes. It was a common thing to have a ball shot through one's hat or clothing. In the rifle-pits we fired from fifty to seventy rounds a day, and death lurked on every hand, whether on or

off duty. Comrade Noah Starcher of Company E was mortally wounded by a musket ball while lying sick on a hospital cot in the regimental hospital, which was quite a distance in the rear of where the regiment was quartered for forty-two days and nights.

This same duty in kind continued until July 3, 1863. On that day Company C was at the head of the trench about thirty feet from one of their forts. A rebel sharpshooter grazed my ear, and about the last cannon they fired, on that part of the line at least, was at our company. We could see they were up to something more than usual, and we watched their port-holes so closely that it was unsafe for them to fire a gun. But they did take the risk and fired a load of grape and canister into the head of our trench, knocking over the gabions we had at the head of the trench and covering several of us with dirt and rubbish. Some of the boys thought we were killed, but none of us was seriously injured. July 4, 1863, dawned bright and gloriously, a day of sacred memories to all who love liberty and freedom, and increasingly so to the Union army before Vicksburg, for, after a most heroic defense, the Confederate General Pemberton surrendered to General Grant his army of 31,600 men, together with 172 cannons, about 60,000 muskets and a large amount of ammunition, it being the largest army ever captured or surrendered on the western hemisphere, or in any part of the world in modern times.

Our line of investment was over fifteen miles, extending from Haines' Bluff to Vicksburg, and on to Warrenton. The enemy's line was about seven miles long. Vicksburg was finely situated for defense. On the north the hills at the highest point rise to about two hundred feet above the Mississippi river, and are cut up by ravines and small streams. The ravines were grown up with cane and brush. The only hope of relief the imprisoned Confederates had in Vicksburg was in the Confederate General Jos. E. Johnston's being able to drive off a portion of our force, so they could withdraw their troops.

By the 25th of June our position was so strong that a less number was required for the investment. Thereupon General Grant detached General W. T. Sherman, with a division from each

of the Thirteenth, Fifteenth and Seventeenth Corps and General Lauman's division to see that General Johnston did not interfere with the siege of Vicksburg. General Johnston had gathered an army of about 24,000 men. General Grant wrote General Sherman that he must defeat General Johnston at least fifteen miles from our works. Most of the troops were not allowed to enter the stronghold they had assisted to capture; but on July 5 the remainder of the Thirteenth and Fifteenth Corps was sent to reinforce the troops already under General Sherman.

General Johnston retreated to Jackson, Mississippi, our forces following him closely, going over nearly the same roads we had marched over in our advance on to Vicksburg. The weather was intensely hot, the roads very dusty and water exceedingly scarce. July 9 our forces reached Jackson, and on the 10th Hovey's division closed up on the line of investment late in the day. On the 11th we had some heavy skirmishing at Lynch's creek, and on the 12th more hard skirmishing along the Raymond road. Our regiment was on the right of Hovey's division, and on our right was Lauman's division, which suffered a heavy loss in an assault upon the enemy's fortifications in their front. This assault was made by a misunderstanding of orders. The siege was prosecuted vigorously until the morning of July 17th, when it was found the enemy had evacuated during the night, after destroying his stores and supplies. Our forces followed them for several miles, but failed to overtake them. The railroads entering Jackson were broken up, and then General Sherman, leaving a garrison in the Capital City, drew back his line to the Big Black. And on the 24th of July, as the regiment was on its way back to Vicksburg, at the crossing of the Big Black river, a violent storm of rain, with thunder and lightning overtook us, and Color Sergeant Wm. Roberts took shelter under a tree, which was struck by lightning, hurling him to the ground and paralyzing his left side, and the flag was stripped from its staff as though cut with a sharp knife. Sergeant Roberts never fully recovered from the shock.

On July 25 our division reached Vicksburg and went into camp below the city, and we then had a chance to see some of the

CHAPLAIN J. E. THOMAS
See page 136

damage and destruction that were caused by the dreadful siege. July 31, 1863, we left with our division on a steamboat for Natchez, Mississippi, and we arrived there the same day and went into camp on the bluffs high above the river. Our camp ground here was fine, and the view grand over that low, flat region of country. We rested at this place until August 31, 1863, when our army corps left for Carrollton, Louisiana, which was about six miles above New Orleans. This was also a fine place and our camping ground was all that could be desired. On September 4 General Grant reviewed our army corps, and after the review the vicious horse he was riding fell on him, hurting him very seriously. On September 11 Colonel Raynor returned from home and brought the regiment a beautiful stand of colors, that was presented to the Fifty-sixth Ohio by the kind hearted and loyal citizens of Portsmouth, Ohio.

While in this camp a funny scene was witnessed one day. One of Company K boys, full of fun and a little reckless, was, for some misconduct, put on extra duty to clean up the camp, etc. But he soon tired of this and refused to work. The Lieutenant of the guard then undertook to make him do so, but he still refused, and ran out on the plain, with the Lieutenant after him, and they made very good time. After he had run a reasonable distance he halted, picked up a stick, and, calling the officer by his given name, said: ''Now, you run ahead of me," and it was great fun to the spectators to see the extra good time the Lieutenant made on the home stretch.

CHAPTER VIII.

THE TECHE CAMPAIGN OF 1863.

September 13, 1863, our army corps crossed the Mississippi river to Algiers, Louisiana, directly opposite New Orleans, going on the cars to Brashier City, Louisiana, about ninety miles in a westerly direction, and on Berwick bay. This was a city in name only. On September 14 we unloaded and went into camp. Here, on September 24, our division formed in line to witness the drumming out of the service of a member of the First Missouri Light Artillery, with his head shaved, the band playing the "Rogue's March," as he passed in review before the division. He presented in truth a pitiable sight. On September 25 we turned over about all of our transportation, and on the Twenty-seventh the Thirteenth Army Corps was reviewed by our corps commander, General E. O. C. Ord.

On September 28 we crossed Berwick bay and lay out all night in a hard rain. We had a miserable time on that low ground, where the mosquitos fairly swarmed, and the misery we endured from them from Helena on down to Louisiana can not be described. They were not the small kind of the North, but were regular gallinippers. Some of them were as large as butterflies, so the boys declared.

October 2, 1863, the United States paymaster called and paid the regiment for two months, and on the 3d we marched up the Teche Bayou about ten miles. The next day we started early and passed through Franklin, a beautiful little town, and went into camp just beyond. Again, on the 6th, we were off early, and camped at noon on a prairie. While marching along this day we saw a never-to-be-forgotten sight. On a fence that ran nearly parallel with our road, and extending as far as we could see, there

were sitting thousands of buzzards. They seemed to be solemnly reviewing us as we passed. They were protected in that section, as they were valuable as being the public scavengers, and consequently of great benefit. While here the news reached us of the battle of Chickamauga, and the cheering by our troops must have greatly astonished the natives. We remained here until October 10, when we moved forward, passing through New Iberia early. The roads were very dusty and the days hot, but the nights fairly cool. We camped after a march of 20 miles. Here we remained until the 22d. We had quite a time politically. The Twenty-fourth and Twenty-eighth Iowa Infantry were in our brigade, and as their state election came off at the same time as it did in Ohio, they held political meetings, and it might be thought an old-time campaign was on. The vote in the Fifty-sixth Ohio stood 167 for Brough and 57 for Vallandigham. This election was held October 13, 1863.

On October 22 we moved forward, going about 14 miles. The weather turned real cold for that latitude, and the 23d we reached Opelusas, having a hard cold rain all day. We remained here until November 1, when we moved back about 12 miles. Having failed to bring the enemy to a stand, our forces fell back leisurely toward our base of supplies. The bushwhackers hung around our column, and on November 2 killed a Captain in the Twenty-fourth Iowa of our brigade, and on November 3 the enemy surprised General Burbridge's brigade. They were in camp some three miles in our rear in a piece of timber. Our division went to their relief on fast time. Burbridge's men rallying, and our forces aiding, the enemy was soon put to flight. While our division was gone the rebel cavalry made a dash to capture our camp, but Captain Thos. W. Kinney, as officer of the day, with the camp guards, drove them off easily. As we gradually fell back, the enemy followed at a distance, but would not accept our repeated offers of battle.

On November 5 we fell back below Vermillionville and camped in a real pretty place. We remained here several days, and on the 11th we had some heavy skirmishing, in fact a small battle, and on the 13th the regiment went out to guard a forage train. On

November 16 we marched back to within six miles of New Iberia and camped, and on the 17th we fell back to New Iberia. The rebels were in sight, but out of reach all day in that level country. They would not attack us, nor stand for us to get at them; but any small body of troops they would attack at once. While here, on the 26th of November, Thanksgiving services were held, and a good time we had.

December 2, 1863, the regiment was sent out after lumber, and on the 3d we received the news of the great victory of our forces at Chattanooga, and it was received with great cheering in all of our camps. There was a great deal of horse racing here among army men, as the country was very suitable for such sport. Here there was much talk of enlisting in the veteran service, a great number doing so.

December 19 we left this place and camped early a short distance below Franklin. On the 21st we marched again and reached Berwick at 4 p. m. Here, on the 22d, the regiment was paid two months' pay. We crossed the bay to Brashier City on the 23d, and, on the 25th, the regiment left on a train of cars for Algiers, reaching there at 2 p. m. Our tents were pitched along the railroad track, and we had rather a dry Christmas. This ended the Teche expedition of 1863.

During this campaign we had many hardships, also many experiences that were funny, ridiculous and outrageous. If there was one place more than another where every officer and enlisted man should have all his powers at command day and night, that place was in the army, and when officers would befog their minds with liquor it was a crime of the gravest character. Not only were the lives of the men under them endangered, but the cause of the country was often in jeopardy. There was hardly a regiment in the army which did not have officers of that kind, and the Fifty-sixth Ohio had its full share. The action of two of our Lieutenants on this expedition shows how unfit they were for such important positions.

On Oct. 14, 1863, near New Iberia, Louisiana, we moved our camp some five or six miles. These two Lieutenants were men

of education and their natural abilities were good, but by the use of liquor they had completely undermined their manhood, and it was an outrage on every self-respecting soldier in the regiment that these two men were ever promoted. On this day Captain ———— was officer of the day, and one of these Lieutenants was officer of the guard and the other Acting Quartermaster. The Captain was a good officer, strict in the performance of duty, and though he would take his bitters, he would not unman himself and lose all self-control, as did the lieutenants. On this day the Captain had secured some liquor, and knowing the infirmities of the Lieutenants he would not share with them, but they found out what the Captain had, and at once set to work to secure a share, as they knew it was useless to ask the Captain to divide with them. The Acting Quartermaster was a smooth talker and suggested that he would draw the Captain into an argument, get him away from his tent, and then the other Lieutenant was to confiscate the liquor. The plot worked like a charm, and the lieutenants took little interest in the war for some hours. The regiment moved up and went into camp before night. Along about midnight the lieutenants came up, found the Quartermaster's tent and turned in, and the next morning they were found with half of their bodies in and half outside of the tent, in a drunken sleep, and to a post was tied a fine horse that they had confiscated from some regiment as they came up. They had some trouble in explaining how the horse got there.

Again, on November 3, the enemy made an attack on General Burbridge's division, and ours went to their relief, a camp guard only being left in charge of the camp. Captain Thos. W. Kinney was officer of the day and one of these Lieutenants officer of guard. The enemy's cavalry made an effort to capture our camps in the absence of the division. Captain Kinney rallied his camp guards, but could not find his officer of the guard. Being told that he was at the Quartermaster's tent, he went in search of him, and there found that these Lieutenants were foolishly drunk on Hostetter's Bitters. The Acting Quartermaster had the empty bottles in a row attempting to show the other Lieutenant some of

the fine points in company drill. Captain Kinney talked to them in plain language; but the Acting Quartermaster waved him off, telling him to go on with the d— war, that they were in no way interested. This was conduct that could not be overlooked, and a few days later, Colonel Raynor notified them to hand in their resignations at once, or charges would be preferred against them. They promptly complied, and were dismissed for the good of the service. They went to New Orleans, got their pay, went on a spree and spent their money, and had to take deck passage up the river for home.

At one point on this trip we were in camp for a few days, near Bayou Teche. Supplies were limited, and especially so in the line of liquor, but some of the officers and men who were fond of it would use every expedient to secure some of the deadly stuff that does no good anywhere, but evil everywhere. One of our Captains, Geo. Wilhelm, well knowing this weakness of his comrades, and to have a little fun, set up a sort of dry joke on half a dozen of his fellow officers. Early one morning he called on them and inquired if they felt like taking a horn before breakfast; and it is to be regretted that they thought they were in need of a horn before breakfast. Shortly after they could be seen wending their way up the levee of the bayou. On its banks, at a short distance from camp, there was a tannery, and near it there had been dumped a large pile of long horns. When the Captain got his squad up to the pile, he in cordial tones, invited each one present to help himself to a choice horn, a long or a short one. They had to laugh at the joke, though more or less disappointed, but it is to be hoped they were benefited by their morning walk.

Christmas day, 1863, the regiment was at Algiers, Louisiana, camped near the town. The last day of 1863 came on with a cold sleet, and it was so cold that most of the regiment went into town for shelter. January 1, 1864, the cold New Year's, so memorable all over the land, was extremely cold as far south as New Orleans.

January 13, the regiment moved into an old mill or foundry, which was a great improvement over the shelter tents. Here we turned over all our teams. The weather continued very cold, and

the mud was everywhere and bottomless. On January 22 we were ordered to leave for Lakeport, on Lake Pontchartrain, a short distance east of New Orleans. We crossed the river and went out to Lakeport on the cars. On the 23d we boarded the steamer General Banks, which took us across to a little place called Madisonville, Louisiana, in a pine woods, and here we went into camp. This was a nice dry place, a great improvement over Algiers. From this place General Grant planned to move on to Mobile, Alabama, but was overruled by General-in-Chief Halleck, and our forces were sent on the disastrous Red River campaign, where nothing was gained, but disaster and great loss in men and material from beginning to end. At this place those who had re-enlisted in the veteran service were mustered in, to date February 1, 1864.

While at this point we had a splendid camping ground, and the weather was extra fine. One of the comrades, noted in his way, was Willis Walker of Company C, who had been detached for service in one of our batteries. He was inclined to fun and jokes, one of which was to try pass the guards on a bogus pass. But at this time he had secured a pass, but the Sergeant of the guard thought he was fooling, and refused to let him out. After some talk, Walker drew his revolver and shot the Sergeant seriously. For this he was courtmartialed and sentenced to the Ohio penitentiary for three years. The provost guards had him in custody at our headquarters; but on a bright moonlight night he came to my tent to say goodby. He had a warm attachment for me, as I had prevented his shooting one of our comrades about two years previous. He told me he had escaped from the guards, and was going out into the Confederacy. After a short talk he started for our picket line. I stood and watched him until he disappeared in the timber. Some two months later he came to the regiment up on Red river, and wanted to stay with us. He said that he secured a rebel suit, made his way to Natchez, Mississippi, and gave himself up as a deserter from the enemy. He then enlisted in our navy and was with the fleet up Red river. He was told by our officers that he could stay to see all the boys, and

then he must go, or he would be arrested. This was the last we ever saw of him.

. February 7, 1864, was Sunday, and we had preaching at Colonel Raynor's headquarters, both morning and evening, by a Chaplain of the Twenty-fourth Iowa Infantry. February 27 we were ordered to Algiers, Louisiana. We crossed Lake Pontchartrain on the steamer Battles, passed through New Orleans, and went into camp the same evening at Algiers. February 29 the non-veterans of the regiment were transferred to the Eighty-third Ohio Infantry, but they did not remain there, as Lieutenant Colonel S. E. Varner was detached and placed in command of the post of Algiers, and a temporary battalion, composed of the non-veterans of the division, numbering about six hundred men, were to perform duty under his command. Major Reiniger was also detached and placed in command of a camp of paroled prisoners. On March 2 we had a review of our brigade, and on the 3d the division was reviewed by General McClernand, who made us a short speech.

Dr. P. M. McFARLAND
See page 137

CHAPTER IX.

THE RED RIVER CAMPAIGN OF 1864.

The regiment was entitled to return to Ohio on the thirty days furlough which was given to those who had re-enlisted to see the end of the war, but instead of the veteran furlough, on March 5, with our division, we were ordered on the ill-fated Red River campaign, which was incompetently managed from beginning to end. We left for Brashier City on the 5th, reaching there the same day, and crossed to Berwick and encamped near our old camp ground of the fall of 1863. March 13 we moved forward and camped above Camp Brisland. We started early on the 14th, and, after a very hard day's march, we camped three miles beyond Franklin, Louisiana. We remained here over the 15th, and on the 16th we marched to within six miles of New Iberia. We reached a little lake at 1 p. m. of the 17th and encamped, and after a short march of 15 miles we camped on the 18th at Vermillion Bayou. On the 19th we reached Carencro Bayou early in the afternoon and camped. We passed through Opelusas and Washington on the 20th, going into camp two miles beyond Washington, Louisiana. On the 21st we lay in camp and the Nineteenth Army Corps passed to the front, and we followed on the 22d, the Fifty-sixth Ohio leading our forces.

On the 23d the regiment was ordered to guard the pontoon train, and we brought it into camp at 8 p. m. The enemy, as usual, was giving us lots of trouble, and the only safety lay in keeping well together. March 26 we reached Alexandria, Louisiana, and camped outside of the town. The 27th was Sunday, and we lay in camp all day. On the 28th we moved forward about 20 miles through a heavy rain most of the day. Our route took us through a pine woods region, and the ground was rough. We reached Cane river on the 29th and camped over the 30th, to wait

for a bridge to be constructed across the river. While waiting here a lot of our boys, in foraging around, secured a large and fine fish net, and as it was made to fish with they concluded to try its qualities. They waded in with the net and soon had ensnared a monster fish that was hard to handle, but after a very dangerous contest with it, as two of them barely escaped being bitten by it, they landed the fish, which proved to be a garfish, or a sea pike, or a sea needle. It was over five feet long and weighed 160 pounds. Its mouth, armed with sharp teeth, was ten inches long at least, but we had a real feast eating it, the meat being sweet and nice.

March 31 we moved forward again, forded a river, and after a march of 17 miles we camped. The wind blew a gale on this day, which made our marching very unpleasant. We reached Nachitoches, Louisiana, on April 1. It was hot and dusty, and more hard wind, which caused the dust to fly in clouds. We went into camp just below town, which was a pretty little place. April 4 General Banks reviewed the troops, about all our forces being present. We remained here until April 6, when our army advanced toward Pleasant Hill, Louisiana. On that night we camped in a thicket of brush after a march of 15 miles.

On April 7 it was 10 a. m. before we started. General A. L. Lee, who commanded our cavalry force of about 5,000 men, held the advance, skirmishing with and developing the enemy, who, continually retreated, regardless of his force. After these troops was the cavalry train of over 200 wagons. After it came the two small divisions of the Thirteenth Corps; then the Nineteenth Corps. From front to rear the line extended from 25 to 30 miles, over a single road, and this difficulty was greatly increased by a rain storm, which, lasting all day of the 7th, rendered that narrow road nearly impassable.

General Franklin had ordered General Lee to push the enemy vigorously, and keep his wagon train well up to the front. General Lee had found his train a source of trouble, being obliged to detach a large portion of his force to guard it. It was General Lee's business to develop the enemy's force and report it to his superior officer. This he failed to do. General Franklin was impressed

with the idea that the enemy would not fight, and that the cavalry was in the way. April 7 we camped at Pleasant Hill after a march of 20 miles. April 8 we started late, and the sharp report of carbine and musket in front was nearly continuous. General Banks arrived at the extreme front at 1 p. m. He found there the whole force of the enemy. He then saw the disadvantage of having a wagon train, filling the only road there for a distance of two or three miles in the rear. If General Banks had withdrawn, declining a general battle, it would have been at some risk to the train; but if he decided upon a battle there, bringing up his scattered infantry to General Lee's support, which he did, the risk was much greater, and made certain his defeat.

General Banks took the greater risk. Our small division had gone into camp some four miles in rear of our advance. We were ordered forward on quick time, and the sound of the conflict was becoming more distinct. General Banks hurried up the infantry in the rear, and brought up fourteen pieces of artillery, in addition to the twelve already with General Lee. In his dispatch to General Franklin, half an hour after he reached the front, he advises that the enemy seems prepared to make a stand, and that he had better bring up his infantry, and concludes: "You had better send back and push up the trains, as manifestly we should be able to rest here." The infantry moved forward quickly, and by 5 p. m. General Cameron's little division, of which the Fifty-sixth Ohio was a part, was on the field. There was less than 2,000 men in the division, and after a forced march of four miles was sent in to action, as General Lauman's troops were driven back. Then, for nearly two hours of desperate fighting, our troops held their line and repulsed the repeated charges of the enemy. In one of these charges the enemy made a desperate effort to capture our colors, and that brave hero, Jack Williams of Company C, the color bearer, with his guards, were having a desperate time to beat them off, when, seeing their danger, Coroporal James M. Halliday of Company F, with superb gallantry, rallied a lot of the boys, and rushed to the rescue and drove the enemy back. Comrade Halliday, though one of the youngest men in the regiment, was placed

in command of his company on the retreat by the commanding officer of the regiment, and he was as competent to command it as any man in the company.

General Banks was present when the battle opened, and as one writer well says, "Fed his army by detachments into this Confederate threshing machine." The desperate situation of our troops nerved every man to the best that was in him, and the veterans, on that battle line, were equal to three times their number of less seasoned troops. The enemy being unable to drive us in front, advanced a large force on the right flank of General Lauman's division, and succeeded in capturing the Forty-eighth Ohio, Nineteenth Kentucky; Seventy-seventh and One Hundred and Thirteenth Illinois regiments, and Captain White's Chicago Battery. And all these, by sundown, with many others captured, were on the way to that vile rebel prison, at Tyler, Texas. This battle was a plain trap, set by the enemy, and our commander had no more gumption than to send his troops into it. There was only one narrow road, with timber and brush on both sides, our wagon train being well to the front, obstructing the movement of troops, and later falling an easy prey to the enemy. Our forces were crowded back slowly and steadily. The men of the Thirteenth Corps could not be stampeded, no difference how desperate the conditions might be. They fell back, stubbornly facing the foe, all feeling that we had not had a fair chance. At this time the writer was Quartermaster Sergeant of the regiment, and, though well up in front, not on the battle line, but when I saw the wounded coming back, and saw the desperate plight my comrades were in, I took my musket and hastened to the firing line, though my superior officer remonstrated with me for going.

About sunset someone called from behind us to run in. On looking around we were greatly rejoiced to see General Emory's division of the Nineteenth Corps, our strong support in our terrible need. They opened ranks for our little force to pass through, the enemy following closely. As soon as we cleared from their front, the Nineteenth Corps fired a volley into them that made the earth shake, as well as the Confederate hosts. Three times they

attacked, but the Nineteenth Corps repulsed their utmost efforts. They tried the flanks, but they were firm, and, night coming on, kept them from making the best use of their greatly superior force. The order was to fall back to Pleasant Hill. No comrade who was there can ever forget the miseries of that night, wagon trains, artillery and the troops, all crowding that narrow road, and some of our comrades had experienced, in the words of the poet:

> "The first dark night of nothingness.
> The last of danger and distress."

At one of our frequent blockades I found Comrade Moses Roberts of Company C, near the road. He had been severely wounded, and was unable to retreat further, but a kind hearted teamster, who had given me a place to ride on his wagon, permitted me to substitute Comrade Roberts, and he escaped with the rest of us.

The loss of the Thirteenth Corps in this action was 1,405. Our regiment had 2 killed, 14 wounded and 19 captured. Admiral Porter, in his history of this action, says: "Even this small force went into battle by detachments." But few in number, the boys of the Thirteenth Corps, held their front. Our entire force was between 6,000 and 7,000 men. The battlefield was about four miles from Mansfield, at a place called Sabine Crossroads. It was about 50 miles south of Shreveport, and 20 miles west of Red river. The Confederate army was under the command of General Dick Taylor, and consisted of Mouton's and Walker's divisions, and General Thos. Green's cavalry, in all amounting to 12,000 men.

General Taylor had been ordered to fall back before our army, leading it on to Shreveport. But the opportunity offered for defeating General Banks was too tempting to be rejected. Out of twenty-six pieces of artillery engaged all but eight were captured by the enemy. But for the position of the train fewer prisoners would have been taken by the enemy, and most of the artillery would have been saved. The loss of our army in this criminally managed battle was over 3,000 men, killed, wounded and prisoners. The Confederates lost about 1,000 men. The enemy captured 220 of our wagons.

General Franklin and Admiral Porter both expressed themselves that the enemy would not fight, but had occasion to reverse their opinion before this campaign was over. There can be but one solution of such a conduct of affairs, and that is, that whoever directed that on our part in this battle was incapable.

At daylight on the 9th of April we reached Pleasant Hill, and that every one of us was about exhausted can well be believed. But we were greatly encouraged to find General A. J. Smith's division of the Sixteenth Corps in line of battle to support us. We all had the greatest confidence in the ability of General Smith to meet and defeat the rebels, and the spirits of all were greatly revived, all feeling that if he commanded we would have an equal or better show than the enemy. Our remnant of the Thirteenth Corps was placed in reserve. Soon after day the enemy advanced upon our forces with great confidence. For over three hours they attacked and charged our troops, but they found in General A. J. Smith a man who was master of the situation at hand. With his gallant division and the troops of the Nineteenth Corps they repulsed every effort of the enemy, who abandoned the attack after over three hours of desperate conflict.

Between 2 and 3 p. m. we continued to retreat on the road to Grand Ecore, on Red river. We marched all night. The road was extremely rough, and it was as dark as it ever gets. April 10 we continued our retreat, and on the 11th of April, at 5 p. m., went into camp near Red river. On the 13th our division moved out a short distance and built fortifications across the road we came in on, the rebels being near and in force. General Franklin passed along as we were at work, and remarked to a squad of Company G boys: "You don't need any protection. We can whip them easily here." Comrade Gil Crabtree replied: "We have been defeated once, and we think we will look out for ourselves." General Franklin was second in command to General Banks.

April 20 General Smith's division of the Sixteenth Corps moved out south on the road to Nachitoches. Our division left this place at 5 p. m. of April 21, and continued to fall back toward

Alexandria, Louisiana. As we departed the few buildings in Grand Ecore were set on fire by some one, and were entirely consumed. We marched all of that night, most of the next day and all of the following night. This service tested the endurance of every comrade there. At daylight on the 23d we found that the Confederates held a strong position on high ground on the south side of Cane river. From this place they had complete command of the low ground to the north, and all approaches to the bridge on the wagon road, and the low ground where we were.

Our troops attacked them in front, and our forces in the rear were heavily engaged. It was a grand sight to see the troops, our forces and the enemy's, moving to attack and counter-attack from every side of that basin where our army was. The rebels seemed to swarm on all sides. Our situation was critical unless the Confederates in our front could be dislodged. While this contest was going on in front and rear, the survivors of the Thirteenth Corps made a detour in the shelter of some woods, forded the river, gained the high ground and swept the rebels from their strong position at the bridge. Our forces in the rear repulsed the enemy at all points, and late in the afternoon all of our troops were safe across Cane River, and camped on the hills in the timber.

April 24 we continued our retreat through the pine woods toward Alexandria, reaching there at dark on the 25th. Here we were in comparative safety.

This campaign was made up of shameful blunders at the hands of officers, who, in some incredible manner, had attained to such responsible command. The ranks of every regiment contained plenty of men who could have handled our army and led them to victory, instead of defeat.

April 27 we received our veteran furlough, and on the 28th we went aboard a steamboat, but at 1 p. m. the rebels made a heavy attack on our works, and it looked as if there would be a general engagement; so we returned and remained in line all night, and we had to remove our things from the boat, as it was ordered

to proceed to New Orleans. On May 2 the Fifty-sixth Ohio, with its division, was sent out on a reconnoissance, but the enemy did not show up with any force that would stand its ground.

SERGEANT GEORGE GRINDLEY
See page 138

CHAPTER X.

The John Warner, Snaggy Point and Our Escape.

May 3, 1864, the regiment was again ordered to depart on its veteran furlough. We embarked on the steamboat John Warner. This was a fine side-wheel boat in good order, and with a brave and loyal Captain. On May 4 the John Warner left Alexandria at 10 o'clock a. m., and we had not gone far beyond our lines when we were fired into from the south side or bank of the river. From behind the levee at the most secure points we were fired into with musketry, but we were not seriously damaged, as our boat was protected by rows of cotton bales around the sides and ends, which secured us with reasonable care against bullets. They began to fire into us at 1 o'clock p. m., and in one of these attacks they killed Tom Morris of Company C, our former brave drummer boy, who, in 1862, in back of Memphis, took the arms and equipments of the fellow who was afraid, and carried them to a good purpose to this eventful day, when, in his daring recklessness, he disdained the good protection afforded by the cotton bales, and stood up fully exposed and fired at the enemy, who lay behind the levee. He was shot through the brain, and in his death a mere boy, that he was, the Union lost one of its bravest defenders.

Our passage so far had been under great difficulties, as the enemy was vigilant as usual, and fired into us from every favorable point, and after running some twenty odd miles we tied up for the night on the north side of the river. Here we thought we were comparatively safe, and all was quiet on the John Warner. The officers and passengers were eating their supper, and the men were partaking of hard-tack, etc.

The river here was rather narrow, and opposite our boat there was a thicket of brush, and about dusk the enemy crept up and

fired a volley into our boat. It was equal to a circus to see those in the cabin at supper rush down the stairs to the stronger protection on the lower deck. On the hurricane roof of the boat Comrade John Henry of Company F was on guard, and how he escaped instant death a kind Providence only knows. The only damage they did was the scare that those at the supper table got.

On the morning of the 5th we were off early, and had gone but a short distance, when we saw a small body of Union troops on the north bank of the river. They were making their way toward Alexandria. We learned they were a part of the One Hundred and Twentieth Ohio Infantry. They reported the rebels in force strongly posted a few miles below; that they had captured the City Belle, the boat they were on, and that they had escaped by the north side of the river.

In a short time after leaving them we were hailed from the north bank. We landed and took aboard a wounded Lieutenant and two soldiers of Company H, One Hundred and Twentieth Ohio Infantry. They were First Lieutenant John M. Baer and Privates Isaac S. Miller and Andrew Manhart.

In a short time we came in sight of their pickets. They fired at us and rode at their best speed for their main force. We had as escorts two light gunboats, the Signal and Covington. On rounding the next bend their battery opened on us. I was standing at the bow of the John Warner, and saw the first ball fired at us strike the water just in front of the boat.

At this place, called Snaggy Point, the river makes a short turn or elbow. The water was low and the channel narrow, and we were coming into the range of their guns. The enemy had two 32-pound Parrott guns, and a 6-gun field battery, with 1,200 cavalry and over 2,000 infantry, securely posted behind the best of fortifications, a high and strong levee. From this secure place they gave us a close and hot fire from the time that we came into range. And we had now entered that concert of all that was horrible. Our gunboats opened fire furiously, but the enemy was too well sheltered to be greatly damaged by it. Nearly every shot they

fired reached our boat, or one of the gunboats. We drifted with the current, the gunboats keeping up a constant bombardment, and the Fifty-sixth Ohio Volunteer Infantry a steady fusillade of musketry.

In the National Tribune of Washington, D. C., under date of February 5, 1885, Lieutenant John M. Baer of the One Hundred and Twentieth Ohio Volunteer Infantry gave the following account of his and our experience in passing through this maelstrom of death and destruction. Coming from a man of some other regiment may add to its worth, and it is here given in his own words:

"Now the time had come for the John Warner to run the blockade. Every preparation had been made, and with the timbers quivering under her immense power of steam, the gallant steamer shot by the first gunboat. Then the Fifty-sixth opened fire. There they stood, the brave Colonel Raynor and his war scarred veterans, looking as if they would conquer fate itself; and that they fought desperately need not be told, for who ever knew them to flinch in the hour of danger? The Colonel rushed back and forth waving his sword. The officers, with sword in one hand and shooting with revolvers with the other, cheered and urged on their men, which was useless, as every man was doing his level best to down a 'Johnny.' Then came a yell from the 'Rebs,' as they mounted the levee. We looked back and saw the boat we had passed all ablaze. Then came the explosion of her magazine. We passed another boat, which was firing very slowly, the 'Rebs' filling its port-holes, when open, so full of shot that they could not use their guns. Then came another yell from the rebels, and, looking ahead, we saw another boat floating disabled down stream. It had swung crosswise in the river, and they were shooting through her lengthwise. Then came a crash and a solid shot went through the wheel-house of the John Warner, disabling her engines and causing her to drift with the current. The noble Captain was then heard calling, 'Help!' 'Tow me out.' We had not reached the point of the bend, consequently our boat almost ran ashore on the rebel side. Cheer after cheer went up from them, thinking they had us in their clutches, but we soon drifted past the bend, and,

fortunately, to the north side of the river. On the refusal of the John Warner's crew to make the boat fast Sergeant Nick Main, Samuel Nickell and J. C. Harper took the rope up the bank and tied the boat up under a shower of bullets. We were in a bad position. The rebels had an enfilading fire on our boat, and they poured their shots into us from three sides. They splintered the light woodwork of the John Warner into slivers. Our cotton bales saved many a life on that boat, as they were a good protection, both on the boat and when we went up the bank. Some of the escapes were marvelous. A citizen passenger sitting in an armchair on the cabin deck in a drunken stupor was not aroused until we had passed the first artillery, when one of our boys dragged him to a safer place. I had left my knapsack where I bunked, outside in the front of the cabin deck, and when I found we had to leave the boat I was very anxious to secure it. I crawled toward it, but they made the splinters fly too close for safety. Securing a long slat, I attempted to draw it within reach, but they had such close range on that point that they knocked the stick out of my hands, and having a desire to enjoy my veteran furlough, I reluctantly left my knapsack for the enemy. The passengers in the cabin lay flat on the floor, the splinters from the light upper woodwork of the cabin and other debris covering them in many places."

At this time I was Quartermaster Sergeant of the regiment, and, being near Colonel Raynor, he directed me to notify the company officers to get their men on shore at once. After performing this duty I returned to Colonel Raynor, and we jumped off the boat behind the wheel-house and scaled the bank under a heavy fire of musketry.

Before our men could get off, a shell from the enemy burst behind the cotton bales in Company D, killing Wm. Bradfield and mortally wounding Sergeant Samuel Wood. They were two exceptionally fine young men, and their loss was greatly deplored. Also James Odle, Thomas Cox and Azariah Arthur were all more or less wounded by the same shell. One extraordinary shot was a shell fired by the enemy that passed through the boat from the

rear end, through every state room on one side, and lodged in a drawer in the Clerk's desk, but did not explode.

As soon as the companies came off the boat a council was held, and it was decided to make an effort to reach the Mississippi river. As this would be quite a long march, we thought it best to secure some rations before starting. A lot of us returned to the John Warner for that purpose. I brought off about a half-bushel of hard-tack and three blankets, and though there was a constant and close fire of musketry I escaped without a scratch. At this same time Comrade Wm. W. Hughes of Company E started up the bank with a box of crackers on his shoulder. When about half way up they knocked it to pieces about him, but he ran back, took up another box and brought it up the bank. Also Comrade Thomas J. Williams of Company E went up on the hurricane roof of the John Warner, and threw off the knapsacks of his company. Surely, the enemy lacked the ball to kill him. These two acts came under my own observation at the time.

Our escorts did their best to dislodge the enemy, but after a most desperate contest failed entirely. A number of the comrades, who were not very well, were under the shelter of the boat, hesitating about taking the risk of going up the bank. I went down to the edge of the bank and urged them to take the risk and come up into the woods, but most of them would not venture, and fell into the enemy's hands and endured a long imprisonment.

The Captain of the Warner sent for Colonel Raynor for consultation. In making the trip the Colonel was shot through the leg. We got him up into the woods as soon as we could, and shortly after the commander of the gunboat Covington sent word to bring the Colonel up stream a short distance, and that he would take him on board, and he thought that he could run by the enemy's batteries. I took my blanket, and, Comrades Samuel Clinger, William Leniger, Samuel Nickel and David Storer assisting, we carried the Colonel up stream, where the Covington landed for him, and we all went aboard. With my musket ready, I stepped to a port hole and fired one shot, when a shell entered over my head, cutting the steampipe and exploded in the ashpit, deal-

4

ing death and destruction on every side. The escaping steam filled our boat, creating quite a panic.

The gunboat Signal at this time lay by the side of the Covington, and nearly every one on the Covington escaped to the Signal. Colonel Raynor was having his wound examined at the time, and was taken with the crowd. When the steam cleared, we discovered only one officer of the Covington and a few of his men, together with us boys of the Fifty-sixth Ohio. The Covington was now a helpless wreck, drifting toward the enemy.

The young officer asked us boys to assist his men with a big gun they were getting ready to fire. We took hold of the rope with the gunboat men. We were now, to all appearances, drifting right into the enemy's hands, and a crowd of them came down to the water's edge to take us in. But to their disappointment our big gun belched its contents in their midst, the recoil sending the Covington back across the river. The young officer told us to make every effort to escape. We did not need any urging on that line. One by one we gathered on the side next the shore, and when the Covington struck the north shore we made our best speed up that bank under a regular shower of bullets. Well, we were not to be killed. They literally mowed the brush over our heads as we crawled away.

As soon as they slacked firing, we started to hunt up the regiment, but found that it had gone down stream a short time before. Near by we found Sergeant J. C. Bingham and the wounded boys of Company D. As we could be of no assistance to them, they urged us to save ourselves if possible, and we took the trail of the regiment and followed in quick time.

Moving on, we soon had a crowd of thirty or forty together, mostly from the gunboats. In the crowd was a Major, a strong, hearty man, and at different times he urged me to stop and surrender. At times we missed the trail of the regiment in the dry woods, and all the crowd sat down and waited until we Fifty-sixth boys and a young colored man from one of the gunboats found it. Our advance guard held a caucus and decided to leave that crowd

as soon as night came, if something better or worse did not intervene.

Some distance out we crossed a road and found that the rebel cavalry had just passed out of sight. They thought we were heading for Alexandria, as many others did, and they were endeavoring to intercept us. Some time after passing this point we heard a boat blow off steam. Then we struck out at our best gait in the direction of the sound, and in a short time reached the river several miles below where we left it. We could see a gunboat quite a distance down stream. We fired our guns and shouted, thus attracting their attention, and the boat landed and waited for us. We thought we had traveled eight or ten miles, and that we were about exhausted can well be believed. This gunboat had taken the regiment on board some distance above, and on learning the condition of affairs at Snaggy Point turned back and took us to the mouth of Red River, and from there the Shreveport, a very heavily loaded steamboat, took us to New Orleans, reaching there May 7, 1864. We were in the worst condition we had ever been.

Here we were quartered in the Virginia warehouse. We drew some much needed clothing and were paid, and received a part of our veteran bounty. Here I will give a short account of what some of our comrades and others endured on this shameful and blundering campaign.

Before we left the Covington the rebels had crossed the river and made a line fast to the John Warner, put the coil into a yawl, and rowed to the south shore, where the line was seized, and, with shouts and cheers, the John Warner was hauled to the opposite shore. The plucky Captain was one of the first to be taken off. Then the rebels swarmed over the boat, drank all the whisky, ransacked the boat and plundered the wounded and dead. They shamefully abused Lieutenant J. M. Baer of the One Hundred and Twentieth Ohio Volunteer Infantry, took his money, stripped off his clothes, leaving him only his undershirt and drawers, and he being badly wounded. The John Warner soon after took fire and was soon consumed.

Colonel Raynor and the other wounded from the City Belle, that the One Hundred and Twentieth Ohio was on, and those from the John Warner and the gunboats, were first taken to a cotton shed nearby, and from there in wagons to Cheneyville, Louisiana.

Captain J. C. Stimmel of the Fifty-sixth Ohio failed to get off the first boat we went on at Alexandria with the regiment, and was captured two days before the mishap to the John Warner, and with a lot of other prisoners was marched toward Tyler, Texas. When the prisoners were near Shreveport Captain Stimmell and another officer broke from the column as they were going through some timber. They ran a short distance and hid in the leaves. The column was halted and a careful search was made. The guards even walked on the log by the side of which they lay. Fortunately they failed to find them. After a long tramp they found a colored man, who kindly fed them and put them on the right course, and also secured them a canoe to travel in, and in that frail craft, after almost incredible hardships and suffering, they reached the mouth of Red river and our fleet. This was some time after our forces had evacuated Alexandria, and the rebels were in full control of Red river.

Captain Ben Roberts of the Fifty-sixth Ohio was captured on the John Warner, and with a later crowd of prisoners was safely imprisoned at Camp Ford, Tyler, Texas. After they had been there for some time they found among their guards a Union man, who agreed to let a squad of them out at the first opportunity, which soon came; and, by twos, ten of them passed out. Captain Roberts and his comrade were the last two out. Shortly after day they heard the bloodhounds on their tracks. Captain Roberts and his chum had followed a water course for a long distance, thereby escaping, but all the others were captured. These two who escaped disguised as rebel soldiers, and with a story of returning to their regiments up in Arkansas got along fairly well, except their long tramp. But as they came near our forces in the region of Little Rock they barely escaped being killed by our soldiers, as some of them had been bushwhacked by the rebels about the time of their arrival, and their gray clothes made things look suspicious. For a

time they were determined to hang them whether or not, but fortunately Captain Roberts' comrade was recognized by some old friends whom he had served with in the past. All in all they had a most desperate experience.

After leaving the Covington we saw no more of the young officer or his men. But in May, 1896, 32 years after this terrible escape, there appeared a notice in The Times-Star of Cincinnati, O., that Dr. Thomas G. Herron would deliver a patriotic address in one of the churches of the city on Memorial day, and among other thing would tell how, during the war, he blew up the United States gunboat Covington to prevent her falling into the enemy's hands. These few lines brought vividly to mind our awful experience on that boat. A short note to Dr. Herron brought in answer the following thrilling letter:

"Cincinnati, O., June 7, 1896.

"Ex-Lieutenant T. J. Williams:

"My Dear Comrade—Thanks. Your very interesting letter of May 30 has been received and contents noted, and as this is Sunday, my day for religious and patriotic duties, I devote this half hour to answering your kind letter. Yes, sir, I am the officer that had command of the Covington the last few hours of its existence. My Captain deserted the boat (Covington) when lying alongside of the United States steamer Signal, and I assumed command and fought until I had lost most of my men. The steam and hot water from the perforated boilers were scalding dead, wounded and fighters, and the gunner's mate had both legs shot off in the magazine door; the master's mate that had charge of the magazine was cut in two by my side; the captain of the gun's crew, by the big gun you mention, had his back shot away, and asked me to put a bullet through him to put him out of his misery. I told the brave sailor I could not, but to make his peace with God, as his moments were very few. He commenced the Lord's prayer, but before he got half way through he gave me a look and his voice ceased and he died. Several scenes like this were too much for me, and so many killed, and with the concentration of fire of General Dick Taylor's men (6,000 men), I ordered the men to arm themselves and get ashore,

first to carry the wounded men off and hide them in the canebrake, and get up the bank. I then spiked all the guns with rat-tail files and broke them off and started ashore, but as I started I looked back, and could not bear the idea of the enemy's capturing those grand guns—30-pound Parrotts and 50-pound Dahlgrens, besides howitzers—with all the ammunition, so I went back and into the fire-room and took seven shovels of hot coals from under the boilers, and carried them back, over my dead boys and bloody deck, and piled them on the pine deck over the magazine. The sixth shovelful burned through the pine deck and the zinc began to melt, and a few hot coals fell into the loose powder and it began to spit. I threw the seventh shovelful into the hole and rushed forward out of the open port and along the casemating and was about fifteen feet from the jumping-off place when the boat blew up, and I was blown up with it and turned several somersaults, circus like, badly burned, and landed in the mud and water. It was awful; my clothes and hair were on fire. I think I was dead for a few moments, but rallied and pulled off my burned clothes and plastered myself with wet, red mud, and got on my feet and went up the bank as fast as my burnt, tired legs would carry me. I was afterward, with a few of my men, chased by bloodhounds, and seven of my men were torn to pieces by them, and I had a terrible experience with them. Tracked and captured by the dogs (five of them) and a company of Johnnies, I was taken out to be hanged, and then to be made a target of afterward. The lasso was ordered and brought to hang me, and the noose made. I saw it all, and heard all the interesting conversation, but I was tired, having run fifteen miles, and so nearly dead that it had little effect upon me. But, thank God, the Johnnies could not find a tree with limbs low enough to hang me on. I, being left alone with the dogs at my feet, saw a woman—an amazon about six feet four inches high. As she drew near I felt that one to save me was near at hand. I asked her if she was a mother. She said 'Yes,' and I said, 'Would you not like to have a Yankee mother save your boy if he were in as bad a fix as I am?' 'Yes, I would,' she said, and she picked me up in her strong hands and carried me about 1,000 yards to her cabin, where I lay two days and nights, buried among a lot of old clothes,

and I was safe." Thus he escaped and still lives to tell of the awful time he had.

The Fifty-sixth Ohio boys who were captured on the Red river fiasco were imprisoned at Camp Ford, near Tyler, Texas, with hundreds of others, among whom was the most of the Forty-eighth Ohio Infantry, captured at Sabine Cross-Roads. When their color-bearer, Isaac Scott, saw that all was lost, he tore the regimental flag from the staff and gave it to his messmate to conceal in his haversack, and after a journey of 150 miles they reached Camp Ford and he delivered the colors to the officers of his regiment. A hole was dug inside of their shanty, and in it they buried their flag. In the stockade were soldiers who had been there nearly two years, and when it was whispered about that there was a Union flag in the prison they could not withstand the pleading of the old prisoners to let them have a glimpse of the old banner of beauty and glory. Time and again it was dug up, and under strict watch the old prisoners were allowed to go in and take a look at Old Glory, and, rough men though they were, with tear-stained eyes they pressed the cherished folds of the old flag to their lips. In the meantime the prison commander got information that led him to believe that there was a Union flag concealed in the prison, so one day they marched a regiment of troops into the prison stockade and made all the Union prisoners fall into line, and after that was done they searched every shanty in the prison pen, and with their bayonets dug up the floors, but did not find the flag. It was a hard matter for them now to find a safe place for the flag, as they were liable to repeat the search at any time. They that night dug the flag up and it was sewed inside the lining of Captain Gunsaulus' blouse, where it remained for about six months. The captain was around among the rebel guards, but they never found out "what a precious charge to keep he had." After seven months of imprisonment the regiment marched to Shreveport, La., and from there by steamboat to the mouth of the Red river, to be exchanged. As the men of the Forty-eighth Ohio stepped on board the Union vessel, the excited soldiers tore the blouse from Captain Gunsaulus' back and hastily tied the flag to a pole, and as the band on our vessel struck up "The Star Spangled Banner," and the dear old flag of the

Forty-eighth Ohio floated in the air, in the presence of the enemy's guards, Captain Birchett, the enemy's officer in command of the guards, spoke of it as being the most exciting scene he had ever witnessed, and that the Forty-eighth Ohio deserve great credit for saving their colors during their imprisonment, it being the only regimental flag that went through a rebel prison during the war. It is now deposited in the statehouse at Columbus, O.

SERGEANT JAMES C. BINGHAM
See page 139

CHAPTER XI.

OUR VETERAN FURLOUGH AND RETURN TO NEW ORLEANS, LA.

The regiment had reached New Orleans on May 7, 1864, and we remained there until May 25, 1864, when we embarked on the steamship Catawba, and at 5 o'clock p. m. we left for home by way of the Gulf of Mexico and the Atlantic ocean to New York. We would not be taken for the same crowd that landed from the Shreveport on May 7, stripped of everything except what we had upon our persons. Our vessel reached the gulf at 1 p. m. of the 26th, and on the 27th we passed the Dry Tortugas Islands at 4 p. m. This place was used as a prison or place for punishment for soldiers of our army, and I believe two or three of our boys were sent there for a short period. On May 28th we passed several vessels, some going in and others going our way. The Catawba was a very fast vessel for that day.

That night the captain of the ship called the attention of some of us to the southern cross, plainly visible in the sky. For his kindness personally I have always been thankful. On May 29 and 30 it was stormy, and many of us had a taste of sea-sickness. We passed stormy Cape Hatteras at 8 p. m. of the 30th. May 31 was very fine and we had lots of amusement in watching the porpoises as they sported about the ship. One large one, a yard ahead, led the ship as though it was hitched to it, for miles upon miles. June 1, 1864, at 5 a. m., we reached New York. We were up early, and will always remember the grand sights on every side as on that bright morning we sailed into that great harbor. It was new and also amusing to us as we marched off the ship to feel that the ground seemed to rise up before us at every step. In New York we were quartered in the Park Barracks, which was close to Barnum's

Museum. We remained here one day and night. June 2, 1864, we crossed to Elizabethport, N. J., and took the cars for Harrisburg, Pa., reaching there at 2 a. m. of the 3d. We left at 5 a. m. and reached Altoona, Pa., at 2 p. m., where our train circled up and over the mountains, where we saw grand and never-to-be-forgotten scenery on every side; passed Johnstown and reached Pittsburg at 10 p. m. Here a delegation met us and we were escorted by them to a hall near the station, where they had the finest supper for us that we had partaken of for over two and a half years at least, and we always feel grateful for the kindness of the good people of that loyal city. We started at midnight for Columbus, O. At some town in northern Ohio we stopped for breakfast. Twenty-minutes was the time allowed. In about nineteen minutes they set the grub before us. Pay had been exacted in advance. Before we had hardly tasted a thing "All aboard!" was called at the door. Most of the boys got out and on the train. Quite a lot of them took their breakfast, dishes and all, but a few remained and finished their meal at leisure, and took passage on the first passenger train for Columbus, O. The conductor tried but failed to collect any fare from them, as they gave him the choice to go on or they would put him off and take charge of the train.

We reached Columbus at noon of the 4th of June, 1864, and were assigned quarters at Tod Barracks. Here we were guarded by some home troops. The boys did not fancy being under guard in their home capital, so taking matters into their own hands, a lot of them captured the guards and went out, taking the sentinels and their arms with them.

June 6 we received our transportation to Portsmouth, Ohio, going by way of Cincinnati, Ohio, and reaching there at 4 a. m. of the 7th. Seventy-six of the boys were placed under my command from Columbus to Portsmouth. On the train to Cincinnati the boys had a jolly, but rather boisterous time of it, having taken on a little too much stimulant. But it is a pleasure to be able to say that they, one and all, instantly obeyed every order from me, and it was useless for any one else to give them orders or tender advice. At one place a truck of our car got off the rails as we crossed a bridge,

but the connections were of good stuff and we were soon on the track again. On the 7th we left for Portsmouth on the Bostona, and arrived there early on the morning of the 8th.

Here we separated for our homes in different directions, and as a general thing we had a pleasant time, and the thirty days seemed to pass at unusual speed to all of us. On July 6 we left Portsmouth for the field, being ordered back to New Orleans, La. The only thing of note on our return trip was the arrest of two of our boys for murder at Cincinnati, O., by a sheriff of an up-river county. The regiment was marching down through the streets to the O. & M. depot when the arrest was made, and the officer had got some distance away before many of the men learned of the transaction, but as soon as they learned of it a crowd of them dropped out of ranks and soon returned with the men arrested, and these comrades went on with us to the end of our service. The sheriff had no heart in the arrest, as he no doubt felt that our comrades had done right under all the circumstances, which were about as follows:

These two men were cousins. The elder had been with us from the beginning, but the younger one volunteered while we were on our veteran furlough. They had gone to a city in their county one day, and as they were returning home, among others on the train was a gang of refugees or deserters from the rebel armies. And some of them took pains to raise a disturbance with our comrade. He was a veteran and with a fair show would meet any man; but being unarmed, except with his pocket knife, and the odds being so largely against him he was watchful, but paid as little apparent attention as possible. No outbreak was made until they reached the station where they were to get off the train. Our comrade was the first to step off. One of the refugees had a new clock, and the leader, who had been hunting for trouble, got off immediately after him. In his hands he had the two clock weights, and with an oath, as he stepped on the platform, he threw with all his power one of these weights at the head of our comrade, barely missing him. There was one of two things for our comrade to do—defend himself or to run; but he had faced too many better men south of the Ohio

river to turn his back on this scoundrel so near his own home. So with his pocket knife he settled the controversy then and there at the cost of his assailant's life. In so far as heard from, the comrades were never after disturbed, the civil authorities feeling, no doubt, that they were justified. We went on by the O. & M. R. R. and connections to Cairo, Ill., and from Cairo by steamboat to New Orleans, La.

LIEUT. COLONEL HENRY E JONES
See page 139

CHAPTER XII.

PATROL DUTY IN NEW ORLEANS AND VICINITY—CONSOLIDATION OF VETERANS INTO THREE COMPANIES AND A ROSTER OF THE VETERANS.

The regiment reached New Orleans on July 20, 1864. On our passage down the river we saw the various places where we had experienced so many hardships and surmounted dangers without number. Soon after our arrival Lieutenant Colonel S. E. Varner and the men of the regiment who did not enter the veteran service rejoined us. After a few days we were assigned to perform patrol duty in the city of New Orleans. Also the First United States Infantry, the First New Orleans Infantry (white), and the Eighty-first United States Infantry (colored) were on duty in and about the city. Here we had good quarters, but the duty was hard and there was a great deal of danger connected with it, and we had a varied and interesting experience, much of it, of course, not worth relating. Oct. 1 the yellow fever broke out near our quarters. On the 2nd a lot of the boys attended Christ church to hear General Pyle preach. Oct. 11 was election day in Ohio, for state officers, and we voted the same as if at home. On Oct. 17, 1864, the non-veterans of Company A, also Captain Manring and Lieutenant William D. Wood were mustered out. These were two very fine men and excellent officers. They and their men had served three years.

A rather unusual and funny episode took place on the 30th of October, and in this department, as well as in others, a great deal of red tape was displayed when a chance to do so offered. On this day a Major on the department staff rode into our quarters and ordered the regiment into line for inspection. As usual there was hustling around, and those that were there were soon in line. Most

of the companies had several men in ranks and made a fair showing, but somehow Company K had only two men and one Sergeant in line. The inspector said nothing much at the time, but in a day or two we received his report, and company by company he passed judgment upon them until he came to Company K, and of this company all he said was "Company K had two men and a dirty Sergeant on inspection." We all thought the joke was on the Sergeant and he was often reminded of it, and it was noticeable that he was more careful after this.

At the close of this month a lot of the young men of the regiment had the pleasure and privilege, under the leadership of Dr. McFarland, of attending the M. E. church on Caroudolet street, to hear Dr. Newman preach. He preached a series of ten sermons to young men, which were of great profit to all who had the good fortune to attend these services. This gifted man, who passed on to the higher life July 5, 1899, was the loved and greatly honored Bishop of the M. E. church.

Nov. 4, 1864, we were ordered to Algiers, La., which was directly across the river from New Orleans. There was also an order issued directing that the veterans of the regiment be consolidated into three companies, and all surplus officers mustered out. On Nov. 7 the regiment was consolidated as ordered, and formed into a battalion of three companies, and the supernumerary officers mustered out as ordered.

A ROSTER OF THE VETERANS.

In letters of gold should be written the names of the comrades who, having taken up arms to save the Union from dissolution, and in their past service had passed through fire and brimstone, would not lay them down or halt in the contest until the last enemy had grounded his arms and bowed in submission to the Union.

THE FIELD AND STAFF.

Lieutenant Colonel Henry E. Jones.................Commander
Dr. P. M. McFarland........ ....Assistant Surgeon

Lieutenant Benjamin Roberts (Promoted) .... Adjutant
Lieutenant Moses Rife .... Quartermaster
Stephen B. Thoburn (Promoted) .... Sergeant-Major
John H. Morris (Discharged)................... Sergeant-Major
William K. Sturgill .... Sergeant-Major
Thomas J. Williams (Promoted) .... Quartermaster Sergeant
John Bevan .... Quartermaster Sergeant
John C. Gross .... Commissary Sergeant
John F. McGrew .... Hospital Steward

Company A of the battalion was composed of the following veterans: Of old Company A, 42 men; of old Company D, 21 men; of old Company F, 16 men; a total of 79 men, as follows:

Benjamin Roberts .... Captain
John K. Combs .... First Lieutenant
Stephen B. Thoburn .... Second Lieutenant
John C. Burk.................... First Sergeant of Company F
James C. Bingham................... Sergeant of Company D
Jesse Wood........................... Sergeant of Company D
Michael Shelton...................... Sergeant of Company A
Hiram McCarley...................... Corporal of Company A
Brittain D. Fry...................... Corporal of Company F
William Bacon....................... Corporal of Company D
Thomas Fee.......................... Corporal of Company A
Henry Hunsucker..................... Corporal of Company A
Gideon M. Hubbard................... Corporal of Company F
David W. Jones...................... Corporal of Company A
Thomas Stafford..................... Corporal of Company A
E. A. Bridwell...................... Musician of Company D

Henry C. Edgington................Wagoner of Company D
Allen, Martin G......................Private of Company A
Allison, Henry D.....................Private of Company A
Bettis, William......................Private of Company A
Bollman, Joseph.....................Private of Company A
Clafflin, John ....Private of Company A
Colly, Samuel........................Private of Company A
Denny, Henry L......................Private of Company A
Farrar, James........................Private of Company A
Gould, Isaac.........................Private of Company A
Hill, Joseph.........................Private of Company A
Hopkins, Matthew....................Private of Company A
Johnson, Elias......................Private of Company A
Jones, Lewis........................Private of Company A
Jones, William D....................Private of Company A
Jones, Thomas W....................Private of Company A
Jones, John D.......................Private of Company A
Lodge, George W....................Private of Company A
Lodge, John.........................Private of Company A
Louks, William A....................Private of Company A
McPhail, Andrew J..................Private of Company A
Manring, William J.................Private of Company A
Manring, Lewis A...................Private of Company A
Morris, James.......................Private of Company A
Norman, John.......................Private of Company A
Owenz, John........................Private of Company A
Ray, George W......................Private of Company A
Reesman, William N................Private of Company A

Slack, Thomas J..........................Private of Company A
Sturgill, James E........................ Private of Company A
Sturgill, Henry H........................Private of Company A
Ward, Craton.............................Private of Company A
White, Thomas............................Private of Company A
Williams, David R........................Private of Company A
Wintersteen, John Q......................Private of Company A
Bacon, William G.........................Private of Company D
Bacon, William...........................Private of Company D
Badger, William..........................Private of Company D
Clifford, Morgan.........................Private of Company D
Cross, Thomas L..........................Private of Company D
Cross, Wilson............................Private of Company D
Golliger, John...........................Private of Company D
Keyser, Abner............................Private of Company D
Lamb, Benoni.............................Private of Company D
Martin, Charles S........................Private of Company D
Odle, James..............................Private of Company D
Page, Lorenzo D..........................Private of Company D
Simpson, William H. H....................Private of Company D
Snively, John............................Private of Company D
Veach, Francis...........................Private of Company D
Venatti, Hezekiah........................Private of Company D
Carrothers, James........................Private of Company F
Cool, William H..........................Private of Company F
Fout, Jasper.............................Private of Company F
Henry, John..............................Private of Company F
Hedgmier, Fred...........................Private of Company F

Jones, Uriah ....Private of Company F
Joice, Michael ....Private of Company F
Lair, William................................Private of Company F
Lingenfelter, Christopher ....Private of Company F
Lord, Ezra F.................................Private of Company F
Martin, Hiram ....Private of Company F
Spencer, Charles ....Private of Company F
Sturgill, William R........................Private of Company F
Truman, Joseph ....Private of Company F

Company B of the battalion was composed of the following veterans: Of old Company B, 3 men; of old Company E, 30 men; of old Company G, 25 men; of old Company H, 17 men; a total of 75 men, as follows:

James C. Stimmell........................Captain of Company G
Thomas J. Williams......................First Lieutenant of Company C
David W. James...........................First Sergeant of Company E
David E. Jones.............................Sergeant of Company E
Lorenzo D. Dalrymple...................Sergeant of Company E
Nicholas D. Main..........................Sergeant of Company G
Daniel L. Bondurant......................Sergeant of Company G
Nathan M. Kent ....Sergeant of Company G
Peter Brown.................................Sergeant of Company H
Robert M. Fulton..........................Corporal of Company E
George Grindley...........................Corporal of Company E
Charles H. Bing............................Corporal of Company E
William Hughes ....Corporal of Company E
Thomas J. Williams ....Corporal of Company E
James Rees ....Corporal of Company E

Francis M. Seth	Corporal of Company G
Calvin McKnight	Corporal of Company H
Henry C. Marshall	Corporal of Company G
Samuel Nickel	Corporal of Company B
Samuel Clinger	Wagoner of Company E
Herder, Jacob	Private of Company B
Reininger, George	Private of Company B
Bing, Joseph M.	Private of Company E
Bing, Joseph E.	Private of Company E
Daniels, David	Private of Company E
Davis, Charles H.	Private of Company E
Evans, Evan E.	Private of Company E
Evans, John E.	Private of Company E
Evans, Evan O.	Private of Company E
Griffith, Rees	Private of Company E
Hickson, Benjamin	Private of Company E
Hughes, George	Private of Company E
Hughes, James	Private of Company E
James, Alfred, Jr.	Private of Company E
Jones, Thomas J.	Private of Company E
Jones, Dennis	Private of Company E
Logue, Ellis	Private of Company E
Radcliff, William H.	Private of Company E
Roush, Newton J.	Private of Company E
Thomas, Rees	Private of Company E
Thomas, Thomas D.	Private of Company E
Williams, Daniel	Private of Company E
Allen, William	Private of Company G

Baker, Charles H.	Private of Company G
Brown, William C.	Private of Company G
Carpenter, Aaron	Private of Company G
Chaffin, George W.	Private of Company G
Comer, Lewis	Private of Company G
Crabtree, Gillen	Private of Company G
Crabtree, Stephen	Private of Company G
Cross, Thomas	Private of Company G
Fasterman, William	Private of Company G
Giles, Dennis	Private of Company G
Giles, Thomas C.	Private of Company C
McCallister George W.	Private of Company G
Morgan, Samuel	Private of Company G
Oberly, Benjamin B.	Private of Company G
Pfuhler, John	Private of Company G
Potts, Hezekiah J.	Private of Company G
Rockwell, John	Private of Company G
Story, Frank	Private of Company G
Titus, John C.	Private of Company G
Carr, William	Private of Company H
Coffman, John	Private of Company H
McIntyre, George W.	Private of Company H
McKeever, Daniel	Private of Company H
McKnight, James	Private of Company H
Newlan, Adam	Private of Company H
Perry, James	Private of Company H
Perry, Jacob	Private of Company H
Phillips, Andrew	Private of Company H

Salliday, George W............ ....Private of Company H
Sanders, Benjamin ....Private of Company H
Sickles, Lafayette...... ....Private of Company H
Spetznagle, Henry ....Private of Company H
Stevenson, Thomas K.... ....Private of Company H
Trailor, Benjamin ....Private of Company H

Company C of the battalion was composed of the following veterans: Of old Company C, 26 men; of old Company I, 21 men; of old Company K, 26 men; a total of 73 men.

William G. Snyder .... Captain
Christian H. Shaefer................ .... First Lieutenant
Harvey N. Bridwell........................ Second Lieutenant
Abram Hibbens................... First Sergeant of Company I
Andrew S. Drennen ....Sergeant of Company C
Samuel Goheen ....Sergeant of Company K
William H. McLaughlin ....Sergeant of Company I
David F. Radcliff.... ....Sergeant of Company K
William H. Wait......... ....Sergeant of Company K
Martin J. Adams...... ....Corporal of Company C
John J. Bussey....... ....Corporal of Company K
Thomas D. Davis.... ....Corporal of Company C
James C. Harper........ ....Corporal of Company K
Luther C. High ....Corporal of Company K
Lafayette Holmes.... ....Corporal of Company K
Thomas S. Jones......... ....Corporal of Company C
Adam Siemon ....Corporal of Company I
George M. Gordy ....Musician of Company K
George W. Lowery......... ....Musician of Company K

Cochran, John J...................Private of Company C
Dalrymple, Smith ....Private of Company C
Davis, Thomas E...................Private of Company C
Davis, Rees.......................Private of Company C
Davis, William D..................Private of Company C
Edwards, Evan ....Private of Company C
Edwards, David E..................Private of Company C
Evans, Daniel J...................Private of Company C
Evans, William T..................Private of Company C
Goudy, Edward ....Private of Company C
Hall, James C.....................Private of Company C
Hunley, Joseph....................Private of Company C
Hunter, Grant B...................Private of Company C
Jones, Evan E.....................Private of Company E
Jones, Daniel.....................Private of Company C
Jones, William J..................Private of Company C
Lewis, Joshua ....Private of Company C
Morris, William ....Private of Company C
Morris, Thomas J..................Private of Company C
Roberts, Moses ....Private of Company C
Samuel, William...................Private of Company C
Schilichter, Christian ....Private of Company C
Williams, John ....Private of Company C
Alexander, Zach T.................Private of Company I
Bland, George H...................Private of Company I
Black, Oscar C ....Private of Company I
Carey, Philip ....Private of Company I
Dolby, James A....................Private of Company I

Desmond, John ....Private of Company I
Ellis, Stephen R................Private of Company I
Hatfield, William ....Private of Company I
Hahn, Lawrence ....Private of Company I
O'Reilly, Martin ....Private of Company I
Sherwood, Jacob................Private of Company I
Sutherland, David ....Private of Company I
Springer, Henry N...............Private of Company I
Stewart, George M..............Private of Company I
Thacker, Fountain ....Private of Company I
Tripp, George ....Private of Company I
Wilson Sylvester ....Private of Company I
Wilson, William A...............Private of Company I
Bennett, Hosea B................Private of Company K
Bowen, William ....Private of Company K
Brooks, John J..................Private of Company K
Burt, Thomas J. ....Private of Company K
Corrill, Thomas J...............Private of Company K
Corrill, Elias ....Private of Company K
Davis, Jonathan ....Private of Company K
Gates, David...................Private of Company K
Knowland, Lutitius ....Private of Company K
Leniger, William ....Private of Company K
Scott, Peter....................Private of Company K
Simer, Andrew J. P.............Private of Company K
Thompson, John ....Private of Company K
Walker, James ....Private of Company K
White, Jacob ....Private of Company K

Yeley, Benjamin ....Private of Company K
Lloyd, Peter ....Private of Company H

On December 3, 1864, Captain L. M. Willets and Lieutenant O. H. Wadsworth reported to us with a company of one-year men, and were assigned to our battalion for duty. They were designated as Company D of the battalion, and the following men were detached for duty in said company, viz:

James Vandervort ....First Lieutenant from Company C
Thomas S. Bennett.... ....First Sergeant from Company G
Thomas H. Cox......... ....Sergeant from Company D
George W. Neff... ....Sergeant from Company F
James U. Pease ....Sergeant from Company F
Samuel L. Wood ....Sergeant from Company D
George W. Cox......... ....Sergeant from Company F
Azariah Arthur ....Corporal from Company D
James Anderson ....Corporal from Company D
John Barr ....Corporal from Company D
Robert Bowles.... ....Corporal from Company F
James Halliday ....Corporal from Company F
James Storer ....Corporal from Company D
William Bradfield ....Private from Company D
Henderson Sturgeon ....Private from Company D
James Sturgeon.... ....Private from Company D

By examining the roster of the regiments it can be seen what became of the veterans, as well also the members of the companies; whether their service was for a long or short period of time.

CHAPTER XIII.

OUR SERVICES IN NEW ORLEANS ETC.

On November 10, 1864, the men in Company D who did not re-enlist as veterans were mustered out, and on the 14th, Captain W. B. Williams of Company C was discharged by order of the war department. He was one of the most competent officers of the regiment, and not excelled by any. He was greatly interested in his men, watchful for their comfort, and energetic in securing the best of everything that could be obtained for them. He was strict in discipline, painstaking in drill. He had confidence in his company and they had the greatest confidence in him as their commander. On the 15th Captain Thomas W. Kinney of Company H, a fine young officer, was mustered out at the expiration of his term of service. November 17 we received news of the re-election of President Lincoln, and about November 23 there was some excitement on account of another outbreak of smallpox in the regiment. Christmas came on at usual time, but our finances were extremely low, so much so that we could not buy presents or give banquets, and though it rained and was dismal outside, in our quarters it was dry and the boys were cheerful in spite of all. December 26 news came of General Thomas' great victory at Nashville; also of the capture of Fort McAllister by General Sherman's army, and on the 31st news came of the fall of Savannah, Ga. January 5, 1865, the regiment received four months' pay. During February a great number of troops arrived from up the river.

February 28 is known as Montegro day. Many went around in masks and dressed in fancy and foolish costumes. The month of March passed with nothing but camp and patrol duties. A great deal of rain fell and the Mississippi was high.

April 8, 1865, news reached us of the fall of Richmond, Va.,

and on the 15th two hundred guns were fired in honor of our recent victories. April 19 the intelligence of the atrocious murder of President Lincoln came.

In New Orleans, on the 22d of April, a great meeting was held, General Banks, General Hulbert and others speaking of the great and sore calamity the country had sustained by the cruel assassination of President Lincoln.

April 24 the rebel gunboat Webb came out of the Red river in an attempt to escape to the Gulf of Mexico. Our quarters at this time were in a large salt warehouse on the river bank. We heard three cannon shots from up stream, which caused us to flock out on the wharf. Presently the Webb came around the bend under a full head of steam. There were several of our war vessels anchored in the river, and we could see that they were making every effort in getting ready for action. About fifty yards from our wharf the powder ship Fearnaught was anchored. The Webb ran as close as it dared in an attempt to attach a torpedo to the Fearnaught and blow her up and scatter death and destruction on every hand, but happily it failed to hit the powder ship. This was another lucky escape for us. Our men-of-war were soon in hot pursuit of the Webb, and forced her crew to run the ram ashore some twenty-eight miles down the river, where they set the Webb on fire and took to the swamps. The river continued very high, and on the 28th a crevasse in the levee three or four miles below Algiers required our attention, and the citizens also were pressed into work to keep it from spreading too much. About this time a squad of men from our battalion were placed upon detached duty to guard the Sparks plantation, up opposite Carrollton, of which the authorities had taken control. Sergeant Peter Brown, Corporals James M. Halliday and James Reed and Private William Hahn and some eight or ten other men composed this detachment. While there they suffered greatly with the terrible break-bone fever, and if any of them survive they feel its effect still.

On April 30 Company B was ordered to guard an officers' prison at No. 21 Rampart street, in New Orleans. May 13 Captain Stimmell was ordered to report to the regiment with the company, but

leaving seventeen men, two Corporals, one Sergeant and myself as Lieutenant, in charge of the prison. On May 28, 1865, our boys, who were captured on the Red river fiasco of 1864, returned from the rebel prison at Tyler, Texas, after more than a year of prison life. June 6 Colonel Smith, Inspector General, and Captain Southwick, inspected the prison. On June 14, 1865, the officers of our battalion were ordered before a board for examination as to qualifications, etc., for commissions in the regular army. The examiners, after consulting Colonel Jones, requested me to remain after the others were dismissed, and upon consultation they informed me that they would recommend my promotion as First Lieutenant in the regular army; but owing to the state of my health I felt it best to decline the honor. June 15 we were ordered to turn our prisoners to the police jail and return to the regiment. On June 16 the battalion was inspected by Colonel Smith of department headquarters. On the 20th Colonel Jones marched the battalion through the streets of Algiers for exercise, and as usual we showed up well. June 23 a large number of troops passed down to Camp Chalmette. July, 1865, was a real hot month, and we were on duty of some kind or other every other day. On the 27th Captain Southwick of headquarters staff inspected the battalion. He called Company B out to see how they could drill, and they were able to and did make a good impression. August 4 a request came that our battalion be consolidated with the Seventy-seventh O. V. I., and on the 17th our battalion was again inspected by Captain Southwick.

During September, 1865, it rained every day, some days a half a dozen hard showers. On September 11 we received four months' pay, and fully four-fifths of our battalion were down sick with the break-bone fever, which left many of them wrecks for life. Dr. McFarland, Captain Willets and Lieutenant Vandivort were the only officers able to be up and around in our battalion.

October 10, 1865, we held an election for our state ticket, **and** on the 13th Companies A, B and C were ordered to move to the Anchor Cotton Press in New Orleans, and Company D to remain on duty in Algiers. October 29 the battalion was inspected by

Major Loring. At this time the following notice appeared in the New Orleans Times:

"To the Editor of the New Orleans Times: Learning that the Fifty-sixth Ohio Veteran Volunteer Infantry were about leaving Algiers to be stationed in New Orleans, there to act in conjunction with the First United States Infantry, we of this town can not permit them to take their departure without testifying our approval of the excellent discipline and conduct of their officers and men while stationed amongst us. It is now some eleven months since Colonel Henry E. Jones and his regiment assumed control of this post, and during that time they have been on the qui vive to prevent any and all unlawful acts that might be attempted by the thousands of troops that have passed through here to their various destinations. Colonel Jones has also placed the civil authorities under many obligations to him, for his prompt and energetic co-operation with them in all matters pertaining to the police and sanitary condition of the right bank of this parish. During the high waters of the last season the gallant Fifty-sixth did yeoman service in stopping the crevasses at McDonoghville and at McGhee's Aurora plantation. At the latter place, were it not for their timely assistance (working day and night), the whole lower coast to Fort Jackson would have been inundated, and many thousands of dollars worth of property been destroyed thereby. In parting with us we sincerely hope the noble 'Buckeye' boys may soon have the pleasure of seeing home again, and bear from us the best of feeling for their future happiness, including all, from the handsome Colonel to the humblest private in the regiment."

"Algiers, October 19, 1865.   ALGERINES."

November 6, 1865, being election day, a detail of twenty men under my command was sent to Algiers to preserve order. The day passed without any serious disturbance. On the 19th a number of us went to hear the celebrated Southern Presbyterian preacher, Dr. Palmer, and on December 22, 1865, Company D was mustered out. December 3 we moved our quarters to the Lower Steam Cotton Press, in the southern part of the city. There we were associated with the First New Orleans Infantry. This was a

regiment of Union men, recruited in the city for duty therein. On December 5, being in charge of the patrol, it became a part of our duty to visit Dan Rice's celebrated circus. The great showman gave us a hearty welcome. Being a true and loyal man, he was glad to see Union soldiers at all times. Christmas day was rather exciting, and we were kept busy in quelling riots between the whites and the blacks; in fact the larger part of our work for months, outside of patrol duty, was in preserving order between these two elements.

December 28, 1865, in charge of a guard, I was detailed to go to Galveston, Texas, to take charge of five hundred recruits from the east for the Fourth and Sixth United States Cavalry, then on duty in Texas. We went over on the steamship St. Mary. The weather was fine and our experience pleasant. We reached Galveston at 9 a. m. on December 30, 1865. Here we were relieved of our recruits by the Forty-eighth O. V. I. January 2, 1866, we left Galveston for New Orleans on the steamship George Peabody. This was a noted ship, having endured many storms and hardships since the war began, but at this time was badly in need of repair. Her pumps were running to keep the water out of her while lying at the dock, on account of her leaking so badly. The vessel had a number of passengers on board for New Orleans. The weather was fine after leaving Galveston until about 9 p. m. of January 3, when there swooped down upon us a mighty storm of wind, the dreaded northwester. The waves seemed to run mountain high. The stoves, tables and chairs broke from their fastenings in the cabin, adding to the confusion of the elements. It was hard work to keep from being dashed about, and many felt that the chances for escape were extremely doubtful. It was curious to observe the action of different individuals under this dreadful trial. Some prayed loud and long; some swore and many cried; in fact some of them did not know what they were doing. I managed to crawl up to the head of the stairs and got a sight of the tempest. The captain informed me that things looked serious and the danger was great, but that he hoped to land us safely but a little behind time. Being anxious about my comrades, who in days past had shared with me so many

dangers, I was glad to notice that on this trying occasion they were doing all they could to encourage the panic-stricken ones, and were taking this trial of their courage without any visible show of fear. On January 4, 1866, we crossed the bar at the mouth of the Mississippi river at 4 a. m., and reached New Orleans at 7 p. m. January 10, 1866, Company B, under my command, was ordered to Greenville, a short distance from the city, to put down a riot between the whites and blacks, which we had no great trouble in settling. We camped on the river bank in tents and remained there on duty until January 21, when we returned to the battalion and took up regular patrol duty again.

February 6, Lieutenant M. Rife, one of our best officers, was mustered out, and on the 8th I received a commission as First Lieutenant, having commanded the company practically from the time of my promotion as Second Lieutenant.

March 4, 1866, was Sunday, and the day of the month and year on which the fire department of the city made its annual parade. With numerous bands added to their great number, they made an animated and imposing display. There was a standing order in that department from the time that General Butler commanded, forbidding the playing of the "Bonny Blue Flag" or any rebel tunes by bands or other instruments of music, as it was done in General Butler's time to insult and aggravate the Union troops. This day, as the parade passed up St. Charles street, when opposite our department headquarters, their fancy band played the "Bonny Blue Flag." An order was sent at once to the Provost Marshal's office to send a guard to arrest that band. Being on duty that day, I was ordered to bring them in. We had only about twenty men there, and the officer who brought the order remarked for our encouragement, "They say that there are not enough Union troops in the city to take a man out of that parade." This band had been with the Army of Northern Virginia and seen lots of hard service. Our squad, with loaded muskets and bayonets fixed, marched down to headquarters. The parade was returning and had passed in part on our arrival. We marched out into the street right up to the edge of the parade, and waited for the band to come up. The win-

dows, balconies and streets were packed and crowded with people. General Sheridan and all of headquarters were closely watching the end of this matter. Not a word was spoken until the band came up, when I stepped before them and ordered them to "File left." In a moment they were surrounded by our squad. Not a man opened his mouth in or out of the parade, though they looked savagely at us as the parade passed. We took them to the Provost Marshal at once and turned them over to him. As far as it extended this was a fine display of the power of the government behind its authorized agents; for what could twenty veteran soldiers have done with the hundreds in that parade, and nearly all of them armed? One thing was sure, not a comrade in that squad hesitated to count the cost for a moment.

On the 17th day of March, 1866, the following order and request were received at our headquarters and a copy given to me, which is as follows:

"State of Louisiana, Executive Department.
"New Orleans, March 17, 1866.
"Brevet Major General T. W. Sherman, Commanding Eastern District of Louisiana:

"General—As some difficulties have arisen in the way of the inauguration of city officers on Monday next, and as I am anxious that no occasion shall be given for any possible collision between the police and the friends of officers-elect in or about the Municipal Hall, I request you to place in charge of that building from Monday morning at 6 a. m. until their service can be dispensed with, a guard of ten men. One to remain at each entrance, six in the interior for relief, to assist the civil power in maintaining the public peace. I have the honor to be, General, your obedient servant,

"J. MADISON WELLS,
"Governor of Louisiana."

Indorse: Official copy confidentially furnished the officer in charge of the detail directed to report to His Excellency, J. Madison Wells, Governor Louisiana.

By order of Brevet Major General Sherman.

Z. K. WOOD, Lieut. A. A. G.

Headquarters Eastern District of Louisiana,
New Orleans, La., March 18, 1866.

Commanding Officer Levee Steam Press Stables: Sir—You will detail from your command a good, faithful and trusty Lieutenant, with ten men, to be selected by you, with directions to report for duty at 6 a. m. tomorrow, at the City Hall, to His Excellency, J. Madison Wells, Governor of Louisiana, or any other official he may have selected, and to carry out the orders given him. The men will be provided with their dinners.

By order of
BREVET MAJOR GENERAL T. W. SHERMAN.
Z. K. Wood, Lieutenant and A. D. C., A. A. A. G. Indorsed.

Headquarters U. S. Forces, Levee Steam Press Stables,
New Orleans, March 18, 1866.

Respectfully referred to First Lieutenant Thomas J. Williams, Company B, Fifty-sixth Ohio Veteran Volunteers, who will report with the within detail as herein directed.

By order of
LIEUTENANT COLONEL TISDALE.
P. DALEY, Second Lieutenant and Acting Post Adjutant.

Our detail reported promptly on time. The entrances were guarded, and though a great crowd of people surged about the building, there was no disturbance. We were all very busy these days; the men on duty 24 out of 48 hours, and some of the officers were busy on boards of survey and other special duties.

March 23, 1866, on returning from 24 hours' patrol duty, I was ordered to take my Company to the Parish Prison to attend a military execution. In prompt and good time we reached the prison, which was a large and strong institution of the kind. On the inside was an open court, and the cells from all sides opened into it. The Company entered and was found facing the front. Four men out of our ranks were selected to carry out the execution. Their muskets were taken by the Provost Marshal. Three were loaded with balls and one with a blank cartridge, and then returned to them. There was a large number of spectators present. The corridors of the second story being crowded, all anxious to witness

the tragedy. The prisoner was brought out and placed at the foot of his coffin. He was calm and apparently cool. On his breast was a large black cross, and with a smile on his face he confronted instant death with as brave a spirit as any man could. The command, "Ready! Aim! Fire!" was given, and the report was like one musket, the victim falling into his coffin. Two balls went through his heart and one through his brain, and the cross on his breast was shattered into fragments.

Glancing along the line and at the crowd of spectators, at the pause before the command "Fire!" I feel safe in saying that not more than one in four looked at the prisoner when the command "Fire!" was given. The comrades who carried out this execution had each good reason to think that his musket contained the blank cartridge. The man executed was paying the penalty for taking the life of a fellow comrade.

They belonged to the Eighty-first United States Colored Troops. This regiment was stationed in the city. It was a common report that the officers of this regiment, who were white men, were all college graduates. They had an extensive and fine field to select their men from, and they took only the best of the young, strong and active men, and by hard work they had brought them up to a high state of discipline. Many of the highest officers of the country who visited the city pronounced this regiment to be the best drilled of any regiment in the service. We had witnessed, as we passed their quarters on various occasions, as many as twenty of their men bucked and gagged, strung along in a row.

On March 26, 1866, the following order was handed to me:

"Headquarters U. S. Forces, Levee Steam Press Stables,
"New Orleans, La., March 26, 1866.
"Special Order No. 4.
"First Lieutenant Thos. J. Williams, Company B, Fifty-sixth Ohio Veteran Volunteers, and Second Lieutenant Frank E. Haggett, Company F, First New Orleans Volunteers, will proceed immediately with their respective companies to Carrrollton, La. The senior officer will report at once to Lieutenant Zeno K. Wood,

A. A. A. General, headquarters East District of Louisiana, for instructions. By order of

"LIEUT. COL. E. TISDALE, Com'g U. S. Forces.

"P. DALEY, Second Lieutenant and Acting Post Adjutant."

On reporting to Lieutenant Wood he directed us to proceed to Carrollton, La., a small town six miles above New Orleans. Our orders were to put an end to a riot then going on there between the white and colored people. We reached there in a short time and found that the trouble was over and had been greatly exaggerated. We remained there over night, and until 3 p. m. of the 27th, when I received the following order:

"Headquarters Eastern District of Louisiana,
"New Orleans, March 27, 1866.

Commanding Officer, Detachment 1, New Orleans Volunteers and Fifty-sixth Ohio Volunteers, Carrollton: Sir—You will at once proceed to this city and report your command to the commanding officer at the Levee Steam Press Stables.

"By order of

"BREVET MAJOR GENERAL SHERMAN.

"Z. K. WOOD, Lieutenant A. A. G."

In obedience to the order we reported at our barracks late that afternoon.

CHAPTER XIV.

THE REGIMENT MUSTERED OUT AND RETURNED HOME, AND A LIST OF THE SURVIVORS AND THEIR POSTOFFICE ADDRESS.

Our patrol duty was very heavy in these days of April, and the rain fell in torrents nearly every day, the streets being flooded in many places, and there was more or less indication that we would be mustered out of the service soon.

While the grateful crowds were showering his subordinates with bouquets, as they rode in the grand parade through the streets of Washington, General Sheridan himself was hastening to a remote region, in obedience to the order requiring him to look after the surrender in the Southwest, and we often saw him while on patrol duty about the city. About this time, while on patrol duty at the St. Charles Theater, while looking in a window at the audience gathering, General Sheridan came up to the window and entered into conversation with me. He was in un-dress uniform, but I was well aware who was talking to me.

On April 17, 1866, we received the following order:

"Headquarters Department of Louisiana,
"New Orleans, La., April 16, 1866.
"Special Order No. 85:

"Extract 2.—Pursuant to instructions from headquarters, Military Division of the Gulf, of this date, the Fifty-sixth Ohio Veteran Volunteers will be immediately mustered out of service in this city, as an entire organization, its service being no longer required. All detached officers and enlisted men of this regiment are hereby relieved, and will rejoin their respective companies without further orders. Immediately upon muster out, as above, the regiment will proceed to Columbus, Ohio (reporting to the chief mustering officer of the State), for payment and final discharge. All

public property (except colors, arms and equipage necessary en route) will be turned over to the proper staff departments in this city. Captain A. McAllister, Commissary of Musters, Department of Louisiana, is charged with the execution of this order, so far as relates to his Department. The Quartermaster's Department will furnish the necessary transportation.

"By order of
"MAJOR GENERAL E. R. CANBY.
"WICKHAM HOFFMAN, Assistant Adjutant General.
"Official Nathaniel Burbank, First Lieutenant, Acting Assistant General."

The following notice appeared in one of the New Orleans papers at this time:

"THE FIFTY-SIXTH OHIO REGIMENT.

"This organization, as previously noticed, is about to be mustered out of the service, and the officers and men are in high spirits at the prospects of soon again visiting home and friends after their long absence.

"The Fifty-sixth was organized by Colonel Peter Kinney, in October, 1861, at Portsmouth, Ohio, and left home with 896 men. During the campaigns in the West, which followed, Colonel W. H. Raynor took command, and the regiment recruited in numbers some 200 men. After the fall of Vicksburg the regiment came to New Orleans. A large proportion of the members then remaining re-enlisted as veterans, and Lieutenant Colonel Henry E. Jones was promoted to the command. Ever since that time the regiment has remained in and around the Crescent City, and we have never known a more orderly and well behaved body of men.

"The officers have formed many warm, and, we trust, lasting friendships among our citizens. There are now left of the Fifty-sixth 180 men and 10 commissioned officers, the latter being: Lieutenant Colonel Henry E. Jones, Assistant Surgeon P. M. McFarland, Captains Benj. Roberts, James C. Stimmell, William G. Snyder, First Lieutenants John R. Combs, Thomas J. Williams, C. H. Shaefer, Second Lieutenants Stephen B. Thoburn and H. N. Bridwell.

"By order of General Sheridan, the names of the following battles are to be inscribed upon regimental banners: Pittsburg Landing, Siege of Corinth, Port Gibson, Champion's Hill, Siege of Vicksburg, Jackson, Carrion Crow Bayou, Sabine Cross Roads, Monnett's Ferry and Snaggy Point.

"The men will start for home in a few days, and we wish them a very pleasant trip, as well as a welcome home, that will equal their brightest anticipations."

For the next few days we were very busy preparing muster-out rolls, and turning over our camp equipage, etc. April 25, 1866, at 10 o'clock a. m., we were all mustered out after over four and a half years of continuous service. On the 26th we went aboard the steamboat Mary E. Forsyth, bound up the Mississippi, for our northern homes, leaving the city at 5 p. m. We passed Natchez, Miss., where we had formerly camped at daylight on the 28th, and we passed Vicksburg just at dark. All was quiet at this time, but we could not forget our terrible experience when in the country back of there in 1863.

We passed Helena, Ark., at 10 a. m. of the 30th. We had good reason to remember this place and the hardships endured there. We passed Memphis at 10 a. m., and could not help thinking of our heroic comrades, who were so foully murdered on the steamboat Sultana, above this city, in 1865. They were most all prisoners, having been long confined at Andersonville and other prisons.

There was this difference between this trip and our former ones. We did not have to keep a constant watch lest we be fired into at every turn. We had a pleasant trip, and reached Cairo, Ills., on May 2, 1866, early in the morning. There was a cold northwest wind blowing, which penetrated through our lightweight clothing, and from our long service in the extreme south we were in poor condition to withstand the cold blasts from the north.

We left Cairo at 4 p. m. of May 2, reached Mattoon, Ills., at 11 a. m., and Indianapolis at 11 p. m. of the 3d, and arrived at

Columbus, O., on the 4th in the afternoon. May 5, 1866, we were paid off for the last time, and early on the morning of the 6th the most of us left for home, by way of Cincinnati, Ohio, and left on the 7th for Portsmouth on the steamboat W. F. Curtis.

We reached Portsmouth on the afternoon of the 8th of May, 1866. There the ranks dissolved into the moving tide of civil life, never more to be re-united, and the Fifty-sixth Ohio Veteran Volunteers were only a memory. It was like sundering family ties. Having been so long together, a strong attachment had grown up between the veterans from long associations and mutual dependence and trust, and that feeling of respect and esteem will never be forgotten in this life. In the busy scenes of active life we lost sight of each other for a time, but in later years old memories returned, and our annual reunions brought us together again to rehearse of the days of trial and danger in the great struggle to preserve the Union.

The Fifty-sixth Ohio Veteran Volunteer Infantry can look back with pride as having been a part of that Grand Army that saved the Union and vindicated the right of liberty to endure forever.

The following notice appeared in the State Journal of Columbus, Ohio, of our arrival there:

"THE FIFTY-SIXTH OHIO VETERANS.

"The Fifty-sixth Regiment, Ohio Veteran Volunteers, arrived in the city on Friday afternoon, and reported at Tod Barracks, where the men will be finally discharged and paid.

"The regiment is in command of Lieutenant Colonel Jones and consists now of three companies, numbering present for duty 145 enlisted men in all, and commanded as follows: Company A, Captain Benjamin Roberts; Company B, First Lieutenant Thomas J. Williams; Company C, Captain W. G. Snyder.

"The regiment left New Orleans April 26 on the steamer Mary E. Forsyth, took the cars at Cairo May 2, and arrived here May 4.

56TH OHIO VOLUNTEER INFANTRY.

"The Fifty-sixth was organized at Portsmouth, Ohio, in October, 1861, by Colonel Peter Kinney, and left for the field with 896 men. The regiment joined the Army of the Tennessee before Fort Donaldson, and remained with that division of the Grand Army until August, 1863, participating in the battle of Shiloh, siege of Corinth, the engagements at Port Gibson, Champion's Hill, and taking part in the ever memorable siege of Vicksburg. During this campaign Colonel W. H. Raynor assumed command of the regiment, and it was increased by two hundred recruits. After the fall of Vicksburg the Fifty-sixth was transferred to the Department of the Gulf, and was commanded by Colonel W. H. Raynor until October 27, 1864.

"In February, 1864, a large number of the men re-enlisted as veterans. On the retirement of Colonel Raynor from the service, Lieutenant Colonel Henry E. Jones, the present commanding officer, took charge of the regiment. After active operations ceased the Fifty-sixth was stationed in or near New Orleans, and the papers of that city state that a more orderly or better behaved body of men was not known during the war experience of New Orleans.

"There are now on the rolls 180 enlisted men and 10 commissioned officers, the latter being: Lieutenant Colonel Henry E. Jones, Assistant Surgeon P. M. McFarland, Captains Benjamin Roberts, James C. Stimmell, Wm. G. Snyder, First Lieutenants John R. Combs, Thomas J. Williams, C. H. Shaefer, and Second Lieutenants Stephen B. Thoburn and Harvey N. Bridwell. In addition to those we named above, the names of the following battles are to be inscribed upon the regimental flags: Jackson, Carrion Crow Bayou, Sabine Cross Roads, Monnette's Ferry and Snaggy Point.

"The conductor of the train and the railroad officials declare the Fifty-sixth the most orderly and quiet body of soldiers that has passed over the road. Our testimony so far must be in their favor. These men were on the streets yesterday, orderly and gentlemanly in their deportment. They will without doubt be paid today and leave for their homes."

The following extract is from one of the Portsmouth, O., papers, of the first reunion of any part of the regiment, which was held at Portsmouth, O., Feb. 12, 1867:

"On Tuesday afternoon, at the call of a committee of officers of the above named regiment, eighteen of the line and field officers of the Fifty-sixth O. V. I., together with invited representatives from the press of the city, met at Varner's Hall to celebrate the day the regiment left for the field, and also to organize a permanent association to meet each year so long as two or more of the officers are alive.

"At this reunion there were present: Colonel Peter Kinney, Colonel Sampson E. Varner, Colonel Henry E. Jones, Major C. F. Reiniger, Captain George Wilhelm, Captain J. C. Stimmell, Captain W. G. Snyder, Captain D. B. Lodwick, Captain Thomas Kinney, Lieutenant H. C. Shump, Lieutenant Henry Lantz, Lieutenant Thomas J. Williams, Lieutenant Charles Seifer and Chaplain J. E. Thomas, and three others whose names we do not recollect. The press of the city was represented by D. C. McFarland of the Tribune, James W. Newman of the Times and S. P. Drake of the Republican. The following were chosen as officers for the ensuing year: Colonel Peter Kinney, president; Colonel Henry E. Jones, Secretary, and Colonel S. E. Varner, Captain George Wilhelm and Chaplain J. E. Thomas, standing committee."

This association did not continue long, as owing to the death of some, and the moving away of others, and its exclusive character, it could of course but survive a short time; buit it merged in later years into that noblest association of all, and every member of the regiment without regard to rank.

The last reunion was held at Portsmouth, O., September 20, 1899, at which there were 70 of the comrades present. Twelve comrades were reported as having died the past year. Captain C. Gillilan was re-elected president, Lieutenant T. J. Williams vice president, and Comrade John D. Jones secretary, and after a very pleasant meeting and a free dinner by the good people of Portsmouth, adjournment was had to meet at Portsmouth in 1900.

While the regiment was at home on their veteran furlough, Colonel Varner and the men who did not enlist as veterans were assigned to perform duty in Algiers, La., and the high esteem in which this excellent officer was held by the citizens of that city is clearly set forth in the following letter to a son of Colonel Varner, and in the extracts from the newspaper of this unprecedented act of presenting him a sword, sash, etc., and in so far as is known is the only instance of the kind during the great civil war, and assuredly will be of interest to all:

"Algiers, La., July 11, 1899.

"Mr. J. H. Varner: Dear Sir—Your favor of the 8th received. I appreciate highly your writing to me. I had the honor of presenting the sword and accoutrements to your honored father on behalf of my fellow-citizens of Algiers, in July, 1864. If my memory is correct you will find engraved on the hilt or scabbard of the sword, 'Colonel S. E. Varner, from the Citizens of Orleans Parish, Right Bank,' or some such similar inscription. Upon my desk lies now a little Algiers newspaper of 1864, with the following:

" 'Military and Civil Directory of the Officials in Algiers.

" 'S. E. Varner, Lieutenant Colonel Commanding Post.

" 'A. Powell, Captain and Provost Marshal.

" 'E. A. Morse (Eighth Vermont), Captain and A. Q. M.

" 'Wm. H. Seymour, Justice of the Peace and President of the Town Council," etc., etc.

"Our official duties brought your father and myself oft together. He was a genial gentleman, and one I loved to know. The sword presentation I believe to be without parallel during the whole civil war; the first case of where the people had been conquered, arose en masse and honored their conqueror. Only a few months before our acquaintance I was a southern soldier, and your dear father knew it—it mattered not.

" 'The blue and the gray are the colors of God,
    They are seen in the sky at even,
And many a noble, gallant soul,
    Has found them passports to heaven.'

"It has been my fortune to meet down here near the gulf, since then, Grant, Sheridan, Garfield and other noted men from your section, but I found none more gentle, kind or truer than your sire. I have often thought of him, and hoped to have the pleasure of meeting him again, but now, like Stonewall Jackson, his spirit voices, 'Come, let us cross over the river, and rest in the shade of the trees.'

"I hope to have the pleasure of meeting you some time during the course of my summer vacation, but if I do not, and you visit our dear old New Orleans, hunt me up. I will send to your address some printed matter for sister to place with the sword and accoutrements. Yours truly, (Signed.) W. H. SEYMOUR."

Note.—The above mentioned sword is now in the possession of Clay Varner Sanford, grandson of Colonel Sampson E. Varner.

(From the New Orleans True Delta, July 1, 1864.)
"COMPLIMENT TO LIEUT. COL. S. E. VARNER — SWORD PRESENTATION AT ALGIERS.

"Yesterday afternoon, when in search of quietness and recreation, we had ourselves transported to the opposite side of the river, and intended to enjoy the breeze across Father Mississippi and a stroll on the grounds where in time of yore the cricket matches were played. Eventually we found that a portion of the ground in the rear of the city was covered with tents. We awakened to the actual state of the country, and were trying the compass to get out of the range of the guns and any accidental smell of gunpowder, but we tacked about, as nautical men say, when we saw strings of civilians wending their way to that same tented field. We joined them, and had a highly intellectual feast and enjoyed ourselves hugely. Judge Seymour presented a sword and accoutrements to Colonel Varner on behalf of the citizens of Gretna, who had just learned that the Colonel was on the eve of departure under orders, as a token of respect. We give the speeches verbatim:

"'Colonel, learning that you were on the eve of your departure to your own native home in Ohio, we have assembled here to say

a few words at parting. A large number of the residents of Algiers have done me the honor to select me as their spokesman on this occasion, deeming that their civil magistrate was the proper person to represent them. It is an honor, Colonel, of which I assure you I indeed feel proud. When I look around me, and see others older in years and in wisdom and more versed in the orator's art, the honor then I feel more deeply.

"'It is now, sir, some four months since the citizens of Algiers formed your acquaintance. Since that time the many obligations you have placed us under, by the faithful performance of your many arduous duties, the valuable assistance you have at all times rendered the civil officers of the parish, behooves us to make suitable acknowledgment of your kindness.

"'For this purpose, Colonel, we are assembled together—an occasion which we will often revert to with manifold pleasure, and one that will indeed be 'a bright spot in our memory's waste,' in future time, when years have passed away. Your mind may perhaps revert to our bright, sunny land, and when it does, think of 'Auld Lang Syne,' and give one stray thought to those who are gathered here to do you honor and to praise. Accept this sword, sash and accoutrements from us, believing them to be a proper gift for a soldier.

"'We place this sword in your possession, Colonel, with the assurance that it never will be drawn without just cause or sheathed without honor, and that its bright blade will never be dimmed by a wrong act of yours.

"'In conclusion, Colonel, allow us also to return our thanks to the gentlemanly and ever courteous officers of your battalion; it is owing to their kind guidance that the men of your command have made so many friends amongst us; and when the day arrives that our bright star spangled banner will again float over our once united, happy land, and our 'wayward sisters' are once more gathered under its beautiful folds,

"'United in spirit, in heart and in song,'
may we not hope to welcome amongst our best citizens the officers and men that were of 'Varner's Battalion?'"

"'Judge Seymour, I accept this magnificent present from a portion of the loyal citizens of Algiers with heartfelt thanks, not that I believe it is a compliment to me alone, but as a token of esteem to the officers and men of this battalion, who have so ably assisted me in carrying out my orders while stationed here. We have simply tried to do our duty, and this occasion is an evidence that you deem us worthy of your approbation. I am glad it is so. If I live years hence, I shall look back with pleasure to the time I spent among you. Your present I shall cherish, and never while in my possession shall it be drawn against the flag of our beloved country, and in whose ever hand may the arm be palsied that draws it in an unjust cause. I soon have to leave you. No matter how unpleasant, orders must be obeyed. Again I thank you for your beautiful present.'"

In the History of the Lower Scioto Valley, the author of the Military History of Jackson county, Ohio, the Hon. H. C. Miller, a gallant comrade of the Eighty-seventh O. V. I. and the First O. H. A., has this to say of our regiment and its service:

"No other men from Jackson county were called to serve so long at such an extreme southern point of latitude, as the regiment passed much of its term of service in the yellow fever district, in the lower Mississippi, and closed by a long garrison duty at New Orleans, and some of its men were not discharged until April, 1866. The Fifty-sixth was a fighting regiment, and in becoming hardened to extreme southern temperature and drinking water from rivers and bayous along the line of its march, the ranks became decimated so that there was not much left of the organization when the war was over, and the few who reached home deserve to be all placed on the pension roll as disabled veterans."

The comrades of the Fifty-sixth Ohio will all remember the Eleventh Indiana Infantry, with whom we served so long; and the following short extracts taken from an address of Colonel Dan Macauley before the Loyal Legion society at Columbus, Ohio, will, I trust, be appreciated by all who may read them. "The Private Soldier as a Forager" was his subject:

CAPT. C. H. SCHAEFER
See page 144

"Camp life, like poverty, made strange companionships, and when we reflect that every hour had its little history, a thousand items spring up to remind us of the peculiar characters who made us laugh in spite of ourselves throughout the entire war. I have in my mind just such an one. I call him 'Sam,' because it really was his name. Tall, very slim, freckled and homely; a born poacher, and his fame as a 'pirooter'—which meant in his vernacuiar, a 'feller that could forage in twelve languages and nary one of them dead'—and his mania for stealing, were only checked by articles too big or hot or wet to carry. It follows naturally that in pure self-defense I detailed him as 'pirooter in chief' of regimental headquarters mess. Some old copies of a comic paper, the Budget of Fun, were much read in camp, and I quietly enjoyed Sam's quaint use of its name as we marched along one afternoon. As we passed a wagon train he sang out to one of the teamsters: 'Say, don't you want a Budget of Fun?' 'Yes,' was promptly answered. 'Take this one,' said Sam, as he shied his heavy knapsack into the wagon for the teamster to carry. One winter we were on a Mississipi river expedition below Helena, Ark., with a fleet of steamers under General Willis A. Gorman. The men suffered from cold and exposure. Sam had taken a violent dislike to General Gorman, because that gallant gentleman had been forced to join in the famous retreat from the first Bull Run battlefield, and several times during this expedition I learned, when our steamers were sufficiently near, Sam would electrify the General by howling at him most derisively: 'Hello, old Bull Run.' Once he made a mistake. Headquarters steamer was alongside of ours, and on the hurricane deck stood the General himself. Sam was on the lower forward deck of our vessel, and bracing himself he yelled up into Gorman's very teeth: 'Hello, old Bull Run!' The General was too quick for him; he shouted down to the guard: 'Throw that man on my boat here, quick!' And sure enough they did. Sam, sprawling through the air like a frog, was pitched on to Gorman's boat, and during the remainder of the day we could see him, long and lank and lean, tied up like a scarecrow to the jack staff of the steamer. It was a cold and gusty day—for Sam. Along towards night he was chucked back to us, stiff as a wooden Indian. It might be supposed the

great irrepressible was squelched. No, not the least in the world. He gathered himself together and chilled, blue as he was, came up stairs to me in the cabin. 'Colonel,' he groaned, 'I wish you'd have my discharge made out right away.' 'Your discharge! your funeral, you mean.' 'No, my discharge, Colonel. I've been put on Gorman's staff.' While we were stationed at Helena, Ark., on the bank of the Mississippi, the Twenty-second and Twenty-fourth Iowa came to us direct from home. They were a gallant set of men, bright and fresh, and possessed of camp outfits of elegance. They had not experienced the miseries of that destroyer of luxury, lack of transportation, and so were fine sport for plucking by old veterans of very little worldly fear and less conscience. My tent, at that time, was up on top of the levee, and one moonlight night about midnight I was aroused by a mysterious shuffling and whispering near the back of the tent, where the new regiments were encamped. 'Easy, boys!' I could hear in stage whispers. 'Easy, thunder! Do you want to wake the Colonel? Steady, now! All together! Easy! Step light—sh-h-h!' and knowing something contraband would pass the door of my tent in a moment I stepped from bed and waited. Some six or eight of our old soldiers came carefully tip-toeing past, lugging a gigantic messbox, just stolen from one of the Iowa camps, the whole enterprise under the management of its natural guide and friend, the redoubtable Sam. 'Good evening, gentlemen!' I said, affectionately; 'much obliged! set it right down here and go to bed. You look tired! Good-night!' Next morning after guard mounting I sent for Sam and had him call up his fellow villains in front of headquarters. Sam eyed me with eager interest as I sent for a guard and the martial band. His eyes opened wider until at last he burst in an agony of supplication: 'Say, Colonel, wot in thunder you goin' to do to me.' The whole camp, out to see the fun, roared with delight as it was announced that they were to march to the Iowa camp with the messbox, under guard, and with the band at the head. 'You'll probably have a warm reception,' I added, encouragingly. 'Oh, Lord!' he groaned, as he turned white at the prospect. 'Oh! say, Colonel, Lord! You wouldn't do that to me, would you, old pard?' was wrung from

the bottom of his heart. It was a fortunate thing for Sam that the guard was along, for the elastic rogue pretended to be in command of the party, issued orders for not marching to suit him, and when in the Iowa camp made a mock presentation speech, which gave both amusement and offense to the recipients. He claimed he had raised the money by subscription to buy the mess-chest presented, and wound up with the remark that whenever, during our marches yet to come, he should see sitting by the roadside tender-hearted stragglers of this regiment, with the 24 on their caps, it would cheer him, for he would know that there wasn't an enemy or a particle of danger within 24 miles. It is more akin to a sorrowful duty than in any spirit of mere fun, that I have evoked from the eventful past, with its distant sounds of drums and marching, this remembrance of Sam. It was thrust upon me the other day by the following item in the Ohio State Journal. It is headed, 'Instantly killed. Nelsonville, O. Today Samuel Irick of Harrisonburg, Va., while painting the newly erected schoolhouse, fell from a ladder 50 feet, killing him instantly.' And so he met his fate at last. In the great hereafter we know not who shall be advanced nor who shall outrank the other. The Colonel may be the last and the 'pirooter' lead the van. And it is around the humblest and weakest of our fellow soldiers who helped us to save a great republic that we need to stand firmest."

"How fast they fall! the men who saved
   The nation in its hour of strife;
Where battle in its fury raved,
   With death and bloody carnage rife!"

On November 27 a sad message was received by the writer, saying your comrade, Henry D. Allison, died suddenly on Sunday morning, November 26, 1899, and will be buried on Tuesday, November 28, and on that beautiful fall day all that was mortal of our noble and brave comrade was laid to final rest at the old Emery church in Jackson county, O., and the high esteem in which he was held was clearly shown by the large number who attended his funeral. Six of the Fifty-sixth Ohio comrades bore his remains to the grave. The largest number of the Fifty-sixth boys that prob-

ably ever attended a comrade's funeral since the war attended this burial. There were present C. Gillilan, David W. Jones, Thomas Stafford, G. A. Ewing and Wm. A. Louks of Company A; R. W. Thomas, James Rees, John C. Gross, Dennis Jones, Thomas J. Williams, Thomas Jenkins, Evan E. Evans, Robert M. Fulton and W. W. Hughes of Company E, and Evan Edwards and T. J. Williams of Company C. And it was well said by one of the four ministers who participated in the service that he was a loyal man—loyal to his God, loyal to his country, his family and his friends, and it can be truthfully said of him he was indeed and in truth one of God's noblemen.

And we can from our hearts exclaim in the language of Comrade F. C. Searl's noble poem:

"O comrades, who have gone before,
   We watched you glide o'er death's dark tide
And camp upon that brighter shore.
   We soon shall hear our last tattoo,
And, one by one, at minute gun,
   Fold up our tents and camp with you."

All here tonight. Our Grand Commander call thou the roll. And may all survivors of the Fifty-sixth Ohio at least answer one by one, with hand on heart, in the grand salute of salvation, "Here! Here!"

All old soldiers of the Union army who are spared should be thankful that they have been permitted to see a thoroughly reunited country, as proved by our late war with Spain. We have seen with what alacrity the men of the south, who during the great civil war fought our forces on hundreds of battlefields, in this late contest vied with those of the north in rushing to the defense of the stars and stripes. General Lee and General Wheeler, two distinguished officers of the old Confederate armies, have in this late war gained additional honors and are still continuing to do so. The nation's standing has been highly exalted among the nations and rulers of the earth. Never before has it seemed so proud a thing to be an American citizen, and for all this we should be duly thankful to the Giver of all good.

And in conclusion, if my comrades find some pleasure in this brief account of the long and dangerous service performed by the regiment, in which I have endeavored not to dwell too much upon the dangers encountered and hardships endured, I shall consider myself well repaid. But I have failed to get far from the dark side of the picture, as there are so many sad scenes painted on our memories that time can not erase. And it is a matter of pride that the regiment never faltered or failed when called on, but promptly assumed the duty assigned, and whether in camp, on the march, on the picket line or the deadly battlefield, the Fifty-sixth Ohio Volunteer Infantry looks back with satisfaction to duty well done.

Though now there is snow in the hair of all of us, and rust in our joints, and wrinkles in our faces, may it never be truthfully said of this dear land:

> "When danger's rife and war is nigh,
> God and the soldier is all the cry;
> When danger's o'er and wrong is righted,
> God is forgot, the soldier slighted!"

POSTOFFICE ADDRESS AND NAMES OF SURVIVORS OF THE FIFTY-SIXTH OHIO VOLUNTEER INFANTRY.

Colonel William H. Raynor......................Toledo, Ohio
Chaplain J. E. Thomas..........................Orpheus, Ohio
Captain M. Manring..............................McFall, Mo.
Captain W. B. Williams.....................Portsmouth, Ohio
Captain J. H. Evans............................Topeka, Kan.
Captain George Wilhelm.....................Greenville, Miss.
Captain Edwin Kinney.......................Chillicothe, Ohio
Captain William G. Snyder ....Bement, Ill.
Captain Thomas W. Kinney..................Portsmouth, Ohio
Captain Benjamin Roberts.....................Covington, Ky.
Lieutenant C. Gillilan.....................Portsmouth, Ohio

Lieutenant J. J. Markham......................Partridge, Kan.
Lieutenant E. W. Veach........................Kingston, Ohio
Lieutenant Henry Lantz.....................Scioto P. O., Ohio
Lieutenant O. J. DeWolf.......................Fostoria, Ohio
Lieutenant H. C. Shump........................Ashland, Ky.
Lieutenant Thomas J. Williams.................Jackson, Ohio
George Grindley ....Washington, D. C.
Abraham Hibbens ....Kinderhook, Ohio
John E. Bevan..................................Mendon, Ohio
David Boring ....Erin, Tenn.
Fred Held..................................Lilly P. O., Ohio
William H. Wait.............................Iowa City, Iowa
John C. Gross..............................Rio Grande, Ohio
John L. Jones..............................Rio Grande, Ohio
Daniel L. Bondurant.....................Wellmansville, Kan.
Lewis Phillips..............................Springfield, Ohio
George M. Salliday ....Sciotoville, Ohio
George L. Steele..............................Wellston, Ohio
James C. Hall................................Portsmouth, Ohio
James Benner ....Portsmouth, Ohio
William H. Lair..................................Lilly, Ohio
Fred Gram ....Ironton, Ohio
Engelbert Nagle ....Sciotoville, Ohio
Morgan Clifford ....Dennis, Ohio
David W. Jones...............................Thurman, Ohio
George J. Reiniger ....Camba, Ohio
Gillem Crabtree ....Lois, Ohio
Jacob Scheely ....Wheelersburg, Ohio

John G. Brown	Beaver, Ohio
Henry Kuglemen	Portsmouth, Ohio
John C. Titus	Indian Run, Ohio
Hiram Martin	Portsmouth, Ohio
Charles Eagan	Jasper, Ohio
John Norman	Portsmouth, Ohio
Gilbert A. Ewing	Jackson, Ohio
John D. Jones	Portsmouth, Ohio
Martin G. Allen	Rushtown, Ohio
Evan Edwards	Gallia, Ohio
Eli Hartley	Wait, Ohio
Joseph Hill	Sciotoville, Ohio
Jonathan Davis	Wellston, Ohio
Ben Wood	Portsmouth, Ohio
George Jones	Jackson, Ohio
George Meixner	Portsmouth, Ohio
Charles Cooper	Pond Run, Ohio
Azariah C. Arthur	Oak Hill, Ohio
Dustan Jones	Portsmouth, Ohio
James Odle	Friendship, Ohio
John Q. Winterstein	Blue Creek, Ohio
B. F. Bennett	Grenup, Ky.
John Brooks	Jackson, Ohio
Robert Bowles	Stuce P. P., Ohio
Nate Brown	Scioto P. O. Ohio
Robert B. Crawford	Ashland, Ky.
John Dimler	Portsmouth, Ohio
Edward A. Dibble	Celina, Ohio

John Fullerton ....Ryan P. O., Ohio
William W. Hughes ....Oak Hill, Ohio
Fred Hedgmyer ....Abashia, Ohio
F. M. Hudson...................................Wellston, Ohio
John Henry ....Pedro P. O., Ohio
Aaron Hammon ....Peniel P. O., Ohio
Thomas D. Jenkins...........................Holcomb P. O., Ohio
Thomas S. Jones ....Oak Hill, Ohio
Nathan M. Kent...............................Scioto P. O., Ohio
George Myers ....Wakefield, Ohio
Nate McGowan ....Abashia, Ohio
John McGarney................................Muff P. O., Ohio
James Rees ....Wales P. O., Ohio
John Rockwell ....Galford, Ohio
Rees W. Thomas ....Jackson, Ohio
George Phillipi................................Portsmouth, Ohio
Joseph Truman ....Rushtown, Ohio
R. H. Slavens ....Flat, P. O., Ohio
Richard Wells ....Galford, Ohio
Thomas J. Williams..........................Thurman, Ohio
Samuel L. Hanes..............................Portsmouth, Ohio
John Pfuhler ....Portsmouth, Ohio
C. C. Schlichter ....Portsmouth, Ohio
Oliver Wirtz ....Portsmouth, Ohio
Samuel Nickel ....Portsmouth, Ohio
Rees Griffith ....Glen Roy, Ohio
John Oney ....Cadmus, Ohio
James B. Sanders ....Lucasville, Ohio
Henry Cline ....Powellsville, Ohio

James J. Jolly ....Gallipolis, Ohio
Martin Roush ....Sarahville, Ohio
Evan E. Evans ....Thurman, Ohio
Smith Dalrymple ....New Orleans, La.
Moses Roberts ....Chase, P. O., Kan.
James B. Dement ....West Union, Ohio
Dennis Jones ....Esop P. O., Ohio
Wm. A. Louks ....Vinton, Ohio
Thomas White ....Pine Grove, Ohio
Joseph White ....Pine Grove, Ohio
John E. Evans ....Kitchen, Ohio
Hiram Lodge ....Wellston, Ohio
Charles Martin ....Vinton, Ohio
Daniel Jones ....Venedocia, Ohio
Robert M. Fulton ....Bulaville, Ohio
Evan O. Evans ....Thurman, Ohio
George Hughes ....Jackson, Ohio
James Hughes ....Oak Hill, Ohio
Hiram McCarley ....Bidwell, Ohio
Wm. W. Mauring ....Byer, P. O., Ohio
Andrew J. McPhail ....Los Angeles, Cal.
Thomas Sims ....Mongula, Mont.
John Daniels ....Pine Grove, Ohio
John Stockham ....Arkansas City, Kan.
Robert H. Jackson ....Hersey P. O., Wis.
Philip Carey ....Fairfield, Iowa
Frank Hammon ....Portsmouth, Ohio
William Fastinau ....Portsmouth, Ohio

Lafayette Sickles	Portsmouth, Ohio
John Cline	Powellsville, Ohio
Ben Yeley	Wait P. O., Ohio
Oliver Nurse	Friendship, Ohio
Aaron Hamilton	Friendship, Ohio
H. G. Blakeman	Friendship, Ohio
John Biggs	Grayson, Ky.
Henry Dunlap	Ashland, Ky.
James Perry	Argentum, Ky.
Lewis Myers	Ironton, Ohio
Samuel Johnson	Bridgeport, Ohio
Thomas Eagan	Jasper, Ohio
Lodwick D. Davis	Columbus, Ohio
Joshua Lewis	Columbus, Ohio
Thomas D. Davis	Columbus, Ohio
S. S. Montgomery	Wapakoneta, Ohio
R. W. Montgomery	Wapakoneta, Ohio
F. M. Lowry	Los Angeles, Cal.
George Lowry	Los Angeles, Cal.
Wm. A. Stephenson	Jackson, Ohio
William Lesser	Beaver, Ohio
Jacob White	Jackson, Ohio
Benjamin Byers	Vigo P. O., Ohio
Philander Bennett	Coalton, Ohio
Thomas Stafford	Gallia, P. O., Ohio
Rees Davis	Tracy P. O., Minn.
Thomas E. Davis	Rio Grande, Ohio
George W. Graves	Washington, Ohio

Peter Petry .... Portsmouth, Ohio
William Samuel .... Columbus, Ohio
Ashley R. Williams .... Goffs P. O., Kan.
John Lasley .... Plymouth, Mo.
Arza Gudgeon .... Otter Vale, Mo.
Henry Kinker .... Bloom P. O., Ohio
George Claar .... Jackson, Ohio
Thomas D. Thomas .... Niles, Ohio
William H. Cool .... Summitville, Ohio
Joseph Aduddle .... Beaver, Ohio
Albert Brown .... Chester, Pa.
Hiram W. Dewitt .... Aid P. O., Ohio
David W. James .... National Military Home, Ohio
John Barrett .... National Military Home, Ohio
Edward Phillips .... National Military Home, Ohio
Edward Goudy .... National Military Home, Ohio
George M. Gordy .... National Military Home, Ohio
Timothy Sullivan .... National Military Home, Ohio
Mike Joyce .... National Military Home, Ohio
Resin Furgeson .... National Military Home, Ohio
Martin Powers .... National Military Home, Ohio
John Lodge .... Ironton, Wis.
Martin J. Adams .... Silverton, Ore.
John G. Siebert .... Reinbeck, Iowa.
Bartholomy Hauser .... Chillicothe, Ohio
David Storer .... Alexandria, Ohio
John Coffman .... Dundas, Ohio
Peter Scott .... Glen Roy, Ohio

William H. Nearman	Oak Hill, Ohio
John Roush	Aid P. O., Ohio
William T. Saxton	Dunlap, Kan.
William H. Brady	Glen Roy, Ohio
Benjamin Rockwell	Kniffin, Iowa
James H. Woolm	Richland, Iowa
David H. Wood	Rooney, Carter County, Ky.
John W. Davis	Elizabeth P. O., Miss.
Nick Barnhart	Cavendish, Mo.
John Shaw	Carrollton, Mo.
Emanuel Russell	Coalton, Ohio
Benjamin Sanders	Steece P. O., Ohio
Geo. W. Harshbarger	Buckland, Ohio
John F. McGrew	Johnstown, Ohio
George M. Tripp	Shelbyville, Ill.
W. H. A. Tripp	Shelbyville, Ill.
Fred Steinmeyer	Wilber, Neb.
David Daniels	Santa Monica, Cal.
Joseph M. Bing	New Orleans, La.
Daniel J. Evans	Pittsburg, Pa.
James Farrar	Sterling, Kan.
Thomas J. Jones	Hiawatha, Kan.
Stephen R. Ellis	Industry, Kan.
Charles H. Bing	Wilmot, Kan.
Frank M. Seth	Parkersville, Kan.
W. C. Bradfield	Augusta, Kan.
William Hahn	Burlington, Kan.
James M. Halliday	Crescent, Oklahoma

William McJunkin .... Liberty, Kan.
Ephraim Phillips .... Salina, Kan.
William H. McLaughlin .... Wichita, Kan.
William Roberts .... Carlisle P. O., Ark.

See page 140

CHAPTER XV.

BIOGRAPHICAL SKETCHES.

William H. Raynor, the son of William and Mary Raynor, was born in Portsmouth, Scioto county, Ohio. In this city he lived during the early years of his life. At the age of 14 he left school and engaged in the mercantile business. At the age of 21 he married Rhoda O. Kendall, of Portsmouth, Ohio, and soon thereafter engaged in the banking business with the late Philander Kinney, and was so engaged when the Civil War began in 1861.

He was at that time Lieutenant in a Portsmouth company of the State militia. The company was under command of Captain Geo. B. Bailey. When the news of the firing on Fort Sumter came Captain Bailey was out of the city. Lieutenant Raynor immediately telegraphed to the Governor of Ohio, offering the services of the company. This message was approved by the Captain.

The next day brought the President's call for troops, and the Portsmouth company was ordered to report at Columbus promptly. Within forty-eight hours the company was in Columbus, and with nine other companies of the State militia was organized into a regiment known as the First Ohio Three Months Volunteers, the Portsmouth company designated as Company G.

The First and Second Ohio started at once for Washington, D. C., and were, with the Second New York Volunteers, assigned to a brigade commanded by General Robert C. Schenck, and Lieutenant Raynor was detached to act as the General's aide. In this capacity he was engaged at the Vienna affair, June 17, 1861, in which Company G of the First Ohio had six killed and four wounded.

At his request, Lieutenant Raynor was returned to his company, and with them was engaged on July 21, 1861, in the first Battle of Bull Run. Here he was slightly wounded in the right instep, was left on the field and became a prisoner; was taken to Richmond and confined in one of the tobacco warehouses on Main street of that city. When his wound had healed so he could walk fairly well he, with two fellow prisoners, Colonel John R. Hurd of Ohio and Colonel Chas. J. Murphy of New York, escaped from the prison, and after thirteen days in the woods and swamps of Virginia they reached the Potomac river, and soon arrived at Washington. As soon as the escape was known the Governor of Ohio offered him a commission as Lieutenant Colonel in a regiment about to be organized at Portsmouth by Colonel Peter Kinney, which was the Fifty-sixth Ohio Volunteer Infantry. This offer was accepted and Colonel Raynor at once engaged energetically in organizing and drilling the regiment, and with it he served full three years.

With the Fifty-sixth Ohio he was present in every engagement, and every important battle they fought was under his command. He was with them in every march they made, with the single exception of the advance on Corinth, at which time he was seriously ill with typhoid fever.

Colonel Kinney resigned April 2, 1863. Lieutenant Colonel Raynor was promoted to Colonel from that date. From November, 1863, until May, 1864, he was in command of the brigade of which the Fifty-sixth formed a part, although there was in the brigade at least one Colonel who, by date of commission, was his superior officer; but the division and corps commanders ordered Colonel Raynor to take the command.

Colonel Raynor was severely wounded at Snaggy Point, La., May 5, 1864, once by a bullet and twice by fragments of shell. The rebel bullet shattered the small bone of his left leg, from which wound he still suffers. At this place he again became a prisoner, and remained in the enemy's hands about six weeks, when he was released on parole. His recovery he ascribes to the unremitting

care and attention of Surgeon Williams and his nurse, John Phuller of the Fifty-sixth, both of whom became voluntary prisoners that they might care for our wounded men in the enemy's hands.

Colonel Raynor was commissioned Brigadier General by brevet, to rank as such from March 13, 1865, by the President of the United States for distinguished and gallant service.

After the war Colonel Raynor engaged in commercial and manufacturing business, and at this writing he is the assistant manager of the Lozier Manufacturing Company, at Toledo, Ohio. No regiment in the army had a more competent commander than Colonel Raynor, and the Fifty-sixth Ohio, under him, was equal to any similar body of men anywhere, and any good work that they performed was due largely to his ability as commander; and he still holds the esteem of every member of the regiment.

A few years ago, at one of our reunions, a veteran of the Fourth West Virginia Infantry, in a talk he gave us, told where he first saw the Fifty-sixth Ohio. As General Grant's army was closing in around Vicksburg he stated that a large number of different commands were near a road watching the troops coming in, when one regiment attracted the attention of all as they marched along. From the fine looking Colonel to the private in the ranks, every man seemed to understand his business, and he felt like shouting when a slight breeze unfolded the flag, displaying upon its folds Fifty-sixth Ohio Volunteer Infantry, a regiment from his native state.

Rev. J. E. Thomas, the son of Enoch and Jane (James) Thomas, was born in Carmarthenshire, Wales, December 25, 1816. He attended college to be educated for the ministry. He began preaching when 16 years of age. In 1835 a number of the brethren came to the United States, and he accompanied them as their pastor. They located in St. Louis, Mo.

In 1846 he came to Jackson county, Ohio, where he has since resided. In 1862 he enlisted in Company C, Fifty-sixth Ohio Infantry, and, after serving nine months as a private, was elected

Chaplain. Three months later he was detailed by General Prentiss as Superintendent of the Freedmen at Helena, Ark., and was in charge of their farm until the summer of 1865. He sent a small bale of cotton to President Lincoln as the first fruits of the labor of the race he had emancipated. He still lives at his home in Jackson County, Ohio., honored and respected by all.

Lieutenant Coleman Gillilan was born in Jackson county, Ohio, November 19, 1837. He received a good common school education, and in schools of a higher grade, thus qualifying himself for the noble work of a teacher; and, notwithstanding his attachment to his profession, he responded to the second call of President Lincoln, and during August and September, 1861, he and Captain M. Manring recruited Company A of the Fifty-sixth Ohio Volunteers Infantry, and on October 8, 1861, he was mustered in as Second Lieutenant and served faithfully until about May 1, 1862, when he was taken very sick at Pittsburg Landing, Tenn. He was sent home with little expectation that he would ever recover, and was mustered out of the service.

The summer of 1863 he spent with the Army in West Virginia. In July, 1864, he recruited a company for the One Hundred and Seventy-third Ohio Volunteer Infantry, of which he was Captain, and served about one year. He has been engaged as a commercial traveler in the shoe trade the greater part of the time since the war. No man is better known or more highly respected in Southern Ohio, and he is worthy of it. He was with the Fifty-sixth but a short time, but no member of the regiment takes a better interest or does more to keep up interest in our annual reunions.

Parker M. McFarland, M. D., Assistant Surgeon of the Fifty-sixth Ohio Volunteer Infantry, passed on to the life beyond in 1890 or 1891, at Centralia, Illinois, and a letter addressed there failed to reach any of his family. This good man was a gentleman in every sense of the word. No other man exerted so much influence for good upon the young men of the regiment. He was a worthy member of the M. E. Church, and well deserved the name of the "beloved physician," who went about doing good in the footsteps of his gracious Master.

Corporal David Evans of Company C, the son of David and Ann Evans, was born in Wales in 1837. The family emigated to the United States when he was quite young. This comrade was a close friend of the writer, and we were attending school at a distance from each other in 1861, but the war spirit was strong in the land, and on September 9, 1861, we started for Portsmouth, Ohio, to enlist; and at a railway station we met, and on September 10 we volunteered, and were never separated until the catastrophe at Champion's Hill, where he was mortally wounded on May 16, 1863, from which he died July 14, 1863. He was a very strong man physically, and few would have survived as long as he did with such a terrible wound.

John Henry Williams, the son of John T. and Elizabeth Williams, was born in Oneida county, New York, in 1843. He volunteered before he was 18 years of age, and was instantly killed at Champion's Hill, Miss., May 16, 1863, a high private in the front rank of Company C. Though young in years, he was an entire stranger to fear. He was an expert forager, and would often make hazardous trips into the enemy's lines.

George Grindley was born March 20, 1841, at Landilo Fawr, Carmarthenshire, Wales. His father was of Scotch lineage and his mother of a very old Welsh family. He arrived in this country with his parents when about 10 years of age. His parents died in 1851, at Cincinnati, Ohio.

When the war commenced he was a farmer boy in Raccoon township, Gallia county, Ohio. He enlisted in Company E, of which company he was a Corporal and a Sergeant, and was transferred to Company B, but never served with it, being on detached service, headquarters, defenses of New Orleans; headquarters, Department of the Gulf; headquarters, Military Division of the Mississippi. He was in all actions and movements of the regiment except from about May 10, 1862, to July 1, 1862, when he was absent sick in the hospital. He served fifty-two months, being mustered out February 7, 1866, as a non-commissioned officer, his services being no longer required.

Comrade Grindley developed into one of the most talented men ever connected with the regiment. He was happily married to a lady of French descent in New Orleans, and now holds an important position in the Pension Bureau at Washington, D. C.

James Cranston Bingham, the son of Royal and Catherine Bingham, was born in Athens county, Ohio, October 4, 1842. At the age of 14 he was thrown upon his own resources. On October 8, 1861, he enlisted in Company D, Fifty-sixth Ohio Volunteer Infantrty, for three years. He was promoted Sergeant August 11, 1863; re-enlisted as a veteran early in 1864, and mustered out April 25, 1866.

In this service he contracted a disease that caused his death. He was with the Fifty-sixth Ohio in all its marches and battles, and in charge of his wounded comrades of Company D, he marvelously escaped when completely surrounded by the enemy on Red river. After the war he attended school for a short time. He moved to Russell, Ky., in 1877, and engaged in the business of florist, etc. He served as Postmaster here for 14 years; was a worthy member of the M. E. Church, holding various official positions, and was Superintendent of the Sunday School for 18 years.

He served as a Lieutenant in the Ohio National Guard while living at Ironton, Ohio. He was a charter member of Russell Castel No. 28, K. G. E., and served as an officer in the order. He was married September 9, 1867, to Rachel Alida Gray, and she, with their eight children, survive him. He passed on to the higher life February 16, 1899. With the love and esteem of all who ever formed his acquaintance, and with "Life's work well done, life's crown well won," he has but passed a little while before us, and family, friends and comrades "know where to find him."

Colonel Henry Ewing Jones was born in Nashville, Tenn., September 28, 1836. His father, David D. Jones, moved to Portsmouth, Ohio, when Henry was but seven months old. He received a common school education at home, and then attended Dennison College at Granville, Ohio, where he graduated with honor about

1860. Returning to his native city, he began the study of law with Hon. Wells A. Hutchins.

At the beginning of the war he enlisted in Company G, First Ohio Volunteer Infantry, and was appointed Sergeant. Upon the expiration of his term of service he re-enlisted in the Fifty-sixth Ohio Volunteer Infantry, and was commissioned Adjutant, in which position he served until February 6, 1863, when he was promoted to Captain, and on August 8, 1863, was detached on brigade and division staff, and served in that capacity until May 8, 1864, and on January 18, 1865, was promoted to Lieutenant Colonel, which rank he held until April 20, 1866, when he was appointed Colonel, but not mustered.

Upon his return from the war he resumed the study of law, and was shortly after admitted to the bar, and by close application and sheer ability, polished and directed by a broad and practical education, he soon attained an enviable eminence as an able advocate.

He was twice elected Prosecuting Attorney of his county, in 1869 and in 1871, and filled the office in a manner highly creditable to himself and friends.

Personally, Colonel Jones was a man of fine appearance and a marvel of health. He died September 13, 1876.

Lieutenant Thomas J. Williams was born November 30, 1840, in Oneida county, New York, a son of John T. and Elizabeth Williams. The family lived in Oneida and Herkimer counties until September, 1854, when they emigrated to Jackson county, Ohio. Here he worked at the iron furnaces, and, as he could, attended the district schools in the winter season. In the spring of 1861 he attended the Ohio University at Athens, Ohio, for one term.

On September 10, 1861, he volunteered, was mustered in October 17, 1861, in Company C, Fifty-sixth Ohio Volunteer Infantry, as a private, but was soon promoted to Corporal, later to Quartermaster Sergeant of the regiment, then to Second Lieutenant, and later to First Lieutenant, and commanded the company the greater

part of the last year in service. Having re-enlisted as a veteran, he was with the regiment for four years six months and eight days. He was hit by a grape-shot and musket ball at Port Gibson, slightly wounded at Champion's Hill, and shot through his blouse at the siege of Vicksburg.

After the war he was engaged in the iron business until 1887. In that year he was elected Clerk of Courts of Jackson county, and re-elected in 1890, and has held other minor offices. He is a member of the G. A. R., also of the Loyal Legion, and of the Masonic Fraternity, and a member of the Presbyterian Church.

Lieutenant Colonel Samson Eagon Varner, son of Christian M. and Elizabeth Eagon Varner, of Scotch-Irish descent, was born in Staunton, Augusta county, Virginia, August 17, 1824. He came to Portsmouth, Ohio, with his parents in the spring of 1838. The journey over the mountains, in company with two other families, was made in wagons, with two carry-alls for the women and youngest children. Colonel Varner early learned the trade of brick-mason, and when he enlisted as Major of the regiment was largely engaged in the manufacture of brick and had become a flourishing building contractor.

He was a born leader, as the many prominent positions accorded to him in the municipal affairs of his city, as well as in the appointment of Post Commandant at Algiers during the closing months of the war, abundantly testify. With limited school opportunities, his habit of reading useful books enriched his mind, and stored it with valuable information. His genial disposition, kindly nature and rare conversational ability rendered him attractive to old and young.

Colonel Varner was married to Maria L. Huston, daughter of Samuel and Elizabeth Huston, two of Scioto county's pioneers, Nov. 26, 1848. Colonel Varner passed away suddenly on the morning of June 5, 1877, of heart disease. Since his death the second son, William E., died of heart disease. Five children are yet living. The oldest, Mrs. Ella Brown, resides at Youngstown; Mrs. Anna Sanford, at Cincinnati; Frank Floyd, the oldest son,

is a building contractor at Portsmouth; James Huston, the youngest son, is connected with his brother-in-law with the firm of Sanford, Varner, Storrs & Co., Cincinnati, Ohio. The youngest daughter, Mrs. Bessie Adams, resides in Portsmouth. These are all filling prominent and responsible positions.

Colonel Varner was for many years a devout attendant at Christ Protestant Episcopal Church. He was an active member of the Street Car Company, and in his memory the cars were draped for thirty days at his death. A whole city mourned the loss of one who was a public, as well as a private, benefactor.

Captain John Yochem was born in Oppenheim, on the Rhine, May 3, 1824. He was of good parentage, and received a careful education. In 1851 he emigrated to America and located in Portsmouth, Ohio. In 1852 he was married to Henrietta Eckenberger, to which union three children were born. In 1867 they moved to Jackson, Ohio. He died October 30, 1897, and the following was read to his memory at the funeral by T. J. Williams:

"As we stand by the remains of our departed comrade, 'the past rises before us as a vision of the night; we see the great assemblages, and hear the fervent appeals of orators; we see the tearful cheeks of women and the determined faces of men.' It was at such a time that I first met our departed comrade. On joining the Fifty-sixth Ohio Volunteer Infantry in the fall of 1861, the greater part of the men being strangers to me, my attention was drawn to one who, by his polished and military appearance, would attract attention in any regiment or gathering of people. I soon learned that this man was Lieutenant John Yochem of Company B, and I feel sure that by his example he inspired many of the younger men of the regiment with a determination to perfect themselves in their military duties.

"He was appointed First Lieutenant November 7, 1861; promoted to Captain April 2, 1863, and discharged November 24, 1864. He participated with the regiment in all of its battles and campaigns, discharging every duty to which he was assigned with fidelity. He had served six years in his Fatherland, in the great

army of Germany. He had the education and talent to hold a much higher position in our service, had it not been for his lack of a command of the English language.

"One of the conspicuous acts of the Captain was at Champion's Hill. When the enemy were forcing us back foot by foot, they made a rush to capture our flags, but the Captain quickly saw the danger, and with a lot of the boys charged and drove them back, thereby saving us from the greatest calamity that could befall any regiment, the loss of their colors.

"The Captain had a kindly feeling for all ex-soldiers, and he loved the Grand Army of the Republic, but his infirmities prevented his attendance of late years. He was a splendid example of our foreign-born citizens, who performed such magnificent service for the land of their adoption in the great war for the preservation of this fair land.

"After passing through so many dangers, seen and unseen, he was spared, and has passed on at a good old age, and we can truly say with our poet comrade, F. C. Searl:

> "One narrow strand is all the land,
> That parts us from our comrades dear;
> O, comrades, who have gone before
> And camp upon the brighter shore,
> We soon shall hear our last tatoo,
> And one by one, at minute gun,
> Fold up our tents and camp with you."

Capt. Christian Henry Schaefer was born at Pittsburg, Pa., June 18, 1840. When quite young his parents moved to Gallipolis, Ohio, where he resided till his death. After coming to Gallipolis he began working in the tin and iron trade, but the war breaking out and being filled with patriotism and love of his country, he was among the first to enlist, which he did with the late Capt. C. C. Aleshire, of Company G, 18th O. V. I., for three months.

After the three months had expired he enlisted for three years with Col. Turley, of Portsmouth, for three (3) years more. During that time he was promoted different times until he was First Lieutenant of his company, which was Company D, 56th O. V. I.

The war having happily ended he was honorably discharged, veteranized and commissioned as Captain and served until July, 1866. During the war he was in the following engagements: Pittsburg Landing, Seige of Corinth, Port Gibson, Champion Hills, Seige of Vicksburg, Jackson, Carrion Bayou, Sabine Cross Roads, Monetts Ferry and Snaggy Point.

After the war he became connected with Halliday & Miles Wholesale Dry Goods house at Gallipolis, and later became a partner in the firm. At the time of his death, which occurred December 28, 1897, he was the Representative of the National Lead Company.

He married Adeline E. Damron, daughter of Hon. John G. Damron, of Gallipolis, Ohio, Jan. 15, 1867, and by their union three children were born, Mrs. H. C. Brown, Edgar G. Schaefer and Dr. Earle Schaefer, of Gallipolis.

He had been an official member of the M. E. Church ever since the present structure was built. He was a good man with a clean heart, void of guile or offense to his fellow man. He was a good boy, an old Academy student, a man of intelligence, genial, warm hearted, generous and kind. His family loose a treasure that will come to them no more. They have our warmest sympathy. The community has lost a good citizen, one of the kind that offered his life freely for his country. That it was not taken was no fault of his. He is gone, but will never be forgotten by those who knew him well and had learned his worth.

LIEUT. THOS. J. WILLIAMS IN 1898
See page 140

56th REGIMENT OHIO VOLUNTEER INFANTRY.

FIELD AND STAFF.

Mustered in from Oct. 1st, 1861, to Jan. 3, 1862, at Portsmouth, O., by R. B. Hull, Captain 18th Infantry, U. S. A. Mustered out April 25, 1866, at New Orleans La., by A. McAllister, Captain 10th U. S. C. Art.

Names.	Rank.	Age.	Date of Entering the Service.	Period of Service.	Remarks.
Peter Kinney	Colonel	56	Sept. 11, 1861	3 yrs.	Resigned April 3, 1863.
William H. Raynor	...do...	27	Sept. 28, 1861	3 yrs.	Promoted from Lieut. Colonel April 2, 1863; wounded and captured May 5, 1864, on steamer John Warner on Red river; discharged Oct. 27, 1864.
Sampson E. Varner	Lt. Col.	....	Sept. 28, 1861	3 yrs.	Promoted from Major April 6, 1863; discharged Nov. 14, 1864.
Harry E. Jones	...do...	25	Sept. 28, 1861	3 yrs.	Promoted Captain Co. A from Adjutant Feb. 6, 1863; to Lieut. Colonel from Captain Co. D Jan. 18, 1865; Colonel April 20, 1866, but not mustered; mustered out with regiment April 25, 1866.
Charles F. Reiniger	Major	55	Aug. 7, 1861	3 yrs.	Promoted from Captain Co. B April 2, 1863; discharged Oct. 27, 1864.
W. N. King	Surgeon	34	Oct. 3, 1861	3 yrs.	Resigned Aug. 28, 1863.
David Williams	...do...	....	Dec. 23, 1863	3 yrs.	Discharged Nov. 25, 1864.
W. C. Payne	As. Surg.	30	Oct. 3, 1861	3 yrs.	Resigned April 8, 1862.
N. W. Fisher	...do...	....	April 1, 1862	3 yrs.	Died Feb. 24, 1863, at ——
Parker M. McFarland	...do...	36	Aug. 21, 1862	3 yrs.	Promoted Surgeon April 20, 1866, but not mustered; mustered out with regiment April 25, 1866.
Benjamin Roberts	Adjutant	25	Oct. 18, 1861	3 yrs.	Appointed from 1st Lieutenant Co. B Sept. 12, 1863; captured May 5, 1864, on board steamer John Warner; escaped July 3, 1864, at Tyler, Tex.; promoted Captain of Co. A, March 29, 1865
W. S. Houston	R. Q. M.	34	Oct. 18, 1861	3 yrs.	Resigned Dec. 17, 1862.
Moses Rife	...do...	24	Nov. 20, 1861	3 yrs.	Appointed from 1st Lieutenant Co. E Sept. 1, 1863; mustered out Feb. 7, 1866.
Jonathan E. Thomas	Chaplain	....	Jan. 10, 1862	3 yrs.	Promoted from private Co. C Sept. 9, 1862; discharged Nov. 5, 1864.
Thomas W. Kinney	Ser. Maj.	20	Oct. 29, 1861	3 yrs.	Promoted from private Co. G Oct. 30, 1861; to 2d Lieutenant Co. H June 10, 1862.
John K. Combs	...do...	24	Nov. 18, 1861	3 yrs.	Promoted from 1st Sergeant Co. H Sept 22, 1862; to 2d Lieutenant Co. B Feb. 14, 1863.
Stephen B. Thoburn	...do...	19	Oct. 8, 1861	3 yrs.	Promoted from Sergeant Co. D July 23, 1863; to 2d Lieutenant Co. A Jan. 18, 1865; veteran.
John H. Morris	...do...	23	Oct. 17, 1861	3 yrs.	Promoted from Sergeant Co. C Feb. 5, 1865; 2d Lieutenant May 31, 1865, but not mustered; discharged Nov. 22, 1865; veteran.
William K. Sturgill	...do...	39	Oct. 17, 1861	3 yrs.	Promoted from 1st Sergeant Co. A Nov. 23, 1865; mustered out with regiment April 25, 1866; veteran.

Names.	Rank.	Age.	Date of Entering the Service.	Period of Service.	Remarks.
Erastus Gates	Q. M. S.	32	Dec. 9, 1861	3 yrs.	Promoted from private Co. H Dec. 9, 1861; to 2d Lieutenant Co. G Sept. 5, 1862.
Henry M. Goldsmith	... do ...	38	Nov. 13, 1861	3 yrs.	Promoted from private of Co. E Sept. 28, 1862; to 2d Lieutenant of Co. H Jan. 1, 1863.
Thomas J. Williams	... do ...	20	Oct. 17, 1861	3 yrs.	Promoted from Corporal Co. C July 4, 1863; 2d Lieutenaut Co. B Jan. 18, 1865; veteran.
John Bevan	... do ..	23	Oct. 15, 1861	3 yrs.	Promoted from Sergeant Co. B Feb. 5, 1865; mustered out with regiment April 25, 1866; veteran.
Joseph S. Patterson	Com.Ser.	30	Oct. 17, 1861	3 yrs.	Promoted from private Co. C Aug. 15, 1862; to 2d Lieutenant Co. K Aug. 31, 1862.
Henry Schump	... do ...	21	Oct. 17, 1861	3 yrs.	Promoted from Corporal Co. C Nov. 1, 1862; to 2d Lieutenant Co. I March 17, 1863
John C. Grass	... do ...	27	Nov. 2, 1861	3 yrs.	Promoted from Corporal Co. E July 4, 1863;discharged Jan. 23,1866;veteran
Lewis H. Hamilton	Hos.St'd.	33	Oct. 15, 1861	3 yrs.	Reduced to ranks and transferred to Co. D ——.
Gilbert A. Ewing	... do ..	....	Dec. 20, 1861	3 yrs.	Promoted from private of Co. A Dec. 20, 1861; discharged Aug. —, 1862, at Columbus, O., of disability.
John F. McGrew	... do ...	....	Oct. 31, 1861	3 yrs.	Promoted from private Co. A Oct. 8, 1862; wounded and captured May 3, 1864, at battle of Snaggy Point, La.;discharged Jan. 2,1866;veteran.
James L. O. Huston	Prin Mus	18	Nov. 13, 1861	3 yrs.	Promoted 2d Lieutenant Co. E Sept. 6, 1862.

COMPANY A.

Mustered in Oct. 29, 1861, at Portsmouth, O., by R. B. Hull, 1st Lieutenant 18th Infantry, U. S. A
Mustered out April 25, 1866, at New Orleans, La., by A. McAllister, Captain 10th U. S. C. Art.

Names.	Rank.	Age.	Date of Entering the Service.	Period of Service.	Remarks.
Maschil Manring	Captain	36	Aug. 8, 1861	3 yrs.	Mustered out Oct. 27, 1864, at New Orleans, La.
Henry E. Jones	... do ...	25	Sept. 28, 1861	3 yrs.	Promoted from Adjutant Feb. 6, 1863; transferred to Co. D Aug. 8, 1863.
Benjamin Roberts	... do ...	25	Oct. 18, 1861	3 yrs.	Promoted from 1st Lieutenant and Adjutant March 29, 1865; mustered out with company April 25, 1866.
William D. Wood	1st Lieut.	33	Nov. 8, 1861	3 yrs.	Promoted Captain May 9, 1864, but not mustered; mustered out Oct. 27, 1864, at New Orleans, La.
William G. Snyder	... do ...	29	Oct. 29, 1861	3 yrs.	Promoted from 2d Lieutenant Co. G May 16, 1863; Captain Co. K Aug. 10, 1864.
John K. Combs	... do ...	24	Nov.18, 1861	3 yrs.	Promoted from 2d Lieutenant Co. B March 29, 1865; to Captain April 20, 1866, but not mustered; mustered out with company April 25, 1866.
Coleman Gillilen	2d Lieut.	24	Nov. 8, 1861	3 yrs	Discharged July 31,1862, of disability.
George W. Manring	... do ...	23	Oct. 17, 1861	3 yrs.	Mustered as private; appointed 1st Sergeant Oct. 29, 1861; promoted 2d Lieutenant July 31, 1862; killed May 16, 1863, in battle of Champion Hills, Miss.
Christian H. Shaefer	... do ...	21	Oct. 5, 1861	3 yrs.	Promoted from 1st Sergeant Co. D May 16, 1863; to 1st Lieutenant Co. C Jan. 18, 1865.

OHIO VOLUNTEER INFANTRY. 147

Names.	Rank.	Age.	Date of Entering the Service.	Period of Service.	Remarks.
Stephen B. Thoburn	2d Lieut.	19	Oct. 8, 1861	3 yrs.	Promoted from Sergt. Major Jan. 18, 1865; to 1st Lieutenant Feb. 24, 1866, but not mustered; mustered out with company April 25, 1866.
William K Sturgill	1st Sergt.	39	Oct. 17, 1861	3 yrs.	Appointed July 31, 1862, promoted Sergt. Major Nov. 23, 1865; veteran.
Harvey N. Bridwell	...do...	25	Oct. 20, 1861	3 yrs.	Transferred from Co. D;: transferred to Co. D Dec. 6, 1864; veteran.
John C. Burk	...do...	32	Oct. 15, 1861	3 yrs.	Transferred from Co. F; appointed 1st Sergeant Nov. 23, 1865; mustered out with company April 25, 1866; veteran.
George W. Thorp	Sergeant	38	Oct. 17, 1861	3 yrs.	Mustered out Oct. 27, 1864, at New Orleans, La.
James Phillips	...do...	44	Oct. 17, 1861	3 yrs.	Mustered out with company April 25, 1866; veteran.
Nicholas Bernhard	.do...	24	Oct. 17, 1861	3 yrs.	Mustered as Nicholas Barnhart; mustered out Oct. 27, 1864, at New Orleans, La.
Samuel J. Blake	do...	23	Oct 17, 1861	3 yrs.	Mustered out Oct. 27, 1864, at New Orleans, La.
Thomas H. Cox	...do...	18	Oct. 5, 1861	3 yrs.	Transferred from Co. D; transferred to Co. D Dec. 6, 1864; veteran.
George W. Cox	...do...	36	Oct. 16, 1861	3 yrs.	Transferred from Co. F; transferred to Co. D Dec. 6, 1864; veteran.
George W. Neff	...do...	22	Oct. 18, 1891	3 yrs.	Transferred from Co. F; captured April 8, 1864, at battle of Sabine Cross Roads, La.; transferred to Co D Dec. 6, 1864; veteran.
James C. Bingham	....do...	19	Oct. 8, 1861	3 yrs.	Transferred from Co. D; appointed from private Feb. 1, 1864; mustered out with company April 25, 1866; veteran.
Jesse Wood	...do...	19	Oct. 8, 1861	3 yrs.	Transferred from Co. D; appointed from private Feb. 1, 1864; mustered out with company April 25, 1866; veteran.
Michael Shelton	...do...	22	Oct. 17, 1861	3 yrs.	Mustered out with company April 25, 1866; veteran.
Hiram Lodge	Corporal	25	Oct. 17, 1861	3 yrs.	Mustered out Oct. 27, 1864, at New Orleans, La.
Francis M. Wheelbarger	...do...	22	Oct. 17, 1861	3 yrs.	Died April 8, 1864, at Halena, Ark.
Thomas Harkinson	...do...	32	Oct. 17, 1861	3 yrs.	Wounded May 16, 1863, in battle of Champion Hills, Miss.; mustered out Oct. 27, 1864.
John Barr	...do..	44	Oct. 21, 1861	3 yrs.	Transferred from Co. D; wounded and captured April 8, 1864, in battle of Sabine Cross Roads, La.; transferred to Co. D Dec. 6, 1864; veteran.
Robert Bowles	...do...	20	Oct. 21, 1861	3 yrs.	Transferred from Co. F; transferred to Co. D Dec. 6, 1864; veteran.
James M. Halliday	..do..	19	Oct. 16, 1861	3 yrs.	Transferred from Co. F; transferred to Co. D Dec. 6, 1864; veteran.
James U. Pease	...do...	27	Oct. 18, 1861	3 yrs.	Transferred from Co. F; transferred to Co. D Dec. 6, 1864; veteran.
David Storer	...do...	23	Nov. 18, 1861	3 yrs.	Transferred from Co. D; transferred to Co. D Dec. 6, 1864; veteran.
Azariah Authors	..do...	21	Oct. 24, 1861	3 yrs.	Transferred from Co D; transferred to Co. D Dec. 6, 1864; veteran.
John Fee	..do...	25	Oct. 17, 1861	3 yrs.	Discharged March 24 1866, at New Orleans, La., of disability; veteran.
Hiram McCarley	...do...	18	Oct. 17, 1861	3 yrs.	Appointed Corporal Feb. 1, 1864; discharged March 24, 1866, at New Orleans, La., of disability; veteran.
Brittain D. Fry	...do...	19	Oct. 19, 1861	3 yrs.	Transferred from Co. F; mustered out with company April 25, 1866; veteran.
William Bacon	...do...	25	Oct. 25, 1861	3 yrs.	Transferred from Co. D; mustered out with company April 25, 1866; veteran.

Names.	Rank.	Age.	Date of Entering the Service	Period of Service.	Remarks.
Thomas Fee............	Corporal	19	Oct. 17, 1861	3 yrs.	Mustered out with company April 25, 1866; veteran.
Henry Hunsucker......	...do...	21	Oct. 21, 1861	3 yrs.	Transferred from Co. D; mustered out with company April 25, 1866; veteran.
Gideon M. Hubbard....	...do...	28	Oct. 17, 1861	3 yrs.	Transferred from Co F; appointed Corporal Feb. 1, 1864; mustered out with company April, 25, 1866; veteran.
David W. Jones..........	...do...	18	Oct. 17, 1861	3 yrs.	Appointed Corporal Jan. 30, 1865; mustered out with company April 25, 1866; veteran.
Thomas Stafford	...do...	32	Oct. 17, 1861	3 yrs.	Appointed Corporal Nov. 30, 1865; mustered out with company April 25, 1866; veteran.
Thomas Sims............	..do...	18	Oct. 17, 1861	3 yrs.	Appointed Corporal March 27, 1866; mustered out with company April 25, 1866; veteran.
William A. Lanks......	...do...	20	Sept. 26, 1861	3 yrs.	Discharged Dec. 15, 1864, at Columbus, O., of disability; veteran.
Elias A. Branham......	Musician	18	Oct. 21, 1861	3 yrs.	Transferred from Co. D——; mustered out with company April 25, 1866; veteran.
Elias A. Bridwell	.do...	....	Oct. 21, 1861	3 yrs.	Transferred from Co. D; mustered out with company April 25, 1866; veteran.
Jesse B. Hart............	...do...	18	Aug. 2, 1864	3 yrs.	Mustered out with company April 25, 1866.
Henry C. Edgington....	Wagoner	21	Aug. 31, 1861	3 yrs.	Transferred from Co. D; veteran.
Allen, William R.......	Private	18	Oct. 17, 1861	3 yrs.	Killed May 16, 1863, in battle of Champion Hills, Miss.
Allen, Martin G	...do...	22	Oct. 17, 1861	3 yrs.	Wounded May 16, 1863, in battle of Champion Hills, Miss.; mustered out with company April 25, 1866; veteran.
Allison, Henry D.......	...do...	20	Oct. 17, 1861	3 yrs.	Wounded July 11, 1863, in action at Jackson, Miss.; mustered out with company April 25, 1866; veteran.
Bacon, William	...do...	41	Nov. 10, 1861	3 yrs	Transferred from Co. D; mustered out with company April 25, 1866; veteran.
Bacon, William G	...do...	19	Oct. 19, 1861	3 yrs.	Transferred from Co. D; mustered out with company April 25, 1866; veteran.
Badger, William	...do...	31	Oct. 8, 1861	3 yrs.	Transferred from Co. D; mustered out with company April 25, 1866; veteran.
Banker, Hiram H	...do...	18	Oct. 17, 1861	3 yrs	Mustered out Oct. 27, 1864, at New Orleans, La.
Bass, William	...do...	....	Oct. 25, 1861	3 yrs.	Killed May 16, 1863, in skirmish at Champion Hills, Miss.
Bass, Joseph..........	...do...	19	Oct. 17. 1861	3 yrs.	
Betlis, William........	..do...	....	Oct. 25, 1861	3 yrs.	Discharged March 5, 1866, at New Orleans, La., of disability; veteran.
Blake, Arius L.........	...do...	21	Oct. 17, 1861	? yrs.	Died July 11, 1863, at Memphis, Tenn., of wounds received June 19, 1863, in battle of Vicksburg, Miss.
Blosser, Charles........	...do...	18	Oct. 17, 1861	3 yrs.	Wounded May 16, 1863, in battle of Champion Hills, Miss.; mustered out Oct. 27, 1864, at New Orleans, La.
Bollman, Joseph	...do...	....	Oct. 25, 1861	3 yrs.	Discharged Oct. 21, 1865, at New Orleans, La., of disability; veteran.
Bowman, George W	...do...	22	Oct. 17, 1861	3 yrs.	Killed May 1, 1863, in battle of Port Gibson, Mississippi.
Brown, Albert..........	...do...	18	Aug. 4, 1864	3 yrs.	Mustered out with company April 25, 1866.

OHIO VOLUNTEER INFANTRY. 149

Names.	Rank.	Age.	Date of Entering the Service.	Period of Service.	Remarks.
Carrothers, James	Private	21	Nov. 20, 1861	3 yrs.	Transferred from Co. F; captured May 5, 1864, on steamer John Warner on Red river, La.; discharged June 30, 1865, at Columbus, O.; veteran.
Chappell, Lineus C	...do...	18	Oct. 17, 1861	3 yrs.	Wounded May 16, 1863, in battle of Champion Hills, Miss.; mustered out with company April 25, 1866; veteran.
Claflin, John	...do...	18	Oct. 17, 1861	3 yrs.	Mustered out with company April, 25, 1866; veteran.
Clefford, Morgan	...do...	19	Oct. 21, 1861	3 yrs.	Transferred from Co. D; mustered out with company April 25, 1866; veteran.
Cosley, Jarvis	...do...	26	Oct. 17, 1861	3 yrs.	Wounded May 16, 1863, in battle of Champion Hills, Miss.; mustered out Oct. 27, 1864, at New Orleans, La.
Colly, Samuel	...do...	22	Oct. 17, 1861	3 yrs.	Wounded April 8, 1864, in battle of Sabine Cross Roads, La.; mustered out with company April 25, 1866; veteran.
Cosley, Francis M	...do...		Oct. 25, 1861	3 yrs.	Died May 18, 1862, near Corinth, Miss.
Cool, William H	...do...		Nov. 20, 1861	3 yrs.	Transferred from Co. F; mustered out with company April 25, 1866; veteran.
Cron, Adam	...do...		Oct. 25, 1861	3 yrs.	Died Oct. 18, 1862, in hospital at Keokuk, Ia.
Cross, Thomas L	...do...	23	Oct. 21, 1861	3 yrs.	Transferred from Co. D; died July 15, 1865, in hospital at Greenville, La.; veteran.
Cross, Wilson	...do...	29	Oct. 21, 1861	3 yrs.	Transferred from Co D; transferred to Veteran Reserve Corps Dec 30, 1864; veteran; mustered out Nov. 16, 1865, at Cairo, Ill.
Davis, William	..do...	42	Oct. 17, 1861	3 yrs.	
Denny, Henry L	...do...	23	Oct. 17, 1861	3 yrs.	Mustered out with company April 25, 1866; veteran.
Dunn, William	...do...	43	Oct. 17, 1861	3 yrs.	Discharged Nov. -, 1862. of disability.
Dunn, William B	...do...	18	Oct. 17, 1861	3 yrs,	
Dunn, Aaron	...do...		Oct. 25, 1861	3 yrs.	Died Oct. 18, 1862, in hospital at Keokuk, Ia.
Ewing, Gilbert A	...do...		Dec. 20, 1861	3 yrs.	Promoted to Hospital Steward Dec. 20, 1861.
Farrar, James	...do...	18	Oct. 17, 1861	3 yrs.	Mustered out with company April 25, 1866; veteran.
Fout, Jasper	...do...	18	Oct. 16, 1861	3 yrs.	Wounded May 16, 1863, in battle of Champion Hills, Miss.; transferred from Co. F; mustered out with company April 25, 1866; veteran.
Golliger, John	...do...	33	Oct. 8, 1861	3 yrs.	Transferred from Co. D; captured May 5, 1864, on steamer John Warner on Red river, La.; discharged June 30, 1865, at Columbus, O.; veteran.
Gould, George	...do...	42	Oct. 17, 1861	3 yrs.	Discharged June —, 1863, at Keokuk, Ia., of disability.
Gould, Isaac	...do...	21	Oct. 17, 1861	3 yrs.	Mustered out with company April 25, 1866; veteran.
Grady, Francis	...do...	22	Oct. 17, 1861	3 yrs.	Mustered out Oct. 27, 1864, at New Orleans, La.
Halfhill, Abraham	...do..	32	Oct. 17, 1861	3 yrs.	Absent, sick in hospital at Raymond, Miss., May 14, 1863; no further record found.
Hammon, Francis	...do...	18	Oct. 17, 1861	3 yrs.	Mustered out Oct. 27, 1864, at New Orleans, La.

Names.	Rank.	Age.	Date of Entering the Service.	Period of Service.	Remarks.
Hammon, Aaron	Private	....	Oct. 24, 1861	3 yrs.	Transferred to 1st Missouri Battery Dec. 6. 1863.
Hedgemier, Frederick	...do..	38	Nov. 18, 1861	3 yrs.	Transferred from Co. F; captured May 5, 1864, on board steamer John Warner, Red River, La.; discharged June 30, 1865, at Columbus, O.; veteran.
Henry, John	...do...	21	Nov. 18, 1861	3 yrs.	Transferred from Co F; discharged Feb. 1, 1866, at New Orleans, La.; veteran.
Hill, Joseph	...do.	25	Oct. 17, 1861	3 yrs	Discharged Sept. 13. 1864, at New Orleans, La., of disability; veteran.
Holecome, Erastus N	...do...	43	Oct. 17, 1861	3 yrs.	Discharged Jan. 13, 1864, at Algiers, La., of disability.
Holesworth, Smith	...do...	41	Oct. 17, 1861	3 yrs.	Discharged ——.
Hopkins, Matthew	...do...	30	Oct. 17, 1861	3 yrs.	Mustered out with company April 25, 1866; veteran.
Irving, Pery L	...do...	20	Oct. 17, 1861	3 yrs.	Mustered out Oct. 27, 1864, at New Orleans, La.
Johnson, Elias	...do...	21	Oct. 17, 1861	3 yrs.	Wounded May 16, 1863, in battle of Champion Hills. Miss.: discharged Sept. 28, 1865, at Camp Dennison, O., of disability; veteran.
Johnson, Josiah	...do...	28	Oct. 17, 1861	3 yrs.	Mustered out Oct. 27, 1864, at New Orleans. La.
Jolly, James I	...do...	21	Oct. 17, 1861	3 yrs.	Discharged ——.
Jones, Lewis	...do...	18	Oct. 17, 1861	3 yrs.	Discharged Oct. 4, 1865. at Camp Dennison, O., of disability; veteran.
Jones William D	...do..	18	Oct. 17, 1861	3 yrs.	Wounded May 16. 1863, in battle of Champion Hills, Miss.; mustered out with company April 25, 1866; veteran.
Jones, Thomas W	...do...	19	Oct. 17, 1861	3 yrs.	Mustered out June 30, 1865, at Columbus. O.; veteran.
Jones, John D	...do...	19	Oct. 17, 1861	3 yrs.	Mustered out with company April 25, 1866; veteran.
Jones, Uriah	...do...	27	Nov. 18, 1861	3 yrs.	Transferred from Co. F; mustered out with company April 25, 1866; veteran.
Joice, Michael	...do...	23	Oct. 20, 1861	3 yrs.	Transferred from Co. F Jan. 26, 1864; captured May 5, 1864, on board steamer John Wagner, Red river, La; mustered out June 30, 1865, at Columbus, O.; veteran.
Keyser, Abner	...do...	20	Oct. 21, 1861	3 yrs.	Transferred from Co. D; mustered out with company April 25, 1866; veteran.
Kiser, Hiram	...do...	24	Oct. 17, 1861	3 yrs.	Wounded May 1, 1863, in battle of Port Gibson, Miss.; discharged——, of disability.
Lair, William	...do...	5	Nov. 20, 1861	3 yrs	Transferred from Co. F; captured April 8, 1864, at battle of Sabine Cross Roads, La.; mustered out June 30, 1865, at Columbus, O.; veteran.
Lamb, Benoni	...do...	35	Oct. 8, 1861	3 yrs.	Transferred from Co. D; mustered out with company April 25, 1866; veteran.
Lesley, John	...do...	18	Oct. 17, 1861	3 yrs.	Discharged June ——, 1862, on Surgeon's certificate of disability.
Lingenfelter, Christ'er.	...do..	38	Oct. 17, 1871	3 yrs.	Transferred from Co. F; discharged July 14, 1865, at Algiers, La., of disability; veteran.
Lodge, George W	...do...	18	Oct. 17, 1861	3 yrs.	Placed on Roll of Honor for meritorious conduct July 16, 1863, at Jackson, Miss.; mustered out with company April 25, 1866; veteran.
Lodge, John	...do...	20	Oct. 17, 1861	3 yrs.	Mustered out with company April 25, 1866; veteran.

OHIO VOLUNTEER INFANTRY.

Names.	Rank.	Age.	Date of Entering the Service.	Period of Service.	Remarks.
Lord, Ezra F	Private	39	Oct. 16, 1861	3 yrs.	Transferred from Co. F; discharged June 30, 1865, at Algiers, La., of disability; veteran.
Lord, William H	... do ...	18	July 14, 1864	3 yrs.	Mustered out with company April 25, 1866.
Louk, William A	... do ...	20	Oct. 17, 1861	3 yrs.	Wounded May 1, 1863, in battle of Port Gibson, Miss.; mustered out with company April 25, 1866; veteran.
McCarty, Richard	... do ...	38	Oct. 17, 1861	3 yrs.	Killed May 1, 1863, in battle of Port Gibson, Mississippi.
McCowan, Nathan	... do ...	39	Nov. 16, 1861	3 yrs.	Transferred from Co. F; discharged Nov. 15, 1865, at New Orleans, La., of disability.
McDonnald, Daniel	... do ...	32	Oct. 17, 1861	3 yrs.	Mustered out Oct. 27, 1864, at New Orleans, La.
McGrew, John F	... do ...		Oct. 31, 1861	3 yrs.	Promoted to Hospital Steward Oct. 8, 1862.
McGrevy, James W	... do ...	35	Oct. 17, 1861	3 yrs.	Died Aug 25, 1864, at New Orleans, La
McPhail, Andrew J	... do ...	18	Oct. 17, 1861	3 yrs.	Mustered out with company April 25, 1866; veteran.
Manring, William W	... do ...	18	Oct. 17, 1861	3 yrs.	Mustered out with company April 25, 1866; veteran.
Manring, Lewis A	... do ...	19	Oct. 17, 1861	3 yrs.	Mustered out with company April 25, 1866; veteran.
Martindale, Andrew M	... do ...	18	Oct. 17, 1861	3 yrs.	Died May 25, 1863, of wounds received May 16, 1863, in battle of Champion Hills, Miss.
Martin, Charles S	... do ...	18	Oct. 5, 1861	3 yrs.	Transferred from Co. D; mustered out with company April 25, 1866; veteran.
Martin, Hiram	... do ...	18	Oct. 30, 1861	3 yrs.	Transferred from Co. F; mustered out with company April 25, 1866; veteran.
Morris, James	... do ...		Oct. 31, 1861	3 yrs	Mustered out with company April 25, 1866; veteran.
Norman, John	... do ...	23	Oct. 17, 1861	3 yrs.	Mustered out with company as private April 25. 1866; veteran.
Nurse, Oliver	... do ...	20	Feb. 20, 1865	3 yrs.	Mustered out Feb. 20, 1866, at New Orleans, La.
Odle, James	... do ...	18	Oct. 21, 1861	3 yrs.	Wounded May 16, 1863, in battle of Champion Hills, Miss., transferred from Co. D; mustered out with company April 25, 1866; veteran.
Ownez, John	... do ...	25	Oct. 17, 1861	3 yrs.	Mustered out April 25, 1866; veteran.
Page, Lorenzo D	... do ...	23	Oct. 8, 1861	3 yrs.	Transferred from Co. D; mustered out with company April 25, 1866; veteran.
Perkins, William	... do ...	44	Oct. 17, 1861	3 yrs.	Died May 4, 1862, while on sick furlough.
Price, Albert E	... do ...	20	Oct. 17, 1861	3 yrs.	Mustered out Nov. 27, 1864.
Ray, George W	... do ...	30	Oct. 17, 1861	3 yrs.	Mustered out with company April 25, 1866; veteran.
Reeseman, William N	... do ...	21	Oct. 17, 1861	3 yrs.	Absent, sick in Hospital at Cairo, Ill., May 16, 1865; mustered out——.
Sanders, Gordon M	... do ...	23	Oct. 17, 1861	3 yrs.	Died March 2, 1863, at Helena, Ark.
Sanders, William	... do ...	19	Oct. 17, 1861	3 yrs.	Discharged Oct. 29, 1862, of disability.
Sexton, William T	... do ...	18	Oct. 17, 1861	3 yrs.	Wounded May 16, 1863, in battle of Champion Hills, Miss.; mustered out Oct. 27, 1864, at New Orleans, La.
Sexton, James	... do ...	28	Oct 17, 1861	3 yrs.	Mustered out Oct. 27, 1864, at New Orleans, La.
Shively, Simon T	... do ...		Sept. 26, 1861	3 yrs.	Discharged Jan. —, 1863, at Jefferson City, Mo., of disability.
Sims, Michael D	... do ...	25	June 7, 1864	3 yrs.	
Simpson, William H. H	... do ...	21	Nov. 5, 1861	3 yrs.	Transferred from Co. D; mustered out June 30, 1865, at Columbus, O.; veteran.

Names.	Rank.	Age.	Date of Entering the Service.	Period of Service.	Remarks.
Slack, William J	Private	29	Oct. 17, 1861	3 yrs.	Died June 19, 1862, at Memphis, Tenn.
Slack, Thomas I	...do...	....	Oct. 25, 1861	3 yrs.	Mustered out with company April 25, 1866; veteran.
Snively, John	...do...	18	Oct. 8, 1861	3 yrs.	Transferred from Co. D; mustered out with company, April 25, 1866; veteran.
Spence, Charles	...do...	18	Oct. 30, 1861	3 yrs.	Transferred from Co. F; wounded and captured April 8, 1864, at battle of Sabine Cross Roads, La.; mustered out June 30, 1865, at Columbus, O.; veteran.
Stover, Henry	...do...	21	Feb. 20, 1865	3 yr.	Mustered out Feb. 20, 1866, at New Orleans, La.
Stratton, Jeremiah	...do...	32	Oct. 17, 1861	3 yrs.	
Sturgill, Joseph E	...do...	18	Oct. 17, 1861	3 yrs.	Captured April 8, 1864, at battle of Sabine Cross Roads, La.; mustered out June 30, 1865, at Columbus, O.; veteran
Sturgill, Henry H	...do...	20	Oct. 17, 1861	3 yrs.	Discharged Dec. 17, 1865, at Granville, La., of disability; veteran.
Sturgill, William R	...do...	39	Oct. 17, 1861	3 yrs.	Transferred from Co. F; mustered out with company April 25, 1866; veteran.
Sturgeon, James	...do...	26	Oct. 8, 1861	3 yrs.	Transferred from Co. D; died Nov. 28, 1864, in hospital at New Orleans, La.
Sturgeon, Henderson	...do...	33	Oct. 8, 1861	3 yrs.	
Truman, Joseph	...do...	22	Oct. 19, 1861	3 yrs.	Transferred from Co. F; mustered out with company April 25, 1866; veteran.
Veach, Francis	...do...	18	Oct. 21, 1861	3 yrs.	Transferred from Co. F; mustered out with company April 25, 1866; veteran.
Veach, William T	...do...	17	Feb. 20, 1865	3 yr.	Mustered out Feb. 20, 1866, at New Orleans, La.
Venatti, Hezekiah	...do...	43	Oct. 8, 1861	3 yrs	Transferred from Co. D; discharged Dec. 23, 1864, at Algiers, La., of disability; veteran.
Ward, Craton	...do...	....	Sept. 1, 1862	3 yrs.	Mustered out with company April 25, 1866; veteran.
White, Thomas	...do...	18	Oct. 17, 1861	3 yrs.	Wounded May 3, 1864, in battle of Snaggy Point, La.; mustered out with company April 25, 1866; veteran.
White, Joseph	...do...	....	Oct. 3, 1861	3 yrs.	Mustered out Oct. 27, 1864, at New Orleans, La.
Williams, David R	...do...	19	Oct. 17, 1861	3 yrs.	Discharged Sept. 28, 1865, at Camp Dennison, O., of disability; veteran.
Wintersteen, John Q	...do...	22	Oct. 21, 1861	3 yrs.	Mustered out with company April 25, 1866; veteran.
Wood, John A	...do...	36	Oct. 17, 1861	3 yrs.	Died Oct. 8, 1862, on board hospital boat D. A. January.
Wood, David	...do...	18	Oct. 17, 1861	3 yrs.	Discharged ——, for wounds received May 16, 1863, in battle of Champion Hills, Miss.
Wood, Samuel L	...do...	24	Oct. 17, 1861	3 yrs.	Died May 5, 1862, at Cincinnati, O.
Wood, William P	...do...	30	Oct. 17, 1861	3 yrs.	Discharged Nov. —, 1862; disability.
Wood, Alfred T	...do...	18	Mch. 17, 1862	3 yrs	Mustered out March 16, 1865, at New Orleans, La.

COMPANY B

Mustered in Oct. 18, 1861, and Nov. 13, 1861, at Portsmouth, O., by R. B. Hull, Captain 18th Infantry, U. S. A. Mustered out April 25, 1866, at New Orleans, La., by A. McAllister, Captain 10th U. S. C. Art.

Names.	Rank.	Age.	Date of Entering the Service.	Period of Service.	Remarks.
Charles F. Reiniger	Captain	55	Aug. 7, 1861	3 yrs.	Promoted to Major April 2, 1863.
John Joehem	... do ...	37	Nov. 7, 1861	3 yrs.	Promoted from 1st Lieutenant April 2, 1863; discharged Nov. 12, 1864.
James C. Stimmel	... do ...	24	Oct. 29, 1861	3 yrs.	Transferred from Co. G; promoted to Lieut. Colonel April 20, 1866, but not mustered; mustered out with company April 25, 1866.
Charles Seifer	1st Lieut.	33	Oct. 18, 1861	3 yrs.	Promoted from 2d Lieutenant May 16, 1863; discharged Nov. 12, 1864, at New Orleans, La.
Benjamin Roberts	... do ...	25	Oct. 18, 1861	3 yrs.	Promoted from 2d Lieutenant Co. C June 18, 1863; appointed Adjutant Sept. 12, 1863.
Thomas J. Williams	... do ...	20	Oct. 17, 1861	3 yrs.	Promoted 2d Lieutenant from Q. M. Sergeant Jan. 18, 1865; to 1st Lieutenant Jan. 30, 1866; mustered out with company April 25, 1866; veteran.
John K. Combs	2d Lieut.	24	Nov. 18, 1861	3 yrs.	Promoted from Sergt. Major Feb. 14, 1863; to 1st Lieutenant Co. A March 29, 1865.
Leopold Sheidlen	1st Sergt.	27	Oct. 17, 1861	3 yrs.	Discharged March 24, 1863, at Moon Lake, Miss., of disability.
Henry Behrens	... do ...	29	Oct. 18, 1861	3 yrs.	Captured June 25, 1862; mustered out Nov. 12, 1864, at New Orleans, La.
David W. James	... do ...	25	Oct. 15, 1861	3 yrs.	Transferred from Co. E; appointed from private June 1, 1864; mustered out with company April 25, 1866; veteran.
Frank Ashenbrenner	Sergeant	42	Oct. 18, 1861	3 yrs.	Discharged Nov. 27, 1862, at Helena, Ark., of disability.
John Dern	... do ...	33	Oct. 18, 1861	3 yrs.	Discharged Nov. 27, 1862, at Helena, Ark., of disability.
John C. Dahler	... do ...	27	Oct. 18, 1861	3 yrs.	Discharged ——, at Memphis, Tenn., of disability.
Frederick Steiber	... do ...	27	Oct. 18, 1861	3 yrs.	Mustered out Nov. 12, 1864, at New Orleans, La.
Frederick Held	... do ...	30	Oct. 18, 1861	3 yrs.	Discharged Nov. 5, 1863, for wounds received May 16, 1863, in battle of Champion Hills, Miss.
Christopher Kraemer	... do ...	40	Nov. 13, 1861	3 yrs.	Mustered out Nov. 12, 1864, at New Orleans, La.
Casper Zipfel	... do ...	29	Oct. 18, 1861	3 yrs.	Mustered out Nov. 12, 1864, at New Orleans, La.
John Bevan	... do ...	23	Oct. 15, 1861	3 yrs.	Transferred from Co. E ——; promoted to Q. M. Sergeant Feb. 5, 1865; veteran.
Thomas S. Bennett	... do ...	27	Oct. 29, 1861	3 yrs.	Transferred from Co. G ——; transferred to Co. D Dec. 5, 1864; veteran.
David E. Jones	... do ...	22	Oct. 15, 1861	3 yrs.	Transferred from Co. E; captured May 5 1864, on board steamer John Warner on Red river, La.; mustered out June 30, 1865, at Columbus O.; veteran.
Lorenzo D. Dalrymple	... do ...	18	Nov. 12, 1861	3 yrs.	Transferred from Co. E; discharged Dec. 27, 1865, of disability; veteran.
Nicholas D. Main	... do ...	24	Oct. 29, 1861	3 yrs.	Transferred from Co. G ——; mustered out with company April 25, 1866; veteran.

Names.	Rank.	Age.	Date of Entering the Service.	Period of Service.	Remarks.
Peter Brown	Sergeant	21	Nov. 21, 1861	3 yrs.	Transferred from Co. H; mustered out with company April 25, 1866; veteran.
Daniel L. Bondurant	...do...	20	Oct. 29, 1861	3 yrs.	Transferred from Co. G; mustered out with company April 25, 1866; veteran.
Nathan. M. Kent	...do...	22	Oct. 29, 1861	3 yrs.	Transferred from Co. G; mustered out with company April 25, 1866; veteran.
Gottleib Sites	...do...	18	Oct. 10, 1861	3 yrs.	Appointed Sergeant Dec. 8, 1863; mustered out Nov. 12, 1864.
August Lange	Corporal	18	Oct. 18, 1861	3 yrs.	Died Sept. 23, 1862, at Helena, Ark.
Henry Hollenback	.do...	29	Oct. 18, 1861	3 yrs.	Mustered out Nov. 12, 1864, at New Orleans, La.
John Deinzer	...do...	28	Oct. 18, 1861	3 yrs.	Mustered out Nov. 12, 1864, at New Orleans, La.
George Reichert	...do...	18	Nov. 13, 1861	3 yrs.	Died Sept. 11, 1862, at Helena, Ark.
Augustus Clemens	...do...	....	Dec. 6, 1861	3 yrs.	Transferred to Veteran Reserve Corps Sept. 12, 1863; mustered out Jan. 5, 1865.
John Dimler	...do...	....	Dec. 10, 1861	3 yrs.	Appointed from Corporal Jan. 22, 1862; mustered out Nov. 12, 1864, at New Orleans, La.
Jacob Petry	...do...	19	Oct. 18, 1861	3 yrs.	Mustered out Nov. 12, 1864, at New Orleans, La.
Henry Seick	...do...	33	Nov. 13, 1861	3 yrs.	Mustered out Nov. 12, 1864, at New Orleans, La.
Henry Dunlap	...do...	18	Nov. 30, 1861	3 yrs.	Transferred from Co. H ——; transferred to Co. D Dec. 5, 1864.
Robert M. Fulton	...do...	21	Nov. 9, 1861	3 yrs.	Transferred from Co. E; wounded and captured April 8, 1864, at battle of Sabine Cross Roads, La.; exchanged June 24, 1864; ——; discharged June 27, 1865, of disability; veteran.
George Grindley	...do...	20	Oct. 15, 1861	3 yrs.	Transferred from Co. E; appointed Corporal ——; mustered out Feb. 7, 1866; veteran.
Charles H. Bing	...do..	21	Nov. 26, 1861	3 yrs.	Transferred from Co. E; mustered out with company April 25, 1866; veteran.
William Hughes	...do...	19	Nov. 15, 1861	3 yrs.	Transferred from Co. E; appointed Corporal June 1, 1864; mustered out with company April 25, 1866; veteran.
Thomas J. Williams	Corporal	21	Oct. 15, 1861	3 yrs.	Transferred from Co. E; appointed Corporal June 1, 1864; mustered out with company April 25, 1866; veteran.
James Rees	...do...	19	Nov. 19, 1861	3 yrs.	Transferred from Co. E; wounded May 1, 1864, in battle of Port Gibson, Miss.; appointed Corporal June 1, 1864; mustered out with company April 25, 1866; veteran.
Francis M. Seth	..do...	21	Oct. 29, 1861	3 yrs.	Transferred from Co. C; mustered out with company April 25, 1866; veteran.
Calvin McKnight	..do...	18	Oct. 31, 1861	3 yrs.	Transferred from Co. H; mustered out with company April 25, 1866; veteran.
Henry C. Marshall	...do...	26	Nov. 5, 1861	3 yrs.	Transferred from Co. B; mustered out with company April 25, 1866; veteran.
Samuel Nickels	...do...	....	Nov. 15, 1861	3 yrs.	Transferred from Co. G ——; appointed Corporal Feb. 14, 1866; mustered out with company April 25, 1866; veteran.
James O. L. Hueston	Musician	18	Nov. 13, 1861	3 yrs.	Promoted to Principal Musician ——.
Charles N. Clinger	...do...	15	Aug. 15, 1864	3 yrs.	Discharged June 27, 1865, of disability.

OHIO VOLUNTEER INFANTRY. 155

Names.	Rank.	Age.	Date of Entering the Service.	Period of Service.	Remarks.
Samuel Clinger	Wagoner	31	Nov. 11, 1861	3 yrs.	Transferred from Co. E; mustered out with company April 25, 1866; veteran.
Allen, William	Private	24	Oct. 22, 1861	3 yrs.	Transferred from Co. G; veteran.
Arman, Henry	...do..	21	Oct. 18, 1861	3 yrs.	Mustered out Nov. 12, 1864 at New Orleans, La.
Auer, Louis	...do..	..	Dec. 10, 1861	3 yrs	Mustered out Nov. 12 1864, at New Orleans, La.
Baker, Charles H	..do.	18	Nov. 23, 1861	3 yrs.	Transferred from Co. G; mustered out with company April 25, 1866; veteran.
Baust, Frank	...do...	40	Oct. 18, 1861	3 yrs.	Discharged Sept. 1, 1862, of disability.
Becker, William	...do...	40	Oct. 18, 1861	3 yrs.	Died July 23, 1864, at New Orleans, La.
Bender, Jacob	...do..	28	Feb. 3, 1862	3 yrs.	Mustered out Feb. 5, 1865, at New Orleans, La.
Benner, John	...do...	24	Oct. 8, 1861	3 yrs.	Mustered as John Bayner.
Bennett, Philander	...do...	24	Jan. 16, 1862	3 yrs.	Transferred from Co. H; mustered out Jan. 16, 1865.
Biebinger, Frederick	...do...	23	Sept. 15, 1861	3 yrs.	Discharged Oct. 18, 1861, at Portsmouth, O., of disability.
Bing, Joseph M	...do...	19	Nov. 2, 1861	3 yrs.	Transferred from Co. E; mustered out with company April 25, 1866; veteran.
Bing, John E	...do...	18	Nov. 2, 1861	3 yrs.	Transferred from Co. E; mustered out with company April 25, 1866; veteran.
Bingham, Levi	...do...	24	Feb. 5, 1862	3 yrs.	Transferred from Co. H; mustered out with company Feb. 5, 1865.
Braun, John George	...do...	27	Oct. 18, 1861	3 yrs.	Dircharged Oct. 18, 1861, at Portsmouth, O., of disability.
Braun, John Gottlieb	...do..	24	Oct. 18, 1861	3 yrs.	Transferred to 1st Missouri Battery April 20, 1863.
Brown, William C	...do...	25	Oct. 29, 1861	3 yrs.	Transferred from Co. G; mustered out with company April 25, 1866; veteran.
Burkholter, Nicholas	...do...	40	Oct. 18, 1861	3 yrs.	Mustered out Nov. 12, 1864, at New Orleans, La.
Carr, William	...do...	40	Nov. 13, 1861	3 yrs.	Transferred from Co. H; discharged Oct. 12, 1865, of disability; veteran.
Carpenter, Aaron	...do...	28	Nov. 21, 1861	3 yrs.	Transferred from Co. G; veteran.
Chaffin, George W	...do...	22	Nov. 6, 1861	3 yrs.	Transferred from Co. G; mustered out with company April 25, 1866; veteran.
Chaffin, Thomas	...do...	26	Jan. 27, 1864	3 yrs.	Transferred from Co. G; mustered out with company April 25, 1866.
Coffman, John	...do...	34	Oct. 26, 1861	3 yrs.	Transferred from Co. H; mustered out with company April 25, 1866; veteran.
Collman, Thomas	...do..	18	July 25, 1864	3 yrs.	Mustered out with company April 25, 1866.
Comer, Lewis	...do...	18	Oct. 29, 1861	3 yrs.	Transferred from Co. G; mustered out with company April 25, 1866; veteran.
Crabtree, Gillen	...do..	28	Oct. 29, 1861	3 yrs.	Transferred from Co. G; wounded April 8, 1864, in battle of Sabine Cross Roads, La., discharged Aug. 16, 1865, of disability; veteran.
Crabtree, Stephen	..do..	25	Oct. 29, 1861	3 yrs.	Transferred from Co. G; mustered out with company April 25, 1866; veteran.
Cross, Thomas	...do...	25	Nov. 25, 1861	3 yrs.	Transferred from Co. G; discharged June 27, 1865, of disability; veteran.
Daloh, Peter	..do...	26	Oct. 18, 1861	3 yrs.	Died July 15, 1862, at Portsmouth, O.
Daniels, David	...do...	19	Oct. 15, 1861	3 yrs.	Transferred from Co. E; captured April 8, 1864, at battle of Sabine Cross Roads, La.; mustered out June 30, 1865, at Columbus, O., veteran.

ROSTER OF FIFTY-SIXTH REGIMENT

Names.	Rank.	Age.	Date of Entering the Service.	Period of Service.	Remarks.
Davis, Thomas J	Private	42	Nov. 15, 1861	3 yrs.	Transferred from Co. E; wounded and captured May 5, 1864, on board steamer John Warner on Red River, La.; mustered out with Company April 25, 1866; veteran.
Davis, Charles H	...do...		Jan. 1, 1862	3 yrs.	Transferred from Co. E; mustered out with company April 25, 1866; veteran.
Deal, William	...do...	18	July 8, 1864	3 yrs.	Transferred from Co. E; mustered out with company April 25, 1866.
Dement, James B	...do...	19	Jan. 29, 1864	3 yrs.	Mustered out with company April 25, 1866.
Deshler, John	...do...	42	Nov. 13, 1861	3 yrs.	Died Jan. 5, 1862, at Portsmouth, O.
Dewitt, Hiram W	...do...	21	Nov. 7, 1862	3 yrs.	Transferred from Co. H; mustered out Nov. 7, 1865.
Donohew, Alvin	...do...	40	Dec. 10, 1861	3 yrs.	Transferred from Co. H Jan. 26, 1864.
Dowler, Francis M	...do...	18	Oct. 15, 1861	3 yrs.	Transferred from Co. E Jan. 26, 1864.
Dumong, Ferdinand	...do...	34	Oct. 18, 1861	3 yrs.	Died Sept. 9, 1862, at Helena, Ark.
Eitner, Peter	...do...	44	Nov. 13, 1861	3 yrs.	Died May —, 1862, at Shiloh, Tenn.
Elberfold, Clemens	...do...	44	Nov. 13, 1861	3 yrs.	Discharged ——, at Memphis, Tenn., of disability.
Emling, George	...do...	37	Feb. 3, 1862	3 yrs.	Wounded May 16, 1863, in Battle of Champion Hills, Miss.; mustered out Feb. 5, 1865.
Evans, Evan E	...do...	18	Oct. 15, 1861	3 yrs.	Transferred from Co. E; mustered out with company April 25, 1866; veteran.
Evans, Evan O	...do...	18	Oct. 15, 1861	3 yrs	Transferred from Co. E; captured April 8, 1864, at battle of Sabine Cross Roads, La., mustered out June 30, 1865, at Columbus, O., veteran.
Evans, John E	...do...	22	Nov. 18, 1861	3 yrs.	Transferred from Co. E; mustered out June 30, 1865, at Columbus, O., veteran.
Farian, John	...do...	36	Oct. 18, 1861	3 yrs.	Mustered out Nov. 12, 1864, at New Orleans, La.
Fasterman, William	...do...	25	Nov. 13, 1861	3 yrs.	Transferred from Co. G Jan. 26, 1864; veteran.
Fluth, William	...do...	40	Oct. 18, 1861	3 yrs.	Mustered out Nov. 12, 1864, at New Orleans, La.
Fouth, Thomas	...do...	29	Oct. 18, 1861	3 yrs.	
Fox, Christian F	...do...	22	July 4, 1864	1 yr.	Mustered out July 6, 1865, at New Orleans, La.
Freudenburg, John	...do...	34	Oct. 18, 1861	3 yrs.	Mustered out Nov. 12, 1864, at New Orleans, La.
Gautsche, Rudolph	...do...	30	Oct. 18, 1861	3 yrs.	Mustered out Nov. 12, 1864.
Georges, Rudolph	...do...	25	Oct. 18, 1861	3 yrs.	
Giles, Dennis	...do...	18	Oct. 29, 1861	3 yrs.	Transferred from Co. G; mustered out with company April 25, 1866; veteran.
Giles, Thomas C	...do...	23	Jan. 31, 1862	3 yrs.	Transferred from Co. G; mustered out with company April 25, 1866; vetern.
Gramme, Frederick	...do...	18	Nov. 13, 1861	3 yrs.	Captured June 25, 1862; exchanged; discharged and joined the navy ——
Griffith, Rees	...do...	19	Oct. 15, 1861	3 yrs.	Transferred from Co. E; mustered out with company April 25, 1866; veteran.
Guy, John W	...do...	43	Nov. 2, 1861	3 yrs.	Transferred from Co. E; discharged Nov. 7, 1865, of disability.
Hauser, Bartholomy	...do...	24	Oct. 18, 1861	3 yrs.	Mustered out Nov. 12, 1864, at New Orleans, La.
Henser, Joseph	...do...	30	Oct. 18, 1861	3 yrs.	Transferred to Veteran Reserve Corps Jan. 16, 1864.
Henser, Samuel	...do...	27	Nov. 13, 1861	3 yrs.	Mustered out Nov. 12, 1864, at New Orleans, La.
Herder, Jacob	...do...		Dec. 8, 1861	3 yrs.	Transferred from Co. G ——; mustered out with company April 25, 1866; veteran.

OHIO VOLUNTEER INFANTRY. 157

Names.	Rank.	Age.	Date of Entering the Service.	Period of Service.	Remarks.
Hepp, Marcus	Private	43	Oct. 18, 1861	3 yrs.	Transferred to Veteran Reserve Corps Sept. 13, 1863.
Hickson, Benjamin	...do...	24	Oct. 25, 1861	3 yrs.	Transferred from Co. E; veteran.
Hoffman, John	...do...	....	Dec. 10, 1861	3 yrs.	Killed May 16, 1863, in battle of Champion Hills, Miss.
Hollenback, Edward	...do...	21	Nov. 13, 1861	3 yrs.	Killed May 16, 1863, in battle of Champion Hills, Miss.
Hughes, George	...do...	26	Oct. 25, 1861	3 yrs.	Transferred from Co. E; mustered out with company April 25, 1866; veteran.
Hughes, James	...do...	20	Nov. 15, 1861	3 yrs.	Transferred from Co. E; mustered out with company April 25, 1866; veteran.
James, Alfred Jr.	...do...	18	Nov. 11, 1861	3 yrs.	Transferred from Co. E; mustered out with company April 25, 1866; veteran.
Jones, Thomas J.	...do...	18	Oct. 15, 1861	3 yrs.	Transferred from Co. E; Captured May 5, 1864, on board steamer John Warner on Red river, La.; mustered out June 30, 1865, at Columbus, O.; veteran
Jones, Dennis	...do...	18	Oct. 15, 1861	3 yrs.	Transferred from Co. E; mustered out June 30, 1865, at Columbus, O.; veteran.
Kintner, Frank	...do...	51	Oct. 18, 1861	3 yrs.	Died June 8, 1863, at Vicksburg, Miss.
Kinker, Henry	...do...	22	Oct. 18, 1861	3 yrs.	Mustered out Nov. 12, 1864, at New Orleans, La.
Krauser, John	...do...	30	Oct. 18, 1861	3 yrs.	Died July 27, 1862, in Asylum, Cincinnati, O.
Kreinbreider, William	...do...	25	Oct. 18, 1861	3 yrs.	Discharged Jan. 27, 1863, at St. Louis, Mo., of disability.
Kunz, Casper	...do...	42	Oct. 15, 1861	3 yrs.	Prisoner of war; discharged April 6, 1863, at Columbus, O.
Landfersick, Ludwick	...do...	26	Sept. 1, 1862	3 yrs.	Detached in 1st Missouri Battery April 16, 1863; mustered out July 6, 1865.
Loesh, John G.	...do...	....	Dec. 2, 1861	3 yrs.	Mustered out Nov. 12, 1864, at New Orleans, La.
Louks, Jacob S.	...do...	27	Nov. 18, 1861	3 yrs.	Transferred from Co. E; mustered out with company April 25, 1866; veteran.
Logue, Ellis	...do...	18	Nov. 11, 1861	3 yrs.	Transferred from Co. E; mustered out with company April 25, 1866; veteran.
Lundrach, Jacob	...do...	44	Nov. 13, 1861	3 yrs.	Discharged Aug. 20, 1862, at Helena, Ark, of disability.
McCallister, George W.	...do...	....	Jan. 2, 1864	3 yrs.	Transferred from Co. G; mustered out with company April 25, 1866; veteran.
McCann, Daniel	...do...	...	June 6, 1864	3 yrs.	Transferred from Co. G ——; mustered out with company April 25, 1866.
McIntire, George W.	...do...	24	Oct. 31, 1861	3 yrs.	Transferred from Co. H; mustered out with company April 25, 1866; veteran.
McKeever, Daniel	...do...	18	Nov. 15, 1861	3 yrs.	Transferred from Co. H; mustered out with company April 25, 1866; veteran.
McKnight, James	...do...	18	Nov. 4, 1861	3 yrs.	Transferred from Co. H; mustered out with company April 25, 1866; veteran.
Marker, Adam	...do...	43	Oct. 18, 1861	3 yrs.	Discharged Aug. 22, 1862, at hospital at Memphis, Tenn., of disability.
Merkle John	...do...	39	Nov. 13, 1861	3 yrs.	Died Aug. 20, 1862, at Helena, Ark.
Moritz, Conrad	...do...	44	Nov. 13, 1861	3 yrs.	Discharged Sept. 1, 1862, at Helena, Ark., of disability.
Meisner, George	...do...	35	Oct. 18, 1861	3 yrs.	Wounded May 16, 1863, in battle of Champion Hills, Miss.; mustered out Nov. 12, 1864, at New Orleans, La.

Names.	Rank.	Age.	Date of Entering the Service	Period of Service.	Remarks.
Mendle, William	Private	....	Nov. 15, 1861	3 yrs.	Discharged Sept. 1, 1862, at Helena, Ark., of disability.
Meyer, Henry	...do...	41	Oct. 18, 1861	3 yrs.	Wounded May 16, 1863, in battle of Champion Hills. Miss.; transferred to Veteran Reserve Corps ——.
Miller, Felix	...do...	31	Oct. 18, 1861	3 yrs.	Died Sept. 3, 1862, at Henela, Ark.
Morgan, Samuel	...do...	....	Dec. 25, 1861	3 yrs.	Transferred from Co. G; mustered out with company April 25, 1866; veteran.
Nannes, Frederick	...do...	40	Nov. 13, 1861	3 yrs.	Discharged Sept. 24, 1863, at Camp Dennison, O., of disability.
Nearman, William H	..do...	18	July 8, 1864	3 yrs.	Transferred from Co. E; mustered out with company April 25, 1866.
Newlan, Adam	...do...	33	Oct. 19, 1861	3 yrs.	Transferred from Co. H; mustered out with company April 25, 1866; veteran.
Oberly, Benjamin B	..do...	21	Oct. 29, 1861	3 yrs.	Transferred from Co. G; mustered out with company April 25, 1866; veteran.
Pepper, Frank	...do...	....	Jan. 11, 1862	3 yrs.	Discharged Sept. 1, 1862, of disability.
Perry, Jacob	...do...	18	Nov. 4, 1861	3 yrs.	Transferred from Co. H; wounded April 8, 1864, in battle of Sabine Cross Roads, La.; mustered out with company April 25, 1866; veteran.
Perry, James	...do...	22	Dec. 9, 1861	3 yrs.	Transferred from Co. H; mustered out with company April 25, 1866; veteran.
Petry, Nicolas	...do...	43	Oct. 18, 1861	3 yrs.	Mustered out Nov. 12, 1864, at New Orleans, La.
Petry, Peter	...do...	26	Oct. 18, 1861	3 yrs.	Mustered out Nov. 12, 1864.
Pfau, Adam	...do...	22	Oct. 18, 1861	3 yrs.	Discharged Sept. 30, 1862, at Memphis, Tenn., of disability.
Pfuhler, John	...do...	35	Oct. 18, 1861	3 yrs.	Transferred from Co. G ——; veteran.
Phillips, Andrew	...do...	29	Oct. 18, 1861	3 yrs.	Transferred from Co. H; mustered out with company April 25, 1866; veteran.
Potts, Hezekiah J	...do...	22	Oct. 29, 1861	3 yrs.	Transferred from Co. G; wounded April 8, 1864, in battle of Sabine Cross Roads, La; mustered out with company April 25, 1866; veteran.
Potts, Abraham W	..do...	22	Nov. 17, 1863	3 yrs.	Transferred from Co. G; mustered out with company April 25, 1866.
Radcliff, William H	...do...	21	Oct. 15, 1861	3 yrs.	Transferred from Co. E; mustered out with company April 25, 1866; veteran.
Rauch, Xavier	...do...	40	Nov. 13, 1861	3 yrs.	Discharged Nov. 23, 1863, at Jefferson City, Mo., of disability.
Reiniger, George	...do...	18	Oct. 18, 1861	3 yrs.	Transferred from Co. G ——; mustered out with company April 25, 1866; veteran.
Reinhard, Henry	...do...	35	Nov. 13, 1861	2 yrs.	Died July 21, 1863, at St. Louis, Mo.
Reller, Henry	...do...	24	Nov. 13, 1861	3 yrs.	Discharged April 6, 1863, at Columbus, O.
Riffelmacher, Michael	...do...	37	Nov. 13, 1861	3 yrs.	Killed May 16, 1863, in battle of Champion Hills, Miss.
Rockwell, John	...do...	43	Oct. 29, 1861	3 yrs.	Transferred from Co. G; mustered out with company April 25, 1866; veteran.
Roush, Newton J	...do...	18	Nov. 18, 1861	3 yrs.	Transferred from Co. E; mustered out with company April 25, 1866; veteran.
Sack, William	...do...	43	Oct. 18, 1861	3 yrs.	Transferred to Veteran Reserve Corps Sept. 13, 1863.
Salliday, George W	...do...	19	Nov. 4, 1861	3 yrs.	Transferred from Co. H; mustered out with company April 25, 1866; veteran.

Names.	Rank.	Age.	Date of Entering the Service.	Period of Service.	Remarks.
Sanders, Benjamin	Private	18	Oct. 22, 1861	3 yrs.	Transferred from Co. H; discharged Jan. 20, 1866, of disability; veteran.
Schaefer, John	do	42	Oct. 18, 1861	3 yrs.	Discharged Aug. 18, 1862, of disability.
Schaefer, Joseph	do	32	Oct. 18, 1861	3 yrs.	Died July 16, 1862, in hospital at Memphis, Tenn.
Schule, Jacob	do		Oct. 1, 1861	3 yrs.	Captured June 25, 1863 ——; joined the Navy ——.
Schwarz, Conrad	do	43	Nov. 13, 1861	3 yrs.	Died June 22, 1863, at Vicksburg, Miss.
Schweinberg, Henry	do	38	Nov. 13, 1861	3 yrs.	Mustered out Nov. 12, 1864, at New Orleans, La.
Seiz, Theophilus	do	28	Oct. 18, 1861	3 yrs.	Mustered out Nov. 12, 1864, at New Orleans, La.
Shety, Jacob	do	18	Nov. 13, 1861	3 yrs.	Captured June 26, 1862; ——; paroled prisoner.
Sickles, Lafayette	do	25	Nov. 29, 1861	3 yrs.	Transferred from Co. H; captured May 3, 1864, at battle of Snaggy Point, La.; mustered out June 30, 1865, at Columbus, O.
Smith, William	do		Dec. 6, 1861	3 yrs.	
Spitznagle, Henry	do	18	Dec. 9, 1861	3 yrs.	Transferred from Co. H; mustered out with company April 25, 1866; veteran.
Stevenson, Thomas K.	do	19	Oct. 29, 1861	3 yrs.	Transferred from Co. H; mustered out with company April 25, 1866; veteran.
Steingle, Joseph	do	21	Nov. 13, 1861	3 yrs.	Mustered out Nov. 12, 1864, at New Orleans, La.
Steinmeier, Frederick	do	20	Oct. 18, 1861	3 yrs.	Mustered out Nov. 12, 1864, at New Orleans, La.
Storz, Frank	do	18	Oct. 18, 1861	3 yrs.	Transferred to Co. G; transferred from Co. G ——; discharged Aug. 16, 1865, for disability; veteran.
Striber, Frederick	do	27	Oct. 18, 1861	3 yrs.	Mustered out Nov. 12, 1864, at New Orleans, La.
Titus, John C.	do	23	Oct. 29, 1861	3 yrs.	Transferred from Co. G; captured April 8, 1864, at battle of Sabine Cross Roads, La.; mustered out June 30, 1865, at Columbus, O.; veteran.
Thomas, Rees	do	29	Nov. 15, 1861	3 yrs.	Transferred from Co. E; captured May 1, 1863, at battle of Port Gibson, Miss.; mustered out with company April 25, 1866; veteran.
Thomas, William	do	21	Oct. 15, 1861	3 yrs.	Mustered out Sept. 6, 1865.
Thomas, Thomas D.	do	20	Oct. 15, 1861	3 yrs.	Transferred from Co. E; mustered out with company April 25, 1866; veteran.
Trailor, Benjamin	do	19	Nov. 17, 1861	3 yrs.	Transferred from Co. H; wounded May 3, 1864, in battle of Snaggy Point, La.; mustered out with company April 25, 1866; veteran.
Vollmer, William	do	36	Nov. 13, 1861	3 yrs.	Died June 16, 1862, at Portsmouth, O.
Weehle, Augustus	do		Jan. 2, 1862	3 yrs.	Discharged Aug. 18, 1862, of disability.
Wegman, Henry	do	18	Oct. 18, 1861	3 yrs.	Mustered out Nov. 12, 1864, at New Orleans, La.
Will, Michael	do	35	Oct. 18, 1861	3 yrs.	Mustered out Nov. 12, 1864, at New Orleans, La.
Welty, John	do	18	Nov. 13, 1861	3 yrs.	Captured June 25, 1862; joined the Navy.
Wetzel, Henry	do	37	Nov. 13, 1861	3 yrs.	Discharged Aug. 15, 1863, at Camp Dennison, O., of disability.

Names.	Rank.	Age.	Date of Entering the Service.	Period of Service.	Remarks.
Weidebrock, Christian.	Private	25	Oct. 16, 1861	3 yrs.	Absent, sick in hospital at Keokuk, Ia.
Williams, Ashley R.	...do...	18	Oct. 15, 1861	3 yrs.	Transferred from Co. E; discharged Dec. 6, 1864, of disability.
Williams, Daniel	...do...	19	Oct. 15, 1861	3 yrs.	Transferred from Co. E; discharged March 7, 1866, of disability; veteran.
Zwilcher, Engelbert	...do...		Feb. 3, 1862	3 yrs.	Captured June 25, 1862; joined the Navy.

COMPANY C.

Mustered in from Oct. 17, 1861, to Nov. 22, 1861, at Portsmouth, O., by R. B. Hull, Captain 18th Infantry, U. S. A. Mustered out April 25, 1866, at New Orleans, La., by A. McAllister, Captain 10th U. S. C. Art.

Names	Rank	Age	Date of Entering the Service	Period of Service	Remarks
William B. Williams	Captain	35	Aug. 7, 1861	3 yrs.	Discharged Nov. 14, 1864, by order of War Department.
William G. Snyder	...do...	29	Oct. 29, 1861	3 yrs.	Transferred from Co. K; mustered out with company April 25, 1866.
Jeremiah P. Wood	1st Lieut	31	Nov. 7, 1861	3 yrs.	Died Sept. 17, 1863, at Portsmouth, O.
Moses Rife	...do...	24	Nov. 20, 1861	3 yrs.	Transferred from Co. E —; appointed Regt. Quartermaster——.
Christian H. Schaefer	...do...	21	Oct. 5, 1861	3 yrs.	Promoted from 2d Lieutenant Co. A, Jan. 18, 1865; mustered out with company April 25, 1866.
Benjamin Roberts	2d Lieut.	25	Oct. 18, 1861	3 yrs.	Promoted to 1st Lieutenant Co. B, June 18, 1863.
James Vandervort	...do...	33	Oct. 17, 1861	3 yrs.	Promoted from 1st Sergeant June 18, 1863; to 1st Lieutenant Co. D May 31, 1865; veteran.
Harvey N. Bridwell	...do...	25	Oct. 21, 1861	3 yrs.	Promoted from 1st Sergeant Co. D May 31, 1865; mustered out with company April 25, 1866.
Abraham Hibbins	1st Sergt.	24	Nov. 19, 1861	3 yrs	Transferred from Co. I as 1st Sergeant; mustered out with company April 25, 1866; veteran.
Henry C. Dare	Sergeant	19	Oct. 17, 1861	3 yrs.	Discharged July 16, 1863, for wounds received May 1, 1863, in battle of Port Gibson, Miss.
Andrew S. Drennen	...do...	22	Oct. 17, 1861	3 yrs.	Appointed Corporal July 25, 1862; Sergeant Aug. 25, 1865; mustered out with company April 25, 1866; veteran.
Thomas L. Evans	...do...	21	Oct. 17, 1861	3 yrs.	Wounded May 1, 1863, in battle o. Port Gibson, Miss.; appointed from Corporal May 1, 1864; mustered out Nov. 14, 1864, at New Orleans, La.
Richard D. Evans	...do...	22	Oct. 17, 1861	3 yrs.	Discharged Dec. 4, 1863, at Helena, Ark., of disability.
Samuel Gohen	...do...	28	Oct. 28, 1861	3 yrs.	Transferred from Co. K; mustered out with company April 25, 1866; veteran.
Henry Kugelman	...do...	19	Oct. 17, 1861	3 yrs.	Appointed from Corporal Jan. 1, 1863; mustered out Nov. 14, 1864, at New Orleans, La.
William H. McLaughlin	...do...	23	Dec. 22, 1861	3 yrs.	Transferred from Co. I; mustered out with company April 25, 1866; veteran.
John H. Morris	...do...	23	Oct. 17, 1861	3 yrs.	Promoted to Sergt. Major Feb. 4, 1865; veteran.
David F. Radcliffe	...do...	23	Oct. 24, 1861	3 yrs.	Transferred from Co. K; wounded April 8, 1864, in battle of Sabine Cross Roads, La.; discharged Aug. 22, 1865, of disability; veteran.

OHIO VOLUNTEER INFANTRY

Names.	Rank.	Age.	Date of Entering the Service.	Period of Service.	Remarks.
William Roberts	Sergeant	23	Oct. 17, 1861	3 yrs.	Mustered out Nov. 14, 1864, at New Orleans, La.
William H. Wait	... do ...	27	Dec. 7, 1861	3 yrs.	Transferred from Co. K; mustered out with company April 25, 1866; veteran.
Martin J. Adams	Corporal	19	Oct. 17, 1861	3 yrs.	Appointed Corporal May 1, 1864; mustered out with company April 25, 1866; veteran.
John J. Bussey	... do ...	18	Dec. 12, 1861	3 yrs.	Transferred from Co. K; mustered out with company April 25, 1866; veteran.
George Caldwell	... do ...	24	Oct. 19, 1861	3 yrs.	Discharged July 24, 1862, at Cincinnati, O., of disability.
Lodwick D. Davis	... do ..	20	Oct. 17, 1861	3 yrs.	Wounded May 16, 1863, in battle of Champion Hills, Miss.; transferred to Veteran Reserve Corps ——.
Thomas D. Davis	... do ...	18	Oct. 17, 1861	3 yrs.	Wounded May 16, 1863, in battle of Champion Hills, Miss.; mustered out with company April 25, 1866; veteran.
David Evans	... do ...	24	Oct. 17, 1861	3 yrs.	Died July 14, 1863, at Chickasaw Bayou, Miss., of wounds received May 16, 1863, in battle of Champion Hills, Miss.
Daniel Friend	... do ...	20	Oct. 19, 1861	3 yrs.	Discharged Sept. 24, 1862, at Helena, Ark., of disability.
James C. Harper	... do ...	18	Nov. 11, 1861	3 yrs.	Transferred from Co. K; mustered out with company April 25, 1866; veteran.
Luther C. High	... do ...	25	Dec. 5, 1861	3 yrs.	Transferred from Co. K; mustered out with company April 25, 1866; veteran.
Lafayette Holmes	... do ...		Jan. 14, 1862	3 yrs.	Transferred from Co. K; mustered out with company April 25, 1866; veteran.
Thomas S. Jones	... do ...	23	Oct. 25, 1861	3 yrs.	Wounded May 16, 1863, in battle of Champion Hills, Miss.; appointed Corporal May, 1, 1864; mustered out with company April 25, 1866; veteran.
Henry Schump	... do ...	21	Oct. 17, 1861	3 yrs.	Promoted to Com. Sergeant Nov. 1, 1862.
Adam Siemon	.. do ...	18	Oct. 31, 1861	3 yrs.	Transferred from Co. I; mustered out with company April 25, 1866; veteran.
William S. Wilcox	... do ...	25	Nov. 26, 1864	1 yr.	Transferred from Co. D; mustered out Nov. 26, 1865, at New Orleans, La.
Thomas J. Williams	... do ...	20	Oct. 17, 1861	3 yrs.	Promoted to Q. M. Sergeant July 4, 1863.
George M. Gordy	Musician	28	Dec. 7, 1861	3 yrs.	Transferred from Co. K; mustered out with company April 25, 1866; veteran.
George W. Lowery	... do ...	21	Dec. 12, 1861	3 yrs.	Transferred from Co. K Jan. 26, 1864; discharged June 19, 1865, at New Orleans, La.; of disability; veteran.
Thomas J. Morris	... do ...	18	Oct. 30, 1861	3 yrs.	Killed May 4, 1864, while on board steamer John Warner on Red river, La.; veteran.
Frank Adams	Wagoner	40	Oct. 17, 1861	3 yrs.	Discharged Feb. 26, 1864, at Madisonville, La., of disability.
Adamson, Thomas G.	Private	39	Oct. 17, 1861	3 yrs.	Discharged Dec. 31, 1861, at Portsmouth, O., of disability.
Alexander, Zachariah T	... do ...	18	Dec. 11, 1861	3 yrs.	Transferred from Company I; mustered out with company April 25, 1866; veteran.
Burwhite, William	... do ...	19	Oct. 24, 1864	1 yr.	Transferred from Co. D; mustered out Dec. 15, 1865, at New Orleans, La.

Names.	Rank.	Age.	Date of Entering the Service.	Period of Service.	Remarks.
Bennett, Hosea B.......	Private	21	Dec. 12, 1861	3 yrs.	Transferred from Co. K; veteran.
Bergman, Andrew J....	... do ...	35	Mch. 19, 1864	3 yrs.	Transferred from Co. K ——; felo-de-see at Gretna, La., May 5, 1865.
Black, Charles B	... do ...	18	Feb. 20, 1865	1 yr.	Mustered out Sept. 5, 1865, at St. Louis, Mo.
Black, Oscar C...........	... do ...	18	Nov. 30, 1861	3 yrs.	Transferred from Co. I; mustered out Feb. 3, 1865, at New Orleans, La.; veteran.
Bland, George H.........	... do ...	19	Oct. 16, 1861	3 yrs.	Transferred from Co. I; died Dec. 20, 1864, at New Orleans, La.; veteran.
Bochar, John K..........	... do ...		Nov. 18, 1863	3 yrs.	Captured April 8, 1864, at battle of Sabine Cross Roads, La.; died June 14, 1864, in Rebel Prison at Tyler, Tex.
Brooks, John J..........	. do ...	35	Dec. 9, 1861	3 yrs.	Transferred from Co. K; mustered out with company April 25, 1866; veteran.
Bowen, William	... do ...		Jan. 14, 1862	3 yrs.	Transferred from Co. K; wounded April 8, 1864, in battle of Sabine Cross Roads, La.; mustered out with company April 25, 1866; veteran.
Brown, Riley.............	... do ...	20	Oct. 17, 1861	3 yrs.	Discharged Oct. 9, 1863, for wounds received May 1, 1863, in battle of Port Gibson, Miss.
Burt, Thomas J.........	... do ...	36	Dec. 14, 1861	3 yrs.	Transferred from Co. K; mustered out with company April 25, 1866; veteran.
Campbell, Alexander....	... do ...	27	Oct. 7, 1861	3 yrs.	Died Nov. 7, 1862, at Helena, Ark.
Carey, Philip.............	... do ...	19	Nov. 10, 1861	3 yrs.	Transferred from Co. I; mustered out with company April 25, 1866; veteran.
Clair, George.............	... do ...	18	Mch. 29, 1864	3 yrs.	Transferred from Co. K ——; mustered out Aug. 19, 1865, at Camp Dennison, O.
Cochran, John J.........	... do ...	22	Oct. 26, 1861	3 yrs.	Mustered out with company April 25, 1866; veteran.
Cole, Charles.............	... do ...	18	Oct. 17, 1861	3 yrs.	Discharged Jan. 2, 1862, at Chillicothe, O.
Collins, James A	... do ...	19	Mch. 27, 1865	1 yr.	Mustered out March 27, 1866, at New Orleans, La.
Coriell, Thomas J.......	... do ...	19	Dec. 16, 1861	3 yrs.	Transferred from Co. K; veteran.
Coriell, Elias.............	... do ...	22	Dec. 19, 1861	3 yrs.	Transferred from Co. K; mustered out June 30, 1865, at Columbus, O.; veteran.
Crabtree, Joseph S......	... do ..	18	Oct. 17, 1861	3 yrs.	Transferred to Veteran Reserve Corps July 1, 1864.
Crabtree, Daniel.........	... do ...	18	Oct. 17, 1861	3 yrs.	Died April 3, 1862, at St. Louis Missouri.
Crabtree, William.......	... do ...	33	Oct. 17, 1861	3 yrs.	Died Aug. 31, 1863, at St. Louis, Mo., of wounds received May 16, 1863, in battle of Champion Hills, Miss.
Crabtree, Disbury S....	... do ...	19	Oct. 17, 1861	3 yrs.	Discharged Dec. 8, 1862.
Cummings, John R......	. . do ...	21	Nov. 15, 1861	3 yrs.	Transferred from Co. K, Jan. 26, 1864; mustered out Nov. 9, 1865, at New Orleans, La.
Dalrymple, Smith........	... do ...	20	Jan. 2, 1862	3 yrs.	Wounded May 16, 1863, in battle of Champion Hills, Miss; mustered out with company April 25, 1866; veteran.
Davis, Richard T........	... do ...	24	Oct. 17, 1861	3 yrs.	Killed May 16, 1863, in battle of Champion Hills, Miss.
Davis, Thomas E........	. . do ...	19	Oct. 17, 1861	3 yrs.	Mustered out Oct. 4, 1865, at Camp Dennison, O; veteran.
Davis, John W...........	... do ...	19	Oct. 17, 1861	3 yrs.	Transferred to Mississippi River Marine Brigade ——.
Davis, Reese.............	... do ...	19	Oct. 17, 1861	3 yrs.	Mustered out with company April 25, 1866; veteran.

OHIO VOLUNTEER INFANTRY. 163

Names.	Rank.	Age.	Date of Entering the Service.	Period of Service.	Remarks.
Davis David F..........	Private	43	Oct. 25, 1861	3 yrs.	Discharged March 26, 1864, at Alexandria, La., of disability; veteran.
Davis, William D.......	...do..	18	Oct. 30, 1861	3 yrs.	Captured April 8, 1864, at battle of Sabine Cross Roads, La.; mustered out June 30, 1865, at Columbus, O; veteran.
Davis, Jonathan.........	...do...	....	Jan. 14, 1862	3 yrs.	Transferred from Co. K; mustered out with company April 25, 1866; veteran.
Deno, Henry............	...do...	22	Nov. 26, 1864	1 yr.	Transferred from Co. D; mustered out Nov. 26, 1865, at New Orleans, La.
Dent, John H...........	...do...	19	Feb. 24, 1865	1 yr.	Mustered out Feb. 25, 1866, at New Orleans, La.
Desmond, John..........	...do...	41	Oct. 18, 1861	3 yrs.	Transferred from Co. I; mustered out with company April 25, 1866; veteran.
Dills, Stephen T........	...do...	25	Oct. 17, 1861	3 yrs.	Mustered out Nov. 14, 1864, at New Orleans, La.
Dodson, Isaac...........	..do...	22	Nov. 3, 1861	3 yrs.	Mustered out Nov. 14, 1864, at New Orleans, La.
Dolby, James A.........	...do...	19	Oct. 26, 1861	3 yrs.	Transferred from Co. I; mustered out with company April 25, 1866; veteran.
Duvall, David D........	..do...	29	Feb. 13, 1865	1 yr.	Mustered out to date Feb. 26, 1865, at Columbus, O.
Edwards, Evan.........	...do...	26	Oct. 18, 1861	3 yrs.	Mustered out with company April 25, 1866; veteran.
Edwards, Evan E.......	...do...	22	Oct. 17, 1861	3 yrs.	Discharged Dec. 18, 1863, for wounds received May 16, 1863, in battle of Champion Hills, Miss.
Edwards, William......	...do...	18	Oct. 17, 1861	3 yrs.	Wounded May 16, 1863, in battle of Champion Hills, Miss.; transferred to Veteran Reserve Corps April 28, 1864.
Edwards, David E......	...do...	18	Oct. 17, 1861	3 yrs.	Wounded May 16, 1863, in battle of Champion Hills. Miss.; mustered out with company April 25, 1866; veteran.
Ellis, Stephen R........	...do...	18	Dec. 11, 1861	3 yrs.	Transferred from Co. I; wounded April 8, 1864, in battle of Sabine Cross Roads, La.; mustered out with company April 25, 1866; veteran.
Evans, Daniel J	...do...	....	Jan. 4, 1862	3 yrs.	Discharged Sept. 22, 1864, at New Orleans, La., of disability; veteran.
Evans, William T......	...do...	35	Oct. 17, 1861	3 yrs.	Mustered out with company April 25, 1866; veteran.
Evans, Evan D.........	...do...	18	Oct. 17, 1861	3 yrs.	Died March 22, 1862, at Crump's Landing, Tennessee.
Fitch, Edward..........	...do...	18	Oct. 17, 1861	3 yrs.	Discharged ——, by order of War Department.
Gates, David...........	...do...	24	Oct. 29, 1861	3 yrs.	Transferred from Co. K; mustered out March 15, 1866, at Columbus, O.; veteran.
Goudy, Edward.........	...do...	21	Oct. 19, 1861	3 yrs.	Mustered out with company April 25, 1866; veteran.
Gephart, Daniel	...do...	....	Dec. 7, 1861	3 yrs.	Transferred from Co. K; discharged Aug. 23, 1863, at Carrolton, La., of disability.
Gratigny, Almond F....	...do...	25	Feb. 15, 1865	1 yr.	Mustered out Feb. 18, 1866, at New Orleans, La.
Guynn, William A......	...do...	25	Feb. 25, 1864	3 yrs.	Transferred from Co. K ——; mustered out with company April 25, 1866.
Hahn, Lawrence........	...do...	21	Oct. 26, 1861	3 yrs.	Transferred from Co. I; mustered out with company April 25, 1866; veteran.

Names.	Rank.	Age.	Date of Entering the Service.	Period of Service.	Remarks.
Hall, James C	Private	25	Oct. 17, 1861	3 yrs.	Captured May 5, 1864, on board steamer John Warner, Red river, La.; mustered out June 30 1865, at Columbus, O.; veteran.
Halbert, John	...do...	43	Oct. 26, 1861	3 yrs.	Discharged Nov. 26, 1862, at Cincinnati, O., of disability.
Harwood, Thomas	...do...	25	Oct. 17, 1861	3 yrs.	Mustered out Nov. 14, 1864, at New Orleans, La.
Hasse, Michael	...do...	36	Oct. 17, 1861	3 yrs.	Discharged Dec. 10, 1862, at Keokuk, Ia., of disability.
Hatfield, William	...do...	27	Oct. 31, 1861	3 yrs.	Transferred from Co. I; mustered out with company April 25, 1866; veteran.
Henesy, Patrick	...do...	30	Nov. 15, 1864	1 yr.	Transferred from Co. D; mustered out Jan. 15, 1866, at New Orleans, La.
Hied, George	...do...	44	Oct. 26, 1861	3 yrs.	Discharged Jan. 16, 1863, at St. Louis, Mo., of disability.
Hill, William S	...do...	18	Oct. 17, 1861	3 yrs.	
Hoyt, William B	...do...	40	Oct. 19, 1861	3 yrs.	Mustered out Nov. 14, 1864, at New Orleans, La.
Hudson, Samuel L	...do...	21	Feb. 20, 1865	1 yr.	Mustered out Feb. 20, 1866, at New Orleans, La.
Hudson Elijah H	...do...	20	Feb. 18, 1865	1 yr.	Mustered out Feb. 18, 1866, at New Orleans, La.
Hunley, Joseph	...do...	32	Oct. 17, 1861	3 yrs.	Mustered out with company April 25, 1866; veteran.
Hunter, Grant B	...do...	36	Oct. 17, 1861	3 yrs.	Mustered out with company April 25, 1866; veteran.
Jackson, Robert H	...do...	16	Sept. 16, 1864	1 yr.	Mustered out July 3, 1865, at New Orleans, La.
Jones, Evans E	...do...	19	Oct. 17, 1861	3 yrs.	Died June 13, 1865, at New Orleans, La.; veteran.
Jones, Daniel	...do...	18	Oct. 17, 1861	3 yrs.	Wounded June 8, 1863, in siege of Vicksburg, Miss.; mustered out with company April 25, 1866; veteran.
Jones, Isaac J	...do...	21	Oct. 17, 1861	3 yrs.	Died April 10, 1862, at St. Louis, Mo.
Jones, William J	...do...	22	Oct. 25, 1861	3 yrs.	Mustered out with company April 25, 1866; veteran.
Kline, Nicholas	...do...	18	Feb. 27, 1864	3 yrs.	Transferred from Co. K——; mustered out with company April 25, 1866.
Knowland, Lutilius	...do...	21	Nov. 30, 1861	3 yrs.	Transferred from Co. K; veteran.
Lacy, Daniel	...do...	25	Oct. 17, 1861	3 yrs.	Killed ——, in an affray at Portsmouth, O.
Leniger, William	...do...	22	Dec. 7, 1861	3 yrs.	Transferred from Co. K; mustered out Jan. 25, 1866, at Columbus, O.; veteran.
Lewis, Henry H	...do...	22	Oct. 25, 1861	3 yrs.	Died Feb. 8, 1864, at Cairo, Ill., of wounds received May 16, 1863, in battle of Champion Hills, Miss.
Lewis, Joshua	...do...	37	Oct. 17, 1861	3 yrs.	Wounded May 16, 1863, in battle of Champion Hills, Miss.; mustered out May 30, 1865, at New Orleans, La.; veteran.
Lloyd, Peter	...do...	44	Oct. 22, 1861	3 yrs.	Transferred from Co. H; mustered out June 30, 1865, at Columbus, O.; veteran.
Lowery, Francis M	...do...	21	Sept. 6, 1864	1 yr.	Mustered out Sept. 6, 1865, at New Orleans, La.
McCann, Thomas J	...do...	18	Nov. 30, 1861	3 yrs.	Transferred from Co. K; captured April 8, 1864, at battle of Sabine Cross Roads, La.; mustered out June 30, 1865, at Columbus, O.
McDonald, Andrew C	...do...	21	Oct. 17, 1861	3 yrs.	Discharged Jan. 26, 1863, at St. Louis, Mo., of disability.
McManaway, Allen	...do...	24	Oct. 17, 1861	3 yrs.	

Names.	Rank.	Age.	Date of Entering the Service.	Period of Service.	Remarks.
Martin, John	Private	29	Oct. 27, 1864	1 yr.	Transferred from Co. D; mustered out Dec. 17, 1865, at New Orleans, La.
Matthews, Thomas	...do..	23	Oct. 17, 1861	3 yrs.	Died April 1ᶜ, 1862, at St. Louis, Mo.
Moore, Samuel H	...do...	24	April 1, 1865	1 yr.	Mustered out March 31, 1866, at New Orleans, La.
Morgan, Evan	...do..	31	Oct. 17, 1861	3 yrs.	Died Dec. 21, 1863, in hospital at Cincinnati, O.
Morris, William	...do...	21	Feb. 10, 1862	3 yrs.	Mustered out Feb. 9, 1865, at New Orleans, La.; veteran.
Morris, James W	...do...	20	Oct. 17, 1861	3 yrs.	Discharged Nov. 15, 1862, at Keokuk, Ia., of disability.
Murray, John P	...do..	43	Oct. 17, 1861	3 yrs.	Discharged Sept. 18, 1862, at Helena, Ark., of disability.
Newcomb, Benjamin F.	...do...	25	Dec. 3, 1861	3 yrs.	Transferred from Co. K; captured May 5, 1864, on Red River Expedition; mustered out June 30, 1865, at Columbus, O.
Nolte, Henry	...do...	33	Oct. 17, 1861	3 yrs.	Discharged Sept. 21, 1863, at St. Louis, Mo., for wounds received May 16, 1863, in battle of Champion Hill, Miss.
O'Reilly, Martin	...do...	21	Oct. 14, 1861	3 yrs.	Transferred from Co. I; mustered out with company April 25, 1866; veteran.
Patterson, Joseph H	...do...	30	Oct. 17, 1861	3 yrs.	Promoted to Com. Sergeant Aug. 15, 1862.
Pearson, William H	...do...	18	Mch. 7, 1865	1 yr.	Mustered out March 7, 1866, at New Orleans, La.
Phillips, Lewis	...do...	18	Nov. 20, 1861	3 yrs.	Discharged Dec. 6, 1862, at Helena, Ark., of disability.
Phillips, Daniel	...do...	....	Dec. 27, 1861	3 yrs.	Died Aug., 25, 1862, at Helena, Ark.
Plummer, Henry C	...do...	18	Feb. 22, 1864	3 yrs.	Transferred from Co. K——.
Richards, Henry	...do...	21	Oct. 17, 1861	3 yrs.	Killed May 16, 1863, in battle of Champion Hills, Miss.
Riggs, Joseph	...do...	18	Oct. 30, 1861	3 yrs.	Died Oct. 17, 1862, at St. Louis, Missouri.
Roberts, Moses	...do...	18	Oct. 17, 1861	3 yrs.	Wounded April 8, 1864, in battle of Sabine Cross Roads, La.; mustered out with company April 25, 1866; veteran.
Roberts, Jeremiah	...do...	26	Jan. 21, 1864	3 yrs.	Mustered out June 30, 1865, at Columbus, O.
Russell, Emanuel	...do...	22	Oct. 26, 1861	3 yrs.	Transferred from Co. K; captured May 5, 1864, on Red River Expedition; mustered out June 30, 1865, at Columbus, O.
Samuel, William	...do...	21	Oct. 17, 1861	3 yrs.	Mustered out with company April 25, 1866; veteran.
Schlichter, Christian	...do...	21	Nov. 16, 1861	3 yrs.	Mustered out with company April 25, 1866; veteran.
Scott, Peter	...do..	....	Jan. 2, 1862	3 yrs.	Transferred from Co. K; wounded April 8, 1864, in battle of Sabine Cross Roads, La.; veteran.
Sherwood, Jacob	...do...	18	Oct. 15, 1861	3 yrs.	Transferred from Co. I; wounded April 8, 1864, in battle of Sabine Cross Roads, La.; mustered out with company April 25, 1866; veteran.
Simer, Andrew J. P	...do..	28	Dec. 16, 1861	3 yrs.	Transferred from Co. K; veteran.
Southerland, David	..do..	18	Nov. 6, 1861	3 yrs.	Transferred from Co. I; mustered out with company April 25, 1866; veteran.
Spekman, Thomas	...do...	33	Oct. 17, 1861	3 yrs.	Wounded May 1, 1863, in battle of Port Gibson, Miss.; transferred to Veteran Reserve Corps ——.
Springer, Henry N	...do...	19	Oct. 26, 1861	3 yrs.	Transferred from Co. I; mustered out with company April 25, 1866; veteran.

Names.	Rank.	Age.	Date of Entering the Service.	Period of Service.	Remarks.
Stamm, Christian	Private	29	Feb. 10, 1864	3 yrs.	Transferred from Co. K——; mustered out with company April 25, 1866.
Stewart, George M	... do ...	20	Nov. 30, 1861	3 yrs.	Transferred from Co. I; mustered out with company April 25, 1866; veteran.
Stewart, Oliver P	... do ...	18	Mch. 27, 1865	1 yr.	Mustered out March 27, 1866, at New Orleans, La.
Thacker, Fountain	... do ...	24	Nov. 7, 1861	3 yrs.	Transferred from Co. I; mustered out June 30, 1865, at Columbus, O.; veteran.
Thomas, Daniel	... do ...		Dec. 13, 1861	3 yrs.	Mustered out Nov. 14, 1864, at New Orleans, La.
Thomas, Jonathan P	... do ...		Jan. 10, 1862	3 yrs.	Promoted to Chaplain Sept. 9, 1862.
Thompson, John	... do ...	25	Dec. 10, 1861	3 yrs.	Transferred from Co. K; mustered out with company April 25, 1866; veteran.
Tripp, George	... do ...	19	Nov. 6, 1861	3 yrs.	Transferred from Co. I; mustered out June 30, 1865, at Columbus, O.; veteran.
Walker, James	... do ...	44	Oct. 26, 1861	3 yrs.	Transferred from Co. K; captured April 8, 1864, at battle of Sabine Cross Roads, La.; mustered out June 30, 1865, at Columbus, O.; veteran.
Walker, Willis D	... do ...	21	Oct. 17, 1861	3 yrs.	
White, Jacob	... do ...	18	Oct. 29, 1861	3 yrs.	Transferred from Co. K; mustered out with company April 25, 1866; veteran.
Williams, John H	... do ...	18	Oct. 17, 1861	3 yrs.	Killed May 16, 1863, in battle of Champion Hills, Miss.
Williams, Evan E	... do ...	18	Oct. 17, 1861	3 yrs.	Discharged Dec. —, 1861, at Portsmouth, O., on writ of habeas corpus.
Williams, John	... do ...	19	Oct. 17, 1861	3 yrs.	Mustered out Feb. 27, 1866, at Columbus, O.; veteran.
Williams, Thoms M	... do ...	26	Nov. 14, 1861	3 yrs.	
Willmer, Philip	... do ...	30	Jan. 3, 1865	1 yr.	Mustered out with company April 25, 1866.
Wilson Sylvester	... do ...	18	Oct. 20, 1861	3 yrs.	Transferred from Co. I; died April 9, 1864 at Camp Ford, Tex., of wound received April 8, 1864, in battle of Sabine Cross Roads, La.; veteran.
Wilson, William A	... do ...	23	Oct. 25, 1861	3 yrs.	Transferred from Co. I; mustered out with company April 25, 1866; veteran.
Yelley, Benjamin	... do ...	18	Dec. 7, 1861	3 yrs.	Transferred from Co. K; mustered out with company April 25, 1866; veteran.
Young, Berry	... do ...	18	Mch. 14, 1865	1 yr.	Mustered out March 17, 1866, at New Orleans, La.

COMPANY D

ORIGINAL COMPANY.—Mustered in from Oct. 8, 1861, to Nov. 7, 1861, at Portsmouth, O., Columbus, O., and Gallipolis, O., by J. R. Edie, Major 15th Infantry, U. S. A.; R. B. Hull, 1st Lieutenant 18th Infantry, U. S. A., and A. B. Dodd, Captain 15th Infantry, U. S. A. Mustered out Nov. 12, 1864, at New Orleans, La., by ——.

NEW COMPANY.—Mustered in Nov. 22, 1864, for one year, at Camp Chase, O., by W. P. Richardson, Colonel 25th O. V. I. Mustered out Nov. 22, 1865, at New Orleans, La., by A. McAllister, Captain 10th U. S. C. Art.

Names.	Rank.	Age.	Date of Entering the Service.	Period of Service.	Remarks.
David B. Lodwick	Captain	21	Aug. 11, 1861	3 yrs.	Resigned July 27, 1863.
Henry E. Jones	... do ...	25	Sept. 23, 1861	3 yrs.	Transferred from Co. A Aug. 8, 1863; detached on Brigade and Division Staff until May 8, 1864; promoted to Lieut. Colonel Jan. 18, 1865.
Levi M. Willits	... do ...	32	Nov. 23, 1864	1 yr.	Mustered out with company Nov. 22, 1865.
Charles W. Veach	1st Lieut.	27	Oct. 18, 1861	3 yrs.	Discharged June 2, 1862.
William L. Porter	... do ...		Sept. 5, 1862	3 yrs.	Detached on Major General Thomas' staff; resigned Nov. 10, 1864.
Orry H. Wadsworth	... do ...	25	Nov. 23, 1864	1 yr.	Resigned May 10, 1865.
James Vandervort	... do ...	33	Oct. 17, 1861	3 yrs.	Promoted from 2d Lieutenant Co. C, May 31, 1865; mustered out with company Nov. 22, 1865; veteran.
Murty W. Lodwick	2d Lieut.	22	Oct. 8, 1861	3 yrs.	Mustered out Sept. 3, 1862.
Augustus S. Chute	... do ...	21	Oct. 8, 1861	3 yrs.	Promoted from 1st Sergeant Oct. 3, 1862; killed May 16, 1863, in battle of Champion Hills, Miss.
Christian H. Schaefer	1st Sergt.	21	Oct. 5, 1861	3 yrs.	Appointed from Sergeant Oct. 3, 1862; promoted to 2d Lieutenant Co. A May 16, 1863.
Harvey N. Bridwell	... do ...	25	Oct. 21, 1861	3 yrs.	Captured May 16, 1863, in battle of Champion Hills, Miss.; 1st Sergeant Aug. 11, 1863; transferred to Co. A Jan. 26, 1864; promoted to 2d Lieutenant Co. C, May 31, 1865; veteran.
Thomas S. Bennett	... do ...	27	Oct. 29, 1861	3 yrs.	Transferred from Co. B, Dec. 5, 1864; mustered out with company Nov. 22, 1865; veteran.
James C. Bingham	Sergeant	19	Oct. 8, 1861	3 yrs.	Appointed from Corporal Aug. 11, 1863; transferred to Co. A Jan. 26, 1864; veteran.
Joseph C. Burriss	... do ...	25	Oct. 21, 1861	3 yrs.	Died Oct. 8, 1862, at St. Louis, Mo..
Thomas H. Cox	... do ...	18	Oct. 5, 1861	3 yrs.	Transferred to Co. A Jan. 26, 1864; veteran.
George W. Cox	... do ...	36	Oct. 16, 1861	3 yrs.	Transferred from Co. A ——; mustered out with company Nov. 22, 1865; veteran.
Henry Dunlap	... do ...	18	Nov. 30, 1861	3 yrs.	Transferred from Co. B; mustered out with company Nov. 22, 1865; veteran.
Aaron Hamilton	... do ...	33	Oct. 21, 1861	3 yrs.	Discharged Oct. —, 1863, at St. Louis, Mo., of disability.
George W. Neff	... do ...	22	Oct. 18, 1861	3 yrs.	Transferred from Co. A; mustered out June 30, 1865, at Columbus, O.
James U. Pease	... do ...	27	Oct. 18, 1861	3 yrs.	Transferred from Co. A; mustered out with company Nov. 22, 1865; veteran.
Stephen B. Toburn	... do ...	19	Oct. 8, 1861	3 yrs.	Promoted to Sergeant Major July 23, 1863.
Amos Fudor	... do ...	18	Sept. 24, 1864	1 yr.	Mustered out July 3, 1865.
Nathan T. Veach	... do ...	37	Oct. 21, 1861	3 yrs.	Discharged Oct. —, 1862, of disability.
Frank Wallace	... do ...	24	Oct. 8, 1861	3 yrs.	Killed Dec. 11, 1862, in camp at Helena, Ark.
Samuel L. Wood	... do ...	18	Oct. 5, 1861	3 yrs.	Died May 19, 1864, of wounds received May 5, 1864, in action at Cheneyville, La.; veteran.

Names.	Rank.	Age.	Date of Entering the Service	Period of Service.	Remarks.
Azariah Arthur	Corporal	21	Oct. 24, 1861	3 yrs.	Transferred to Co. A; from Co. A Dec. 1864 ——; mustered out with company Nov. 22, 1865; veteran.
James Anderson	...do...	22	Oct. 8, 1861	3 yrs.	Wounded May 16, 1863, in battle of Champion Hills, Miss.; killed April 8, 1864, in battle of Sabine Cross Roads, La.; veteran.
William Bacon	...do...	41	Nov. 10, 1861	3 yrs.	Appointed Corporal Nov. —, 1862; transferred to Co. A Jan. 26, 1864; veteran.
John Barr	...do...	44	Oct. 21, 1861	3 yrs.	Wounded and captured May 16, 1863, at battle of Champion Hills, Miss.; transferred from Co. A, Battalion, Dec. 6, 1864; mustered out Jan. 30, 1865, at Columbus, O.; veteran.
Robert Bowles	...do...	20	Oct. 21, 1861	3 yrs.	Transferred from Co. A ——; mustered out June 30, 1865, at Columbus, O.; veteran.
Francis M. Cole	...do...	22	Oct. 21, 1861	3 yrs	Appointed Corporal ——, 1863; mustered out Nov. 12, 1864, at New Orleans, La.
Lewis Comer	...do...	36	Nov. 7, 1861	3 yrs.	Discharged April, 4, 1863, of disability.
Joseph R. Cross	...do...	35	Oct. 21, 1861	3 yrs.	Died March 31, 1862, at Crump's Landing, Tenn.
Silas A. Dickens	...do...	18	Oct. 11, 1864	1 yr.	Mustered out Nov. 10, 1865, at New Orleans, La.
James M. Holliday	...do...	19	Oct. 16, 1861	3 yrs.	Transferred from Co. A Dec. 6, 1864 ——; mustered out with company Nov. 22, 1865; veteran.
David A. Loveland	...do...	21	Oct. 21, 1861	3 yrs.	Died June 3, 1863, of wounds received May 16, 1863, in battle of Champion Hills Miss.
Ezra Miller	...do...	19	Nov. 11, 1864	1 yr.	Mustered out Nov. 11, 1865, at New Orleans, La.
Silas R. Moon	...do...	30	Oct. 27, 1864	1 yr.	Mustered out Oct. 27, 1865, at New Orleans, La.
John C. Seamon	...do...	20	Nov. 4, 1864	1 yr.	Mustered out Oct. 12, 1865, at New Orleans, La.
David Storer	...do...	23	Nov. 18, 1861	3 yrs.	Captured June 5, 1863, at Champion Hills, Miss.; transferred from Co. A Dec. 6 1864; mustered out with company Nov. 22, 1865; veteran.
John C. Teaman	...do...	34	Oct. 13, 1864	1 yr.	Mustered out Oct. 12, 1865, at New Orleans, La.
William S. Wilcox	...do...	25	Nov. 26, 1864	1 yr.	Transferred to Co. C Nov. 21, 1865.
Oliver Wirtz	...do...	19	Oct. 8, 1861	3 yrs.	Discharged Nov. 8, 1862, at Keokuk, Ia., of disability.
Jesse Wood	...do...	19	Oct. 8, 1861	3 yrs.	Appointed Corporal Nov. —, 1863; transferred to Co. A Jan. 26, 1864; veteran.
Elias A. Branham	Musician	18	Oct. 21, 1861	3 yrs.	Transferred to Co. A ——.
Elias A. Bridwell	...do...	18	Oct. 21, 1861	3 yrs.	Transferred to Co. A, Jan. 26, 1864; veteran.
Jeremiah M. Howell	...do...	45	Oct. 11, 1861	3 yrs.	Died March 27, 1862, at Crump's Landing, Tenn.
Charles H. Nelson	...do...	18	Nov. 17, 1864	1 yr.	Mustered out Nov. 17, 1865, at New Orleans, La.
David M. Sigman	...do...	18	Nov. 22, 1864	1 yr.	Mustered out with company Nov. 22, 1865.
Henry C. Edgington	Wagoner	21	Oct. 21, 1861	3 yrs.	Captured May 16, 1863, at battle of Champion Hills, Miss.; transferred to Co. A Jan. 26, 1864; veteran.
Adams, Jacob L.	Private	34	Oct. 8, 1861	3 yrs.	
Adams, William	...do...	21	Oct. 14, 1864	1 yr.	
Allen, Robert	...do...	26	Oct. 24, 1861	3 yrs.	Died July 1, 1863, at Memphis, Tenn.
Altman, Solomon	...do...	30	Oct. 8, 1861	3 yrs.	Transferred to Veteran Reserve Corps ——.
Atkinson, John	...do...	27	Oct. 10, 1864	1 yr.	Mustered out Oct. 9, 1865, at New Orleans, La.

OHIO VOLUNTEER INFANTRY.

Names.	Rank.	Age.	Date of Entering the Service.	Period of Service.	Remarks.
Avery, Joseph J	Private	19	Sept. 22, 1864	1 yr.	Mustered out July 3, 1865, at New Orleans, La.
Avery, John M	... do ...	18	Oct. 1, 1864	1 yr.	Mustered out July 3, 1865, at New Orleans, La.
Bacon, John A	... do ...	19	Oct. 21, 1861	3 yrs.	Discharged May 8, 1862, at St. Louis, Mo., of disability.
Bacon, William G	... do ...	25	Oct. 21, 1861	3 yrs.	Transferred to Co. A Jan. 26, 1864; veteran.
Badger, William	. do ...	31	Oct. 8, 1861	3 yrs.	Transferred to Co. A Jan. 26, 1864; veteran.
Barhite, William	... do ...	19	Oct. 24, 1864	1 yr.	Transferred to Co. C, Nov. 21, 1865.
Bates, John	... do ...	21	Nov. 4, 1864	1 yr.	
Beavers, Andrew	... do ...	42	Oct. 21, 1861	3 yrs.	Died May 30, 1862, in Scioto county, Ohio.
Berger, Martin L	... do ...	36	Oct. 12, 1864	1 yr.	Mustered out Oct. 11, 1865, at New Orleans, La.
Bradfield, Washington	... do ...	20	Oct 5, 1861	3 yrs.	Mustered out Nov. 12, 1864, at New Orleans, La.
Bradfield, William	... do ...	22	Oct. 5, 1861	3 yrs	Killed May 5, 1864, on board steamer John Warner on Red river, La.; veteran.
Brawham, Edward	... do ...	42	Oct. 21, 1861	3 yrs.	Discharged Nov. —, 1862, of disability.
Brenner, Frederick	... do ...	28	Nov. 7, 1864	1 yr.	Discharged May 19, 1865, at New Orleans, La., of disability.
Cadwell, Garrett	... do ...	25	Oct. 14, 1864	1 yr.	
Cadwell, Jesse F	... do ...	24	Oct. 9, 1864	1 yr.	
Carr, Anthony	... do ...	19	Oct. 13, 1864	1 yr.	
Casey, James	... do ...	28	Nov. 11, 1864	1 yr.	
Choquett, Henry	. do ...	22	Nov. 22, 1864	1 yr.	Mustered out Nov. 22, 1865, at New Orleans, La.
Clarke, William J	... do ...	21	Oct. 14, 1864	1 yr.	
Clefford, John M	... do ...	22	Oct. 21, 1861	3 yrs.	Mustered out Nov. 12, 1864, at New Orleans, La.
Clefford, Morgan	... do ...	19	Oct. 21, 1861	3 yrs.	Transferred to Co. A Jan. 26, 1864; veteran.
Clefford, Luke	... do ...	35	Oct. 21, 1861	3 yrs.	Killed May 16, 1863, in battle of Champion Hills, Miss.
Cochran, Hiram C	... do ...	38	Oct. 15, 1864	1 yr.	Mustered out Oct. 15, 1865, at New Orleans, La.
Colvin, John	... do ...	33	Oct. 21, 1861	3 yrs.	Died April 17, 1862, at St. Louis, Mo.
Cook, Joseph	... do ...	34	Nov. 17, 1864	1 yr.	
Cook, Benjamin F	... do ...	43	Sept. 28, 1864	1 yr.	Mustered out June 10, 1865, at New Orleans, La.
Conwell, Thomas D	... do ...	18	Oct. 20, 1864	1 yr.	Mustered out June 21, 1865, at New Orleans, La.
Crab, Hale	... do ...	29	Oct. 24, 1864	1 yr.	
Crogman, Antone	... do ...	30	Oct. 11, 1864	1 yr.	Discharged Aug. 16, 1865, at New Orleans, La., of disability.
Cross, Thomas L	... do ...	23	Oct. 21, 1861	3 yrs.	Transferred to Co. A, Jan. 26, 1864; veteran.
Cross, Wilson	... do ...	29	Oct. 21, 1861	3 yrs.	Transferred to Co. A, Jan. 26, 1864; veteran.
Cross, Allen R	... do ...	22	Oct. 21, 1861	3 yrs.	Discharged Jan. 19, 1864, at Algiers, La. of disability.
Daniels, John	... do ...	18	Oct. 5, 1861	3 yrs.	Captured May 16, 1863, at battle of Champion Hills, Miss.
Deno, Henry	... do ...	22	Nov. 26, 1864	1 yr.	Transferred to Co. C, Nov. 21, 1865.
Devine, James A	. do ...	25	Nov. 11, 1864	1 yr.	Mustered out Nov. 11, 1865, at New Orleans, La.
Dodds, Thomas B	... do ...	44	Oct. 8, 1861	3 yrs.	Killed May 16, 1863, in battle of Champion Hills, Miss.
Eaton, Turner	... do ...	31	Oct. 8, 1861	3 yrs.	Killed May 16, 1863, in battle of Champion Hills, Miss.
Ellison, William G. L	... do ...	22	Oct. 8, 1861	3 yrs.	Wounded May 1, 1863, in battle of Port Gibson, Miss.; mustered out Nov. 12, 1864, at New Orleans, La.
Eno, Cleophius	... do ...	23	Oct. 5, 1861	3 yrs.	Discharged Feb. —, 1863, of disability.
Estill, William	... do ...	45	Oct. 8, 1861	3 yrs.	Discharged Dec. 13, 1862, at Helena, Ark., of disability.

Names.	Rank.	Age.	Date of Entering the Service.	Period of Service.	Remarks.
Evans, Perminius	Private	44	Oct. 22, 1864	1 yr.	Mustered out Oct. 25, 1865, at New Orleans, La.
Farrell, George W	...do...	23	Nov. 4, 1864	1 yr.	
Ferguson, Reason	...do...	23	Oct. 5, 1861	3 yrs.	Discharged August 3, 1864, at New Orleans, La., for wounds received May 16, 1863, in battle of Champion Hills, Miss.
Ferris, James	...do...	23	Oct. 20, 1864	1 yr.	
Flanagan, Michael	...do...	22	Nov. 3, 1864	1 yr.	
Fricks, John	...do...	34	Oct. 10, 1864	1 yr.	Mustered out Oct. 10, 1865, at New Orleans, La.
Gilmore, Andrew	...do...	43	Oct. 8, 1861	3 yrs.	Died May 3, 1862, at Vinton Furnace, O.
Galliger, John	...do...	33	Oct. 8, 1861	3 yrs.	Transferred to Co. A, Jan. 26, 1864; veteran.
Goldsby, John	...do...	29	Oct. 14, 1864	1 yr.	
Graves, George W	...do...	26	Oct. 5, 1861	3 yrs.	Discharged May 3, 1862, at Louisville, Ky., of disability.
Gregor, Thomas	...do...	29	Nov. 5, 1864	1 yr.	
Grenle, Aaron	...do...	24	Oct. 12, 1864	1 yr.	Mustered out Oct. 11, 1865, at New Orleans, La.
Hahn, William	...do...	18	Oct. 10, 1864	1 yr.	Mustered out Oct. 9, 1865, at New Orleans, La.
Hamilton, Lewis H	...do...	32	Oct. 15, 1861	3 yrs.	Reduced from Hospital Steward —; discharged June —, 1863, at Gallipolis, O., of disability.
Hammond, John G	...do...	27	Nov. 17, 1864	1 yr.	Mustered out Nov. 17, 1865, at New Orleans, La.
Harrington, George	...do...	28	Nov. 4, 1864	1 yr.	Mustered out Nov. 4, 1865, at New Orleans, La.
Hays, Henry	...do...	18	Oct. 13, 1864	1 yr.	Mustered out Oct. 13, 1865, at New Orleans, La.
Henesy, Patrick	...do...	30	Nov. 15, 1864	1 yr.	Transferred to Co. C, Nov. 21, 1865.
Henderson, William	...do...	25	Oct. 1, 1864	1 yr.	
Henry, William	...do...	22	Oct. 8, 1861	3 yrs.	
Hemenis, Matthew	...do...	29	Nov. 1, 1864	1 yr.	Mustered out Nov. 1, 1865, at New Orleans, La.
Herr, Peter F	...do...	19	Oct. 15, 1864	1 yr.	Mustered out Nov. 22, 1865.
Hildebrand, James	...do...	18	Sept. 30, 1864	1 yr.	Mustered out July 3, 1865, at New Orleans, La.
Hoffman, Albert	...do...	24	Nov. 5, 1864	1 yr.	
Hoffman, Ogden	...do...	22	Nov. 22, 1864	1 yr.	Mustered out Nov. 22, 1865, at New Orleans, La.
Hunsucker, Henry	...do...	21	Oct. 21, 1861	3 yrs.	Transferred to Co. A, Jan. 26, 1864; veteran.
Hutton, Milton	...do...	23	Oct. 21, 1861	3 yrs.	
Hutton, John	...do...	18	Oct. 21, 1861	3 yrs.	Died Sept. 15, 1862, at Helena, Ark.
Irwin, Albert	...do...	23	Oct. 5, 1861	3 yrs.	Discharged Sept. 30, 1862, at Helena, Ark., of disability.
Jeckel, Bernard	...do...	21	Oct. 11, 1864	1 yr.	Mustered out Oct. 11, 1865, at New Orleans, La.
Jones, Charles	...do...	18	Sept. 20, 1864	1 yr.	Mustered out July 3, 1865, at New Orleans, La.
Jones, John	...do...	18	Nov. 10, 1864	1 yr.	Mustered out Nov. 10, 1865, at New Orleans, La.
Kantz, Lewis P	...do...	19	Sept. 24, 1864	1 yr.	Died April 21, 1865, at St. Louis, Mo.
Keyser, Abner	...do...	20	Oct. 21, 1861	3 yrs.	Transferred to Co. A Jan. 26, 1864; veteran.
King, Robert H	...do...	28	Nov. 14, 1864	1 yr.	Mustered out May 30, 1865, at Mobile, Ala.
Lamb, Benoni	...do...	35	Oct. 8, 1861	3 yrs.	Transferred to Co. A Jan. 26, 1864; veteran.
Leonard, George	...do...	38	Nov. 3, 1864	1 yr.	
Lenning, Britton	...do...	20	Sept. 26, 1864	1 yr.	Mustered out July 3, 1865, at New Orleans, La.
Lenning, Melancthon	...do...	24	Oct. 1, 1864	1 yr.	Mustered out July 3, 1865, at New Orleans, La.
Long, Charles	...do...	21	Oct. 25, 1864	1 yr.	
Long, Isaac N	...do...	22	Sept. 24, 1864	1 yr.	Mustered out July 3, 1865, at New Orleans, La.

OHIO VOLUNTEER INFANTRY. 171

Names.	Rank.	Age.	Date of Entering the Service.	Period of Service.	Remarks.
Lukemire, John	Private	44	Oct. 1, 1864	1 yr.	Mustered out Oct. 6, 1865, at New Orleans, La.
McCormick, John	... do ...	18	Oct. 1, 1864	1 yr.	Mustered out July 3, 1865, at St. Louis, Mo.
McDonald, George	... do ..	43	Oct. 18, 1864	1 yr.	Mustered out Oct. 18, 1865, at New Orleans, La.
McFadden, Philomen B.	... do ...	30	Nov. 17, 1864	1 yr.	Mustered out Nov. 17, 1865, at New Orleans, La.
McMahon, Thomas	... do ...	27	Oct. 30, 1864	1 yr.	
McNurry, Samuel W	... do ...	45	Oct. 8, 1861	3 yrs.	Discharged ——, 1862, of disability.
Madden, William	... do ...	20	Nov. 30, 1864	1 yr.	
Maloney, John	... do ...	18	Oct. 20, 1864	1 yr.	Mustered out Oct. 20, 1865, at New Orleans, La.
Marshall, Alpheus	.. do .	18	Oct. 8, 1861	3 yrs	Mustered out Nov. 12, 1864, at New Orleans, La.
Martin, John	... do ...	29	Oct. 27, 1864	1 yr.	Transferred to Co. C Nov. 21, 1865.
Martin, Charles S.	... do ...	18	Oct. 5, 1861	3 yrs.	Wounded ——, 1863. in siege of Vicksburg, Miss.; transferred to Co. A Jan. 26, 1864; veteran.
Millirons, Thomas J.	... do ...	23	Oct. 8, 1861	3 yrs.	Mustered out Nov. 12, 1864, at New Orleans, La.
Mills, Zachariah	... do ...	24	Oct. 8, 1861	3 yrs.	Wounded May 1, 1863, in battle of Port Gibson, Miss.; mustered out Nov. 12, 1864, at New Orleans, La.
Moyer, Wilber C.	... do ...	18	Oct. 19, 1864	1 yr.	Mustered out Nov. 22, 1865.
Mulford, Jasper	... do ...	18	Oct. 8, 1864	1 yr.	Mustered out Oct. 8, 1865, at New Orleans, La.
Murphy, Samuel	... do ...	22	Oct. 8, 1861	3 yrs.	Mustered out Nov. 12, 1864, at New Orleans, La.
Neff, Eli	... do ...	37	Nov. 7, 1861	3 yrs.	Discharged ——, 1862, of disability.
Ocans, William	... do ..	21	Oct. 20, 1864	1 yr.	
Odle, James	.. do ..	18	Oct. 21, 1861	3 yrs.	Wounded May 16, 1863, in battle of Champion Hills. Miss.; transferred to Co A Jan. 26, 1864; veteran.
Owens, John	... do ...	20	Oct. 18, 1864	1 yr.	Mustered out Oct. 18, 1865, at New Orleans, La.
Page, William	... do ...	23	Oct. 8, 1861	3 yrs.	Died April 10, 1862, at West Union, O.
Page, Lorenzo D	... do ...	33	Oct. 8, 1861	3 yrs.	Transferred to Co. A Jan. 26, 1864; veteran.
Park, Rufus H	... do ...	34	Oct. 9, 1864	1 yr.	Discharged Nov. 18. 1864, at Camp Chase, O., of disability.
Parr, William	... do ...	30	Nov. 2, 1864	1 yr.	Mustered out Nov. 2, 1865, at New Orleans, La.
Pickle, Russell	... do ...	20	Nov. 5, 1864	1 yr.	Discharged Jan. 26, 1865, at New Orleans, La., of disability.
Pickle, Rosemond	... do ...	28	Nov. 5, 1864	1 yr.	
Phalwine, Jacob	... do ...	18	Oct. 17, 1864	1 yr.	Died Aug. 26, 1865, in Granville, La.
Pieman, John C	... do ...	34	Oct. 13, 1864	1 yr.	Mustered out Nov. 22, 1865, at New Orleans, La.
Price, James C	... do ...	25	Sept. 30, 1864	1 yr.	Died April 21, 1865, at New Orleans, La.
Rankin, Enoch P	... do ...	26	Nov. 14, 1864	1 yr.	Mustered out Aug. 16, 1865, at New Orleans, La.
Reinkie, John	... do ...	20	Oct. 11, 1864	1 yr.	Mustered out Oct. 11, 1865, at New Orleans. La.
Russell, James N	.. do ..	30	Oct. 5, 1861	3 yrs.	Discharged Dec. 4, 1862, at Keokuk, Ia., of sability.
Sands, James	... do ...	20	Nov. 5, 1864	1 yr.	
Sayers, John	... do ...	19	Nov. 1, 1864	1 yr.	
Schimansky, Lewis	... do ...	18	Oct. 3, 1864	1 yr.	Mustered out Oct. 12, 1865, at New Orleans, La.
Shaw, Jonathan	... do ...	34	Oct. 21, 1861	3 yrs.	Mustered out Nov. 12, 1864, at New Orleans, La.
Sheahan, John	... do ...	26	Nov. 4, 1864	1 yr.	
Sheppard, Leonard	... do ...	23	Oct. 8, 1861	3 yrs.	Discharged Jan. 20, 1863, at St. Louis, Mo., of disability.
Sheppard, Alexander	... do ...	38	Oct. 8, 1861	3 yrs.	Discharged —, 1862, of disability.
Shidler, John L	... do ...	27	Oct. 21, 1864	1 yr.	Mustered out Oct. 21, 1865, at New Orleans, La.

Names.	Rank.	Age.	Date of Entering the Service	Period of Service.	Remarks.
Shrader, Frederick	Private	18	Oct. 3, 1864	1 yr.	Mustered out Oct. 11, 1865, at New Orleans, La.
Simpkins, Albert	...do...	25	Oct. 7, 1864	1 yr.	Mustered out Oct. 7, 1865, at New Orleans, La.
Simpson, Wm. H. H	...do...	21	Nov. 5, 1861	3 yrs.	Captured May 16, 1863, at battle of Champion Hills, Miss.; transferred to Co. A Jan. 26, 1864; veteran.
Slamaker, George	...do...	23	Oct. 27, 1864	1 yr.	
Slaymaker, George	...do...	23	Oct. 27, 1864	1 yr.	
Smith, Allen G	...do...	19	Oct. 21, 1861	3 yrs.	Died March 11, 1862, at Cincinnati, O.
Smith, Judson	...do...	37	Oct. 27, 1864	1 yr.	Mustered out May 25, 1865, at New Orleans, La.
Smith, Henry	...do...	22	Nov. 4, 1864	1 yr.	Mustered out Aug. 3, 1865, at St. Louis, Mo.
Smith, William	...do...	22	Oct. 15, 1864	1 yr.	
Smith, William	...do...	21	Oct. 18, 1864	1 yr.	
Snively, John	...do...	18	Oct. 8, 1861	3 yrs.	Transferred to Co. A Jan. 26, 1864; veteran.
Somers, Charles	...do...	18	Oct. 8, 1861	3 yrs.	Discharged ——, 1861, by civil authority.
Sorley, James	...do...	21	Oct. 14, 1864	1 yr.	
Spence, Thomas	...do...	28	Nov. 3, 1864	1 yr.	
Stephens, Wm. H	...do...	18	Oct. 10, 1864	1 yr.	Mustered out Oct. 10, 1865, at New Orleans, La.
Stephens, James E	...do...	20	Oct. 28, 1864	1 yr.	
Stockham, John	...do...	18	Oct. 21, 1861	3 yrs.	Captured May 16, 1863, at battle of Champion Hills, Miss.; mustered out Nov. 12, 1864, at New Orleans, La.
Storer, Charles V	...do...		Nov. 18, 1861	3 yrs.	Discharged Nov. 13, 1862, at Keokuk, Ia., of disability.
Sturgeon, Henderson	...do...	33	Oct. 8, 1861	3 yrs.	Transferred to Co. A Jan. 26, 1864; veteran.
Sturgeon, James	...do...	26	Oct. 8, 1861	3 yrs.	Transferred to Co. A Jan. 26, 1864; veteran.
Sutton, Oswell	...do...	44	Sept. 27, 1864	1 yr.	Mustered out July 3, 1865, at New Orleans, La.
Thompson, Charles	...do...	21	Nov. 3, 1864	1 yr.	
Tucker, William	...do...	18	Oct. 29, 1861	3 yrs.	Discharged ——, 1862, of disability.
Veach, George W	...do...	23	Oct. 21, 1861	3 yrs.	Discharged May 3, 1862, at Louisville, Ky., of disability.
Veach, John E	...do...	18	Oct 21, 1861	3 yrs.	Died May 20, 1863, of wounds received May 16, 1863, in battle of Champion Hills, Miss.
Veach, Francis	...do...	18	Oct. 21, 1861	3 yrs.	Transferred to Co. A Jan. 26, 1864; veteran.
Vennatti, Hezekiah	...do...	43	Oct. 8, 1861	3 yrs.	Transferred to Co. A Jan. 26, 1864; veteran.
Walker, Charles	...do...	27	Nov. 5, 1864	1 yr.	
Walker, James	...do...	27	Nov. 4, 1864	1 yr.	
Wallace, Elisha S	...do...	27	Oct. 8, 1861	3 yrs.	Mustered out Nov. 14, 1864, at New Orleans, La.
Walter, John	...do...	19	Oct. 25, 1864	1 yr.	
Ward, Barney	...do...	23	Oct. 13, 1864	1 yr.	
Watson, Albert	...do...	21	Nov. 3, 1864	1 yr.	
Wesley, William	...do...	17	Oct. 12, 1864	1 yr.	Mustered out Oct. 12, 1865, at New Orleans, La.
West, Robert	...do...	25	Oct. 15, 1864	1 yr.	Mustered out Oct. 15, 1865, at New Orleans, La.
Whittaker, Henry	...do...	35	Sept. 28, 1864	1 yr.	Mustered out Aug. 9, 1865, at St. Louis, Mo.
Williams, Henry	...do...	19	Oct. 8, 1861	3 yrs.	Died Jan. 25, 1862, at Portsmouth, O.
Wilson, Robert	...do...	18	Oct. 19, 1864	1 yr.	
Williams, John	...do...	23	Nov. 17, 1864	1 yr.	
Wilson, James	...do...	21	Nov. 4, 1864	1 yr.	
Wilson, James	...do...	27	Oct. 10, 1864	1 yr.	
Winchell, Israel	...do...		Oct. 8, 1861	3 yrs.	Discharged ——, 1861, by civil authority.

OHIO VOLUNTEER INFANTRY 173

Names.	Rank.	Age.	Date of Entering the Service.	Period of Service.	Remarks.
Winterstein, John	Private	19	Oct. 21, 1861	3 yrs.	Discharged ——, 1862, of disability.
Wood, Alfred T	do	....	Mch. 17, 1862	3 yrs.	Discharged Nov. 12, 1864, at New Orleans, La., of disability; veteran.
Woods, William	do	23	Oct. 7, 1864	1 yr.	Mustered out Oct. 7, 1865, at New Orleans, La.
Wyatt, Benjamin F	do	18	Sept. 22, 1864	1 yr.	Mustered out July 3, 1865, at New Orleans, La.

COMPANY E.

Mustered in Nov. 28, 1861, at Portsmouth, O., by R. B. Hull, Captain 18th Infantry, U. S. A.
Mustered out Nov. 12, 1864, at New Orleans, La., by Thomas R. Rodman, A. C. M.

Names	Rank	Age	Date of Entering the Service	Period of Service	Remarks
John Herbert Evans	Captain	25	Aug. 20, 1861	3 yrs.	Mustered out Nov. 19, 1864, at New Orleans, La.
Moses Rife	1st Lieut.	24	Oct. 31, 1861	3 yrs.	Wounded May 16, 1863, in battle of Champion Hills, Miss.; appointed Regt. Quartermaster Sept. 1, 1863.
John J. Markham	do	25	Oct. 15, 1861	3 yrs.	Promoted to 2d Lieutenant from 1st Sergeant March 18, 1863; to 1st Lieutenant May 9, 1864; mustered out Nov. 19, 1864, at New Orleans, La.
James K. Campbell	d Lieut.	25	Oct. 15, 1861	3 yrs.	Resigned Aug. 5, 1862.
James L. O. Huston	do	18	Nov. 13, 1861	3 yrs.	Promoted from Principal Musician Sept. 6, 1862; resigned April 17, 1863.
David W. James	1st Sergt	25	Oct. 15, 1861	3 yrs	Appointed from Sergeant June 1, 1864; transferred to Co. B ——; veteran.
George L. Rife	Sergeant	22	Nov. 2, 1861	3 yrs.	Killed May 16, 1863, in battle of Champion Hills, Miss.
David E. Jones	do	21	Oct. 15, 1861	3 yrs.	Transferred to Co. B Jan. 26, 1864; veteran.
John E. Bevan	do	23	Oct. 15, 1861	3 yrs.	Transferred to Co. B Jan. 26, 1864; veteran.
James H. Evans	Corporal	23	Oct. 15, 1861	3 yrs.	Killed May 1, 1863, in battle of Port Gibson, Mississippi.
Robert M. Fulton	do	21	Nov. 9, 1861	3 yrs.	Transferred to Co. B Jan. 26, 1864; veteran.
George Grindley	do	20	Oct. 15, 1861	3 yrs.	Transferred to Co. B Jan. 26, 1864; veteran.
John C. Gross	do	27	Nov. 2, 1861	3 yrs.	Promoted to Com. Sergeant July 4, 1863.
Philip D. Jenkins	do	21	Oct. 15, 1861	3 yrs.	Discharged ——, of disability.
Thomas D. Jones	do	20	Oct. 15, 1861	3 yrs.	Died Sept. 24, 1862, at Helena, Ark.
Henry Martin	do	24	Oct. 15, 1861	3 yrs.	Died July 29, 1863, at Evansville, Ind., of wounds received May 16, 1863, in battle of Champion Hills, Miss.
David Mulholland	do	27	Nov. 2, 1861	3 yrs.	Discharged Sept. 3, 1862, of disability.
J. Melvin Bing	Musician	19	Nov. 2, 1861	3 yrs.	Transferred to Co. B, Jan. 26, 1864; veteran.
J. Ernest Bing	do	18	Nov. 2, 1861	3 yrs.	Transferred to Co. B Jan. 26, 1864; veteran.
Charles N. Clinger	do	15	Aug 15, 1864	3 yrs.	Transferred to Co. B ——.
Allen, Isaac	Private	40	Oct. 25, 1861	3 yrs.	Discharged Feb. 8, 1863, at Helena, Ark., of disability.
Allen, William	do	....	Jan. 2, 1862	3 yrs.	Died Oct. 22, 1862, at Helena, Ark.
Barneatt, John	do	19	Oct. 15, 1861	3 yrs.	Discharged ——, 1862, of disability.
Bevan, Benjamin	do	19	Oct. 15, 1861	3 yrs.	Died Oct. 17, 1862, at St. Louis, Mo.
Bing, Charles H	do	21	Nov. 2, 1861	3 yrs.	Transferred to Co. B Jan. 26, 1864; veteran.

Names.	Rank.	Age.	Date of Entering the Service.	Period of Service.	Remarks.
Brown, John	Private	18	Oct. 15, 1861	3 yrs.	Mustered out Nov. 12, 1864, at New Orleans, La.
Brown, George	...do...	44	Oct. 15, 1861	3 yrs.	Mustered out Nov. 12, 1864, at New Orleans, La.
Chafings, Richard	...do...	21	Oct. 15, 1861	3 yrs.	Discharged Jan. 13, 1864, at Algiers, La., of disability.
Clinger, Samuel	...do...	31	Nov. 11, 1861	3 yrs.	Transferred to Co. B Jan. 26, 1864; veteran.
Cook, Leonard	...do...		Oct. 15, 1861	3 yrs.	Discharged ——, 1861, by writ of habeas corbus.
Dairymple, Lorenzo D.	...do...	18	Nov. 12, 1861	3 yrs.	Transferred to Co. B Jan. 26, 1864; veteran.
Daniels, David	...do...	19	Oct. 15, 1861	3 yrs.	Transferred to Co. B Jan. 26, 1864; veteran.
Davis, Jenkin	...do...	22	Nov. 15, 1861	3 yrs.	Died Feb. 25, 1863, at Helena, Ark.
Davis, Thomas J.	...do...	42	Nov. 15, 1861	3 yrs.	Captured May 16, 1863, at battle of Champion Hills, Miss.; ——; transferred to Co. B Jan. 26, 1864; veteran.
Davis, Charles H.	...do...		Jan. 1, 1862	3 yrs.	Transferred to Co. B Jan. 26, 1864; veteran.
Deal, William	...do...	18	July 8, 1864	3 yrs.	Transferred to Co B Nov. 19 1864.
Dickason, John W.	...do...	44	Oct. 15, 1861	3 yrs.	Died Oct 14, 1862, at St. Louis, Mo.
Dickey, William	...do...	38	Nov. 2, 1861	3 yrs.	
Dowler, Francis M.	...do...	18	Oct. 15, 1861	3 yrs.	Transferred to Co. B Jan. 26, 1864; veteran.
Edwards, Abram	...do...	20	Nov. 18, 1861	3 yrs.	Discharged May 18, 1863, at St. Louis, Mo., of disability.
Erwin, Francis	...do...		Dec. 5, 1861	3 yrs.	Discharged ——, 1862, of disability.
Evans, John E.	...do...	22	Nov. 18, 1861	3 yrs.	Transferred to Co. B, Jan. 26, 1864; veteran.
Evans, Evan E.	...do...	18	Oct. 15, 1861	3 yrs.	Transferred to Co. B, Jan. 26, 1864; veteran.
Evans, Wm. E.	...do...	21	Oct. 15, 1861	3 yrs.	Discharged Aug. 24, 1863, at Camp Dennison, O., of disability.
Evans, John H.	...do...	20	Oct. 15, 1861	3 yrs.	Died March 15, 1863, at St. Louis, Mo.
Evans, Evan O.	...do...	18	Oct. 15, 1861	3 yrs.	Transferred to Co. B, Jan. 26, 1864; veteran.
Evans, Daniel J.	...do...	21	Oct. 15, 1861	3 yrs.	Died Oct. 4, 1862, at Helena, Ark.
Ferris, Joshua A.	...do...	18	Oct. 15, 1861	3 yrs.	Died May 31, 1862, at Cincinnati, O.
Fulton, Oliver	...do...	18	Nov. 2, 1861	3 yrs.	Died Nov. 4, 1862, at Helena, Ark.
George, Archibald	...do...	21	Nov. 2, 1861	3 yrs.	Died June 5, 1863, of wounds received May 16, 1863, in battle of Champion Hills, Miss.
Goldsmith, Henry M.	...do...	38	Nov. 13, 1861	3 yrs.	Promoted to Q. M. Sergeant Sept. 28, 1862.
Gordon, John	...do...		Nov. 18, 1861	3 yrs.	Died Feb. 9, 1862, at Portsmouth, O.
Griffiths, Rees	...do...	19	Oct. 15, 1861	3 yrs.	Wounded May 16, 1863, in battle of Champion Hills, Miss.; transferred to Co. B, Jan. 26, 1864; veteran.
Gross, Abner	...do...	23	Nov. 9, 1861	3 yrs.	Discharged Jan. 17, 1863, at St. Louis, Mo., of disability.
Guy, John W.	...do...	43	Nov. 2, 1861	3 yrs.	Transferred to Co. B, Jan. 26, 1864; veteran.
Guy, Alvah	...do...		Dec. 5, 1861	3 yrs.	Discharged Nov. 14, 1862, at Keokuk, Ia., of disability.
Harris, William	...do...	41	Nov. 15, 1861	3 yrs.	Discharged Feb. 9, 1864, at Madisonville, La., of disability.
Hickson, Benjamin	...do...	24	Oct. 25, 1861	3 yrs.	Transferred to Co. B, Jan. 26, 1864; veteran.
Hix, Eli	...do...	18	Nov. 28, 1861	3 yrs.	Died Sept. 29, 1863, at Helena, Ark.
Hughes, George	...do...	26	Oct. 25, 1861	3 yrs.	Transferred to Co. B, Jan. 26, 1864; veteran.
Hughes, William	...do...	19	Nov. 15, 1861	3 yrs.	Transferred to Co. B, Jan. 26, 1864; veteran.
Hughes, James	...do...	20	Nov. 15, 1861	3 yrs.	Transferred to Co. B, Jan. 26, 1864; veteran.
James, Alfred, Jr.	...do...	18	Nov. 11, 1861	3 yrs.	Transferred to Co. B, Jan. 26, 1864; veteran.
Jenkins, Thomas	...do...	25	Oct. 15, 1861	3 yrs.	Discharged Jan. 21, 1863, at St. Louis, Mo., of disability.

Names.	Rank.	Age.	Date of Entering the Service.	Period of Service.	Remarks.
Johnson, Thomas	Private	18	Oct. 15, 1861	3 yrs.	Discharged Nov. 27, 1862, at Keokuk, Ia., of disability.
Jones, John G	...do...	18	Oct. 15, 1861	3 yrs.	Mustered out Nov. 12, 1864, at New Orleans, La.
Jones, Thomas J	...do...	18	Oct. 15, 1861	3 yrs.	Transferred to Co. B, Jan. 26, 1864; veteran.
Jones, John L	...do...	22	Oct. 15, 1861	3 yrs.	Detached with 1st Missouri Light Artillery ——; mustered out Nov. 12, 1864, at New Orleans, La.
Jones, Dennis	...do...	18	Oct. 15, 1861	3 yrs.	Transferred to Co. B, Jan. 26, 1864; veteran.
Jones, William	...do...	24	Nov. 15, 1861	3 yrs.	Died July 8, 1863, at Van Buren Hospital, La., of wounds received May 16, 1863, in battle of Champion Hills, Miss.
Logue, Ellis	...do...	18	Nov. 11, 1861	3 yrs.	Transferred to Co. B, Jan. 26, 1864; veteran.
Louks, Jacob	...do...	27	Nov. 18, 1861	3 yrs.	Transferred to Co. B, Jan. 26, 1864; veteran.
McGhee, A. J	...do...	43	Nov. 11, 1861	3 yrs.	Discharged——, 1862, of disability.
Nearman, William H	...do...	18	July 8, 1864	3 yrs.	Transferred to Co. B, Nov. 19, 1864.
Radcliff, Wm. H	...do...	21	Oct. 25, 1861	3 yrs.	Captured May 16, 1863, at battle of Champion Hills, Miss.; ——; transferred to Co. B, Jan. 26, 1864; veteran.
Radcliff, Julius A	...do...	18	Oct. 25, 1861	3 yrs.	Discharged——, 1862, of disability.
Ralston, David D	...do...	44	Nov. 11, 1861	3 yrs.	Discharged ——, 1862, of disability.
Ratekin, John	...do...	19	Oct. 15, 1861	3 yrs.	Died Nov. 9, 1862, at Keokuk, Ia.
Ratekin, John B	...do...	20	Oct. 15, 1861	3 yrs.	Discharged Nov. 28, 1862, at Keokuk, Ia., of disability.
Reese, James	...do...	19	Nov. 19, 1861	3 yrs.	Transferred to Co. B, Jan. 26, 1864; veteran.
Reynolds, Charles B	...do...		Jan. 1, 1862	3 yrs.	Discharged Nov. 27, 1862, at Keokuk, Ia., of disability.
Roush, Newton J	...do...	18	Nov. 18, 1861	3 yrs.	Transferred to Co. B, Jan. 26, 1864; veteran.
Russell, Aaron	...do...	27	Nov. 2, 1861	3 yrs.	Discharged Dec. 10, 1862, at Keokuk, Ia., of disability.
Russell, George	...do...	44	Nov. 9, 1861	3 yrs.	Transferred to Veteran Reserve Corps———
Scott, John M	...do...	26	Nov. 25, 1861	3 yrs.	Mustered out Nov. 12, 1864, at New Orleans, La.
Siebert, John G	...do...		Nov. 20, 1863	3 yrs.	Discharged March 20, 1863, of disability.
Starcher, Noah	...do...	27	Nov. 19, 1861	3 yrs.	Died July 2, 1863, of wounds received in siege of Vicksburg, Miss.
Thaxton, Levi A	...do...	25	Nov. 2, 1861	3 yrs.	Died June 1, 1862, at Covington, Ky.
Thomas, William J	...do...	21	Nov. 15, 1861	3 yrs.	Discharged——, 1862, of disability.
Thomas, Rees	...do...	19	Nov. 15, 1861	3 yrs.	Transferred to Co. B, Jan. 26, 1864; veteran.
Thomas, Thomas D	...do...	20	Oct. 15, 1861	3 yrs.	Transferred to Co. B, Jan. 26, 1864; veteran.
Williams, Thomas J	...do...	21	Oct. 15, 1861	3 yrs.	Transferred to Co. B, Jan. 26, 1864; veteran.
Williams, Ashley R	...do...	18	Oct. 15, 1861	3 yrs.	Transferred to Co. B, Jan. 26, 1864; veteran.
Williams, Daniel	...do...	19	Oct. 15, 1861	3 yrs.	Wounded May 16, 1863, in battle of Champion Hills, Miss.; transferred to Co. B, Jan. 26, 1864; veteran.
Woodruff, Enoch E	...do...	18	Oct. 15, 1861	3 yrs.	Mustered out Nov. 12, 1864, at New Orleans, La.

ROSTER OF FIFTY-SIXTH REGIMENT

COMPANY F.

Mustered in from Oct. 15, 1861, to Nov. 7, 1861, at Portsmouth, O., and McArthur, O., by John R. Edie, Major 15th Infantry, U. S. A., and A. B. Dodd, Captain 15th Infantry, U. S. A. Mustered out Nov. 14, 1864, at New Orleans, La., by Thomas R. Rodman, A. C. M.

Names.	Rank.	Age.	Date of Entering the Service.	Period of Service.	Remarks.
George Wilhelm	Captain	30	Aug. 21, 1861	3 yrs.	Wounded and captured May 16, 1863, at battle of Champion Hills, Miss.; captured his guard, escaped and returned to Union lines; mustered out Nov. 14, 1864, at New Orleans, La.
Henry Lautz	1st Lieut.	28	Nov. 21, 1861	3 yrs.	Mustered out Nov. 21, 1864, at New Orleans, La.
John F. Morton	2d Lieut.	25	Nov. 21, 1861	3 yrs.	Discharged Aug. 19. 1862.
Oration J. DeWolf	...do...	20	Oct. 16, 1861	3 yrs.	Promoted from 1st Sergeant June 2, 1862; to 1st Lieutenant May 9, 1864, but not mustered; mustered out Nov. 13, 1864, at New Orleans, La.
John D. Markell	1st Sergt.	24	Oct. 18, 1861	3 yrs.	Died July 9, 1863, of wounds received May 16, 1863, in battle of Champion Hills, Miss.
John C. Burke	...do...	32	Oct. 19, 1861	3 yrs.	Transferred to Co. A, Jan. 26, 1864; veteran.
Joel Burnett	Sergeant	33	Oct. 16, 1861	3 yrs.	Discharged ——, for wounds received May 16, 1863, in battle of Champion Hills, Miss.
George W. Cox	...do...	36	Oct. 16, 1861	3 yrs.	Wounded May 16, 1863, in battle of Champion Hills, Miss.; transferred to Co. A, Jan. 26, 1864; veteran.
Irvin Drake	...do...	25	Oct. 16, 1861	3 yrs.	Mustered out Nov. 14, 1864, at New Orleans, La.
James P. Lowery	...do...	28	Nov. 18, 1861	3 yrs.	Mustered out Oct. 14, 1864, at New Orleans, La.
George W. Neff	...do...	22	Oct 18, 1861	3 yrs.	Transferred to Co. A, Jan. 26, 1864; veteran.
William H. Patton	...do...	30	Nov. 20, 1861	3 yrs.	Discharged Dec. 1, 1862, of disability.
Robert Bowles	Corporal	41	Oct. 20, 1861	3 yrs.	Transferred to Co. A, Jan. 26, 1864; veteran.
C. F. Ford	...do...	29	Oct. 16, 1861	3 yrs.	Discharged March —, 1864, of disability.
Jasper Fout	...do...	18	Oct. 16, 1861	3 yrs.	Wounded May 16, 1863, in battle of Champion Hills, Miss.; transferred to Co. A, Jan. 26, 1864; veteran.
Britton D. Fry	...do...	19	Oct. 19, 1861	3 yrs.	Transferred to Co. A, Jan. 26, 1864; veteran.
James M. Halliday	...do...	19	Oct. 15, 1861	3 yrs.	Transferred to Co. A Jan. 26, 1864; veteran.
Irvin Jennings	...do...	35	Nov. 9, 1861	3 yrs.	Died Aug. 3, 1863, at Helena, Ark.
James U. Pease	...do...	27	Oct. 18, 1861	3 yrs.	Wounded May 16, 1863, in battle of Champion Hills, Miss.; transferred to Co. A Jan. 26, 1864; veteran.
Timothy Sullivan	...do...	21	Nov. 19, 1861	3 yrs.	
William E. Williams	...do...	44	Nov. 20, 1861	3 yrs.	Discharged Dec. 1, 1862, of disability.
James W. Truman	...do...	23	Oct. 19, 1861	3 yrs.	Transferred to Veteran Reserve Corps ——, 1864.
Allen, John C	Private	27	Oct. 19, 1861	3 yrs.	Died Jan. 5, 1862, at St. Louis, Mo.
Bennett, Ephraim	...do...	44	Nov. 20, 1861	3 yrs.	Discharged Feb. 6, 1863, at St. Louis, Mo., of disability.
Bowles, Jacob	...do...	40	Oct. 20, 1861	3 yrs.	Discharged Dec. 18, 1861, at Portsmouth, O., of disability.
Bradshaw, Levi	...do...	35	Nov. 20, 1861	3 yrs.	Discharged Dec. 1, 1862, of disability.
Branon, L. D	...do...	41	Oct. 16, 1861	3 yrs.	Discharged Feb. 6, 1863, at St. Louis, Mo., of disability.
Brown, Sandford	...do...	18	Oct. 20, 1861	3 yrs.	
Carry, Timothy F	...do...	40	Oct. 31, 1861	3 yrs.	Drowned July 23, 1862, in Ohio river at Cincinnati, O.

Names.	Rank.	Age.	Date of Entering the Service.	Period of Service.	Remarks.
Cline, John	Private	23	Oct. 31, 1861	3 yrs.	Mustered out Nov. 14, 1864, at New Orleans, La.
Collier, Erastus S	...do...	37	Oct. 21, 1861	3 yrs.	Transferred to 1st Missouri Light Artillery Jan. 1, 1864; veteran.
Cool, William H	...do...	....	Nov. 20, 1861	3 yrs.	Transferred to Co. A Jan. 26, 1864; veteran.
Cooper, Charles	...do...	....	Nov. 20, 1861	3 yrs.	Mustered out Nov. 14, 1864, at New Orleans, La.
Carrothers, James	.do...	21	Nov. 20, 1861	3 yrs	Transferred to Co. A Jan. 26, 1864; veteran.
Devoir, Edward	...do...	19	Oct. 20, 1861	3 yrs.	Died July 21, 1862, at Memphis, Tennessee.
Dibble, Edward A	...do...	33	Oct. 8, 1862	9 mos	Drafted; mustered out July 8, 1863, at Vicksburg, Miss.
Dodge, John C	...do...	35	Oct. 16, 1861	3 yrs.	Died Oct. 20, 1862, at Helena, Ark.
Fry, Freeman W	...do...	31	Oct. 1, 1861	3 yrs.	Discharged Oct. 15, 1862, of disability.
Fuller, James M	...do...	27	Oct. 19, 1861	3 yrs.	Died June 10, 1862, at Shiloh, Tenn.
Glascow, John P	...do...	39	Oct. 19, 1861	3 yrs.	Discharged May 9, 1863, of disability.
Graham, James	...do...	31	Oct. 18, 1861	3 yrs.	Discharged Feb. 6, 1865, of disability.
Hawkins, Charles D	...do...	23	Oct. 8, 1862	9 mos	Drafted; mustered out July 8, 1863, at Vicksburg, Miss.
Henry, John	.do...	21	Nov. 18, 1861	3 yrs.	Transferred to Co. A Jan. 26, 1864; veteran.
Hedgmier, Frederick	...do...	38	Nov. 18, 1861	3 yrs.	Transferred to Co. A Jan. 26, 1864; veteran.
Hindman, David	...do...	23	Oct. 19, 1861	3 yrs.	Died March 5, 1862, at Fort Donelson, Tenn.
Houser, John	...do...	25	Oct. 8, 1862	9 mos	Drafted; mustered out July 8, 1863, at Vicksburg, Miss.
Hubbard, Gideon	...do...	28	Oct. 17, 1861	3 yrs.	Transferred to Co. A Jan. 26, 1864; veteran.
Hubbard, Clement D	...do...	26	Oct. 16, 1861	3 yrs.	Killed May 16, 1863, in battle of Champion Hills, Miss.
Johnson, George N	...do...	36	Oct. 8, 1862	9 mos	Drafted; mustered out July 8, 1863, at Vicksburg, Miss.
Joice, Michael	...do...	23	Oct. 20, 1861	3 yrs.	Transferred to Co. A Jan. 26, 1864; veteran.
Jones, David	...do...	28	Nov. 4, 1861	3 yrs.	Died July 4, 1864, at New Orleans, Louisiana.
Jones, Jesse	...do...	22	Oct. 18, 1861	3 yrs.	Died Aug. 2, 1863, of wounds received July 9, 1863, in battle of Jackson, Miss.
Jones, Robert	...do...	20	Oct. 18, 1861	3 yrs.	Died Sept. 20, 1862, at Helena, Ark.
Jones, Dustan	...do...	22	Oct. 18, 1861	3 yrs.	Mustered out Nov. 14, 1864, at New Orleans, La.
Jones, George	...do...	31	Oct. 16, 1861	3 yrs.	Mustered out Nov. 14, 1864, at New Orleans, La.
Jones, Uriah	...do...	27	Nov. 18, 1861	3 yrs.	Transferred to Co. A Jan. 26, 1864; veteran.
Justice, George	...do...	29	Oct. 19, 1861	3 yrs.	Died July 30, 1864, at Cario, Ill.; veteran.
Knapp, Edwin	...do...	37	Oct. 17, 1861	3 yrs.	Transferred to 1st Missouri Battery Jan. 1, 1864; veteran.
Lair, William	...do...	25	Nov. 20, 1861	3 yrs.	Transferred to Co. A Jan. 26, 1864; veteran.
Lindsey, Levi	...do...	40	Oct. 17, 1861	3 yrs.	Discharged Feb. 6, 1863, of disability.
Lingenfelter, Christian	...do...	38	Oct. 17, 1861	3 yrs.	Transferred to Co. A Jan. 26, 1864; veteran.
Lord, Ezra F	...do...	39	Oct. 16, 1861	3 yrs.	Transferred to Co. A Jan. 26, 1864; veteran.
McCowen, Nathan	...do...	39	Nov. 16, 1861	3 yrs.	Transferred to Co. A Jan. 20, 1864; veteran.
McElvany, Robert	...do...	44	Nov. 7, 1861	3 yrs.	Discharged ——, by order of War Department.
McGarvey, John	...do...	26	Oct. 30, 1861	3 yrs.	Mustered out Nov. 14, 1864, at New Orleans, La.
Martin, Hiram	...do...	18	Oct. 30, 1861	3 yrs.	Transferred to Co. A Jan. 26, 1864; veteran.
Morton, Josiah H	...do...	18	Nov. 16, 1861	3 yrs.	

Names.	Rank.	Age.	Date of Entering the Service.	Period of Service.	Remarks.
Nall, William	Private	29	Oct. 19, 1861	3 yrs.	Discharged —, 1863, at St. Louis, Mo., of disability.
Nall, Wesley	...do...	23	Oct. 20, 1861	3 yrs.	Died Jan. 26, 1862, at Portsmouth, O.
Nelson, William	...do...	37	Nov. 10, 1861	3 yrs.	
O'Brien, Patrick	...do...	32	Oct. 21, 1861	3 yrs.	Transferred to Veteran Reserve Corps, —, 1863.
Ogan, John	...do...	25	Nov. 8, 1861	3 yrs.	Mustered out Nov. 14, 1864, at New Orleans, La.
Patterson, James	...do...		Nov. 25, 1861	3 yrs.	Discharged April 1, 1862, at Helena, Ark., of disability.
Petty, William M	...do...		April 1, 1862	3 yrs.	Discharged Aug. —, 1864, at New Orleans, La., of disability; veteran.
Pierson, David B	...do...	25	Oct. 18, 1861	3 yrs.	Discharged July 1, 1862, of disability.
Pounds, William	...do...		Nov. 10, 1861	3 yrs.	Died Nov. 17, 1862, at Cincinnati, Ohio.
Price, George	...do...	19	Nov. 8, 1861	3 yrs.	Died Nov. 14, 1862, at Helena, Ark.
Pugh, Jesse B	...do...	38	Oct. 18, 1861	3 yrs.	Died Sept. 5, 1863, at New Orleans, La.
Radford, William	...do...	44	Nov. 20, 1861	3 yrs.	Discharged Dec. 1, 1862, of disability.
Santy, Wilbert	...do...	25	Oct. 17, 1861	3 yrs.	Discharged April 1, 1863, of disability.
Scott, William	...do...	35	Oct. 19, 1861	3 yrs.	Discharged May 9, 1862, of disability.
Scott, John R	...do...	33	Nov. 19, 1861	3 yrs.	Discharged Aug 3, 1862, of disability.
Sisler, William S	...do...	25	Nov. 7, 1861	3 yrs.	Died —, of wounds received April 8, 1864, in battle of Sabine Cross Roads, La ; veteran.
Slaughter, Stephen	...do...	44	Oct. 20, 1861	3 yrs	Discharged Dec. 1, 1862, of disability.
Smith, Reuben	...do...	24	Oct. 19, 1861	3 yrs.	Discharged May 9 1862, of disability.
Spence, Thomas J	...do...	24	Oct. 30, 1861	3 yrs.	Died — 1862, at Columbus, Ky.
Spence, Charles	...do...	18	Oct. 30, 1861	3 yrs.	Transferred to Co. A Jan. 26, 1864; veteran.
Spriggs, Benjamin F	...do...	20	Oct. 20, 1861	3 yrs.	Wounded June 18, 1863, in siege of Vicksburg, Miss.; transferred to Veteran Reserve Corps Nov. 18, 1863; mustered out Oct. 22, 1864, at St. Louis, Mo.
Sturgill, William R	...do...	23	Nov. 18, 1861	3 yrs.	Transferred to Co. A Jan. 26, 1864; veteran.
Sturgill, John M	...do...		Nov. 20, 1861	3 yrs.	
Taylor, George S	...do...	18	Oct. 18, 1861	3 yrs.	Discharged Jan. 15, 1863, at St. Louis, Mo. of disability.
Trevary, Francis P	...do...	26	Oct. 8, 1862	9 mos	Drafted; mustered out July 8, 1863, at Vicksburg, Miss.
Truman, Joseph	...do...	22	Oct. 19, 1861	3 yrs.	Transferred to Co. A, Jan. 26, 1864; veteran.
Welch, Michael G	...do...	32	Oct. 30, 1861	3 yrs	Died Dec. 2, 1862, at Helena, Ark.
Wishon, David	...do...	29	Oct. 17, 1861	3 yrs.	Died May 5, 1863, at Grand Gulf, Miss.
Woods, Benjamin	...do...	33	Oct. 30, 1861	3 yrs.	Discharged Dec. 1, 1862, of disability.

COMPANY G.

Mustered in Oct. 29, 1861, and Dec. 3, 1861, at Portsmouth, O., by R. B. Hull, Captain 18th Infantry, U. S. A. Mustered out Nov. 14, 1864, at New Orleans, La., by Thomas R. Rodman, A. C. M.

Names	Rank	Age	Date	Period	Remarks
Isaac Fullerton	Captain	52	Aug. 25, 1861	3 yrs.	Resigned Feb. 14, 1863.
James C. Stimmel	...do...	24	Oct. 29, 1861	3 yrs.	Promoted from 1st Lieutenant May 16, 1863; captured May 1, 1864, on Red River Expedition, La.; escaped May 16, 1864, at Marshall, Tex.; reached Union lines on Mississippi river June 7, 1864, having traveled 600 miles; transferred to Co. B Dec. —, 1864.

OHIO VOLUNTEER INFANTRY.

Names.	Rank.	Age.	Date of Entering the Service.	Period of Service.	Remarks.
Erastus Gates	1st Lieut.	32	Dec. 9, 1861	3 yrs.	Promoted to 1st Lieutenant April 2, 1863; resigned July 26, 1863.
Benjamin B. Allen	2d Lieut.	28	Oct. 29, 1861	3 yrs.	Resigned Sept. 21, 1862.
William G. Snyder	...do...	29	Oct. 29, 186.	3 yrs.	Promoted from 1st Sergeant Sept. 7, 1862; to 1st Lieutenant Co. A May 16, 1863.
Duncan McKinsie	1st Sergt.	24	Oct. 29, 1861	3 yrs.	Died July 15, 1863, of wounds received May 16, 1863, in battle of Champion Hills, Miss.
William B. Matson	...do...	26	Oct. 29, 1861	3 yrs.	Mustered out Nov. 14, 1864, at New Orleans, La.
William Adams	Sergeant	25	Oct. 29, 1861	3 yrs.	Died Nov. 28, 1862, in Scioto county, Ohio.
Thomas S. Bennett	...do...	27	Oct. 29, 1861	3 yrs.	Transferred to Co. B, Jan. 26, 1864; veteran.
Benjamin F. Bennett	...do...	32	Sept. 12, 1861	3 yrs.	Discharged July —, 1862, at Cincinnati, O., of disability.
Henry F. Cline	...do...	24	Nov. 5, 1861	3 yrs.	Mustered out Nov. 14, 1864, at New Orleans, La.
Robert B. Crawford	...do...	18	Nov. 19, 1861	3 yrs.	Mustered out Nov. 14, 1864, at New Orleans, La.
John S. Eakins	...do...	22	Nov. 25, 1861	3 yrs.	Mustered out Nov. 14, 1864, at New Orleans, La.
Charles F. Hudson	...do...	30	Nov. 5, 1861	3 yrs.	Captured May 16, 1863, at battle of Champion Hills, Miss.; ——; mustered out Nov. 14, 1864, at New Orleans, La.
Nicholas D. Maine	...do...	24	Oct. 29, 1861	3 yrs.	Appointed from Corporal July 16, 1863; transferred to Co. B, Jan. 26, 1864; veteran.
Thomas Cross	Corporal	25	Nov. 26, 1861	3 yrs.	Appointed Corporal Nov. 25, 1863; transferred to Co. B, Jan. 26, 1864; veteran.
Martin Downey	...do...	39	Nov. 8, 1861	3 yrs.	Appointed Corporal April 17, 1862; killed May 16, 1863, in battle Champion Hills, Miss.
James C. Galford	...do...	42	Oct. 29, 1861	3 yrs.	Discharged Feb 8, 1863, at Helena, Ark., of disability.
Andrew Greaser	...do...	26	Oct. 29, 1861	3 yrs.	Discharged Oct. 3, 1863, of disability.
George Hadaway	...do...	33	Oct. 29, 1861	3 yrs.	Discharged April —, 1863, at Memphis, Tenn, of disability.
Francis M. Hudson	...do...	26	Nov. 5, 1861	3 yrs.	Appointed Corporal Nov. 25, 1863; mustered out Nov. 14, 1864, at New Orleans, La.
Nathan M. Kent	...do...	22	Oct. 29, 1861	3 yrs.	Transferred to Co. B, Jan. 26, 1864; veteran.
John Rockwell	...do...	43	Oct. 29, 1861	3 yrs.	Transferred to Co. B, Jan. 26, 1864; veteran.
George W. Rockwell	...do...	30	Oct. 29, 1861	3 yrs.	Died July 7, 1863, of wounds received May 16, 1863, in battle of Champion Hills, Miss.
Reuben H. Slavens	...do...	25	Oct. 29, 1861	3 yrs.	Captured May 16, 1863, at battle of Champion Hills, Miss; mustered out Nov. 14, 1864, at New Orleans, La.
Allen, William	Private	24	Oct. 22, 1861	3 yrs.	Transferred to Co. B, Jan. 26, 1864; veteran.
Anderson, Henry F.	...do...	18	Nov. 25, 1861	3 yrs.	Discharged Feb. 1, 1862, at Portsmouth, O., by civil authority.
Anderson, Thomas L.	...do...	41	Nov. 10, 1861	3 yrs.	Discharged Feb. 8, 1863, of disability.
Anderson, George	...do...	18	Nov. 27, 1861	3 yrs.	Mustered out Nov. 14, 1864, at New Orleans, La.
Baker, Charles B	...do...	29	Nov. 23, 1861	3 yrs.	Transferred to Co. A, Jan. 26, 1864; veteran.
Bennett, James F	...do...	27	Oct. 29, 1861	3 yrs.	Mustered out Nov. 14, 1864, at New Orleans, La.
Bennett, Joseph	...do...	23	Oct. 29, 1861	3 yrs.	Discharged Dec. —, 1863, at Cincinnati, O., of disability.

Names.	Rank.	Age.	Date of Entering the Service	Period of Service.	Remarks.
Bendurant, Daniel L..	Private	20	Oct. 29, 1861	3 yrs.	Transferred to Co. B, Jan 26, 1864; veteran.
Blakeman, Andrew J..	... do ...	27	Oct. 29, 1861	3 yrs.	Discharged Feb. 8, 1863, at Cincinnati, O., of disability.
Blout, Henry	... do ...	25	Nov. 24, 1861	3 yrs.	
Bouser, Isaac	... do .	43	Oct. 22, 1861	3 yrs	Discharged Feb. 6, 1863, at Helena, Ark., of disability.
Brown, Nathaniel	... do ...	38	Oct. 22, 1861	3 yrs.	Captured May 16, 1863, at battle of Champion Hills, Miss.; mustered out Nov. 14, 1864, at New Orleans, La.
Brown, William C.	... do ...	25	Oct. 29, 1861	3 yrs.	Transferred to Co. B, Jan. 26, 1864; veteran.
Carpenter, Aaron	... do ...	28	Nov. 21, 1861	3 yrs.	Transferred to Co. B, Jan. 26, 1864; veteran.
Chaffin, George W.	... do ...	22	Nov. 6, 1861	3 yrs	Transferred to Co. B, Jan. 26, 1864; veteran.
Chaffin, Thomas	... do ...	26	Jan. 27, 1864	3 yrs	Transferred to Co. B, - —.
Comer, Lewis	... do ...	18	Oct. 29, 1861	3 yrs.	Transferred to Co. B, Jan. 26, 1864; veteran
Crabtree, Stephen	... do ...	25	Oct. 29, 1861	3 yrs.	Transferred to Co. B, Jan. 26, 1864; veteran.
Crabtree, Gillen	... do ...	28	Oct 29, 1861	3 yrs.	Transferred to Co. B, Jan. 26, 1864; veteran
Crum, Isaac	... do ...	....	Dec. 20, 1861	3 yrs.	Died Sept. 4, 1862, at Helena, Ark.
Dement, James B	... do ...	19	Jan. 29, 1864	3 yrs.	Tran-ferred to Co. B, ——.
Eakins, Fletcher R.	... do ...	20	Nov. 25, 1861	3 yrs.	Discharged Dec. 18, 1862 at Keokuk, Ia., of disability.
Fasterman, Wm. G.	... do ...	25	Nov. 13, 1861	3 yrs.	Transferred to Co. B, Jan. 26, 1864; veteran.
Field James	... do ...	21	Oct. 29, 1861	3 yrs.	Died ——, of wounds received May 16, 1863, in battle of Champion Hills, Miss.
Freeland, Middleton	... do ...	43	Nov. 27, 1861	3 yrs.	Transferred from Co. K, Dec.—, 1861; killed May 16, 1863. in battle of Champion Hills, Miss.
Fullerton, John	... do ...	18	Oct. 29, 1861	3 yrs.	Discharged Aug. —, 1863, at Helena, Ark., of disibility.
Galford, James	... do ...	19	Oct. 29, 1861	3 yrs.	Died Sept. 7, 1862, at Memphis, Tenn.
Giles, Thomas C.	... do ...	23	Jan. 31, 1862	3 yrs	Transferred to Co. B, Jan. 26, 1864; veteran.
Giles, Dennis	... do ...	18	Oct. 29, 1861	3 yrs.	Transferred to Co, B, Jan. 26, 1864; veteran.
Gaw, Barnett	... do ...	18	Nov. 1, 1861	3 yrs.	Discharged Dec. 3, 1861, by civil authority.
Graham, Wellington	... do ...	22	Oct. 29, 1861	3 yrs.	Killed June 23, 1863, in siege of Vicksburg, Miss.
Hartley, Eli	... do ...	....	Feb. 10, 1862	3 yrs.	Discharged May 9, 1862, of disability
Hays Robert	... do ...	42	Oct. 29, 1861	3 yrs.	Died May 30, 1862, at Cincinnati, O.
Herder, Jacob	... do ...	....	Dec. 8, 1861	3 yrs.	Transferred to Co. B, ——; veteran.
Hill, Charles W.	... do ...	18	Oct. 29, 1861	3 yrs.	Died ——, of wounds received May 16, 1863, in battle of Champion Hills, Mississippi.
Hill, Levi J.	... do ...	33	Oct. 29, 1861	3 yrs.	Died Oct. 5, 1863, at New Orleans, Louisiana.
Kent, Emanuel	... do ...	....	Dec. 10, 1861	3 yrs.	Died May 22, 1863, at Milliken's Bend, Louisiana.
Kent, Oliver	... do ...	....	Dec. 17, 1861	3 yrs.	Discharged Dec. 10, 1862, of disability.
Kent, Alfred	... do ..	21	Oct. 29, 1861	3 yrs.	Died July 18, 1863, at Haine's Bluff, Mississippi.
Kinney, Thomas W.	... do ...	19	Oct. 30, 1861	3 yrs	Promoted to Sergeant Major Oct. 30, 1861.
Lambert, James	... do ...	43	Nov. 9, 1861	3 yrs.	Discharged Feb. 6, 1863, at Helena, Ark., of disability.
Lindsey, William	... do ...	18	Nov. 27, 1861	3 yrs.	Discharged Dec. 3, 1861, by civil authority.
McCallister, George W.	... do ...	....	Jan. 2, 1862	3 yrs.	Transferred to Co. B. Jan. 26, 1864; veteran.

OHIO VOLUNTEER INFANTRY.

Names.	Rank.	Age.	Date of Entering the Service.	Period of Service.	Remarks.
McCann, Daniel	Private		June 6, 1864	3 yrs.	Transferred to Co. B, ——.
McCowen, Henry H	...do ...	34	Nov. 22, 1861	3 yrs.	Killed May 16, 1863, in battle of Champion Hills, Miss.
McJunkin, William	...do ...	28	Oct. 29, 1861	3 yrs.	Wounded May 1, 1863, in battle of Port Gibson, Miss.; mustered out Nov. 14, 1864.
McNally, Thomas D	...do ...	19	Oct. 29, 1861	3 yrs.	Died Feb. 12, 1863, at St. Louis, Mo.
Marshall, Henry C	...do ...	26	Nov. 5, 1861	3 yrs.	Transferred to Co. B, Jan. 26, 1864; veteran.
Meed, Ebenezer	...do ...	24	Oct. 29, 1861	3 yrs.	Died May 15, 1862, in hospital at Shiloh, Tenn.
Morgan, Samuel J	...do ...		Dec. 25, 1861	3 yrs.	Transferred to Co. B, Jan. 26, 1864; veteran.
Myers, James M	...do ...	26	Nov. 25, 1861	3 yrs.	Died May 16, 1864, at New Orleans, La.; veteran.
Myers, John M	...do ...		Dec. 9, 1861	3 yrs.	Died April 7. 1862, at Cincinnati, O.
Nickels, Samuel	...do ...		Nov 15, 1861	3 yrs.	Transferred to Co. B ——; veteran.
Nagle, Englebert	...do ...		Nov. 5, 1861	3 yrs.	Transferred to Veteran Reserve Corps April 22, 1 64.
Oberly, Benjamin	...do ...	21	Oct. 29, 1861	3 yrs.	Transferred to Co. B, Jan. 26, 1864; veteran.
Pfuhler, John	...do ...	35	Oct. 18, 1861	3 yrs.	Transferred to Co. B.
Piggott, Wm. H	...do ...	22	Oct. 29, 1861	3 yrs.	Discharged Oct. —, 1862, at Helena, Ark., of disability.
Porter, William F	...do ...	24	Oct. 5, 1861	3 yrs	Killed May 16, 1863, in battle of Champion Hills, Miss.
Potts, Abraham W	...do ...	22	Nov. 17, 1863	3 yrs.	Transferred to Co. B Jan 26. 1864.
Potts, Hezekiah J	...do ...	22	Oct. 29, 1861	2 yrs.	Captured May 16, 1863, at battle of Champion Hills, Miss.; transferred to Co. B Jan 26, 1864; veteran.
Quartz, Samuel B	...do ...	18	Oct. 29, 1861	3 yrs.	Killed May 16, 1863, in battle of Champion Hills, Miss.
Reeves, Ephraim	...do ...	22	Nov. 30, 1861	3 yrs.	Captured May 16, 1863, at battle of Champion Hills, Miss.; mustered out Nov. 14, 1864, at New Orleans, La.
Rickey, Isaac M	...do ...	28	Oct. 29, 1861	3 yrs.	Discharged April 29, 1863, at Brum's Landing. Miss., of disability.
Rieneger, George W	...do ...	18	Oct. 18, 1861	3 yrs.	Transferred from Co. B Feb. 23, 1864; to Co. B ——; veteran.
Roberts, Jeremiah	...do ...		Jan. 22, 1864	3 yrs.	Missing April 8, 1864, at battle of Sabine Cross Roads, La.
Rockwell, John	...do ...	43	Oct. 29, 1861	3 yrs.	Transferred to Co. B Jan. 26, 1864; veteran.
Rockwell, Benjamin	...do ...	29	Oct. 29, 1861	3 yrs.	Discharged Feb. 12, 1863, of disability.
Sample, Joseph H	...do ...	42	Oct. 30, 1861	3 yrs.	Discharged Feb. 8, 1863, of disability.
Seth, Francis M	...do ...	21	Oct. 29, 1861	3 yrs.	Wounded May 16, 1863, in battle of Champion Hills, Miss.; transferred to Co. B Jan 26, 1864; veteran.
Sikes, Isaac W	...do ...	19	Oct. 29, 1861	3 yrs.	Died Feb. 19, 1863, at Helena, Ark.
Sites, Peter	...do ...	44	Nov. 19, 1861	3 yrs.	Discharged Aug. 14, 1862, at Helena, Ark.
Slavens, John W	...do ...	18	Oct. 29, 1861	3 yrs.	Discharged Feb 12, 1863, at St. Louis, Mo., of disability.
Snyder, Judah M	...do ...	39	Oct. 29, 1861	3 yrs.	Died Jan 24, 1863, at Helena, Ark.
Southworth, Leonard	...do ...	21	Oct. 29, 1861	3 yrs.	Discharged March 29, 1863, at Helena, Ark., of disability.
Storz, Frank	...do ...	18	Oct. 18, 1861	3 yrs.	Transferred to Co. B ——; veteran.
Titus, William	...do ...	21	Oct. 29, 1861	3 yrs.	Wounded May 1, 1863, in battle of Port Gibson, Miss.; mustered out Nov. 14, 1864, at New Orleans, La.
Titus, John C	...do ...	23	Oct. 29, 1861	3 yrs.	Transferred to Co. B Jan. 26, 1864; veteran.
Vangerder, Green B	...do ...	35	Oct. 29, 1861	3 yrs.	Discharged Sept. —, 1863, at Carrollton, La., of disability.
Wells, Richard	...do ...	18	Oct. 29, 1861	3 yrs.	Discharged Feb. 12, 1863, at St. Louis, Mo., of disability.

COMPANY H.

Mustered in from Oct. 16, 1861, to Dec. 9, 1861, at Portsmouth, O., and Columbus, O., by John R. Edie, Major 15th Infantry, U. S. A., and R. B. Hull, Captain 18th Infantry, U. S. A. Mustered out Nov. 15, 1864, at New Orleans, La , by Thomas R. Rodman, A. C. M.

Names.	Rank.	Age.	Date of Entering the Service.	Period of Service.	Remarks.
Lansing V. Applegate	Captain	40	Oct. 16, 1861	3 yrs.	Resigned Feb. 6, 1863.
Thomas W. Kinney	... do ...	20	Oct. 29, 1861	3 yrs.	Promoted to 2d Lieutenant from Sergt. Major June 10, 1862; 1st Lieutenant Dec. 27, 1862; Capt. Feb. 14, 1863; mustered out Nov. 15, 1864, at New Orleans, La.
Charles Soule, Jr	1st Lieut.	26	Oct. 16, 1861	3 yrs.	Resigned June 10, 1862.
Charles W. Veach	... do ...	27	Oct. 18, 1861	3 yrs.	Transferred from Co. D July 15, 1863; resigned Sept 22, 1864.
Thomas Brown	2d Lieut.	28	Oct. 18, 1861	3 yrs.	Promoted to 1st Lieutenant June 20, 1862, but not mustered; resigned June 20, 1863.
Henry M. Goldsmith	... do ...	38	Nov. 13, 1861	3 yrs.	Promoted from Q. M. Sergeant Jan. 1, 1863; resigned Nov. 27, 1863.
John K. Combs	1st Sergt.	24	Nov. 18, 1861	3 yrs.	Promoted to Sergt. Major Sept. 22, 1862.
William H. Brady	... do ...	23	Nov. 12, 1861	3 yrs.	Appointed from Sergeant Sept. 12, 1861; captured May 16, 1863, at battle of Champion Hills, Miss., mustered out Nov. 15, 1864, at New Orleans, La.
Clarence P. Bliss	Sergeant	21	Oct. 21, 1861	3 yrs.	Discharged Nov. 9, 1862, at Keokuk, Ia., of disability.
John Brady	.. do ...	21	Nov. 13, 1861	3 yrs.	Discharged Nov. 9, 1862, at Keokuk. Ia., of disability.
Philip Cahill	... do ...	38	Oct. 22, 1861	3 yrs.	Discharged Nov. —, 1862, at St. Louis, Mo., of disability.
Samuel Johnston	... do ...	36	Oct. 22, 1861	3 yrs.	Mustered out Nov. 15, 1864.
Ephraim Phillips	... do .	19	Oct. 25, 1861	3 yrs.	Mustered out Nov. 15, 1864.
John Shaw	... do ...	24	Oct. 22, 1861	3 yrs.	Wounded May 16, 1863, in battle of Champion Hills, Miss.; mustered out Nov. 15, 1864.
Peter Brown	Corporal	31	Nov. 21, 1861	3 yrs.	Captured May 16, 1863, at battle of Champion Hills, Miss.; transferred to Co. B Jan. 26, 1864; veteran.
Alonzo B. Cole	... do ...	18	Oct. 25, 1861	3 yrs.	Mustered out Nov. 23, 1864, at Columbus, O.
Henry Dunlap	... do ...	18	Nov. 30, 1861	3 yrs.	Appointed Corporal Sept. 3, 1863; transferred to Co. B Jan. 26, 1864; veteran.
George Myers	... do ...	18	Oct. 22, 1861	3 yrs.	Mustered out Nov. 15, 1864, at New Orleans, La.
Newell L. Nicholas	... do ...	24	Nov. 15, 1861	3 yrs.	Mustered out Nov. 15, 1864, at New Orleans, La.
Martin Phillips	... do ...	27	Oct. 10, 1861	3 yrs.	Mustered out Oct. 10, 1864, at Columbus, O.
Bass, Byron	Private		Nov. 27, 1861	3 yrs.	Killed May 16, 1863, in battle of Champion Hills, Miss.
Bassett, Gilbert B	... do ...	19	Oct. 3, 1862	9 mos	Drafted; mustered out July 8, 1863.
Bennett, Philander	... do ...	24	Jan 16, 1862	3 yrs.	Transferred to Co. B Jan. 26, 1864.
Biggs, John H	... do ...	26	Nov. 18, 1861	3 yrs	Mustered out Nov. 15, 1864.
Black, Adam	... do ...	20	Oct. 8, 1862	9 mos	Drafted; died March 31, 1863, in hospital at Helena, Ark.
Boren, Abram H	... do ..	45	Nov. 4, 1861	3 yrs.	Died Sept. 13, 1863, at Columbus. O.
Boren, James D	... do ..	18	Oct. 23, 1861	3 yrs.	Died ——, of wounds received May 16, 1863, in battle of Champion Hills, Miss.
Bowens, John	... do ...	24	Nov. 15, 1861	3 yrs.	Died Jan. 25, 1862, at St. Louis, Mo.
Boyd, William P	... do ...	45	Oct. 22, 1861	3 yrs.	Mustered out Nov. 27, 1864.
Brown, Alfred	... do ...	22	Nov. 21, 1861	3 yrs.	Returned to 5th Virginia Cavalry——.

OHIO VOLUNTEER INFANTRY 183

Names.	Rank.	Age.	Date of Entering the Service.	Period of Service.	Remarks.
Brown, Isaac	Private	24	Nov. 21, 1861	3 yrs.	Died April 3, 1862, at Crump's Landing, Tenn.
Bingham, Levi	...do...	24	Feb. 5, 1862	3 yrs.	Transferred to Co. B Jan. 26, 1864; veteran.
Bragdon, Solomon	...do...	20	Nov. 22, 1861	3 yrs.	Killed May 1, 1863, in battle of Port Gibson, Mississippi.
Burch, Robinson G	...do...	20	Oct. 8, 1862	9 mos	Drafted; wounded May 18, 1863, in action near Vicksburg, Miss.; mustered out July 8, 1863.
Byers, Benjamin	...do...	21	Oct. 21, 1861	3 yrs.	Mustered out Dec. 23, 1864, at Columbus, O.
Camp, John	...do...	45	Oct. 18, 1861	3 yrs.	Discharged Sept. 1, 1863, at Carrollton, La. of disability.
Campbell, Merit	...do...	26	Oct. 19, 1861	3 yrs.	Died ——, of wounds received May 16, 1863, in battle of Champion Hills, Miss.
Carr, William	...do...	40	Nov. 13, 1861	3 yrs.	Reduced from Corporal ——; transferred to Co. B Jan. 26, 1864; veteran.
Carr, Robert	...do...	22	Oct. 21, 1861	3 yrs.	
Christie, James E	...do...	24	Dec. 3, 1861	3 yrs.	Returned to 23d Kentucky Regiment Infantry Jan. 7, 1862.
Coffman, John	...do...	34	Oct. 26, 1861	3 yrs.	Transferred to Co. B Jan. 26, 1864; veteran.
Cross, Wilson	...do...	29	Oct. 21, 1861	3 yrs.	Transferred to Co. A ——.
Dean, Eli	...do...	43	Oct. 19, 1861	3 yrs.	Mustered out Nov. 15, 1864.
Dewit, Hiram	...do...	21	Nov. 7, 1862	3 yrs.	Transferred to Co. B Jan. 26, 1864; veteran.
Donohew, Alvin	...do...	40	Dec. 10, 1861	3 yrs.	Transferred to Co. B Jan. 26, 1864; veteran.
Eagle, William	...do...	43	Oct. 29, 1861	3 yrs.	Died Sept. —, 1862, at Memphis, Tenn.
Friley, William	...do...	27	Feb. 4, 1862	3 yrs.	Killed May 1, 1863, in battle of Port Gibson, Mississippi.
Gates, Erastus	...do...	32	Dec. 9, 1861	3 yrs.	Promoted to Q. M. Sergeant Dec. 9, 1861.
Gray, James	...do...	44	Nov. 2, 1861	3 yrs	Discharged July 25, 1862, at Cincinnati, O., of disability.
Gudgeon, Dixon	...do...	19	Oct. 19, 1861	3 yrs.	Wounded and captured April 8, 1864, at battle of Sabine Cross Roads, La.; died ——, in Rebel Prison; veteran.
Gudeon, Arza	...do...	21	Oct. 19, 1861	3 yrs.	Discharged Nov. 20, 1862, at St. Louis, Mo., of disability.
Haines, Archibald	...do...	28	Oct. 23, 1861	3 yrs.	Mustered out Nov. 15, 1864.
Haines, James W	...do...	18	Nov. 18, 1861	3 yrs.	Died April 28, 1862, at Pittsburg Landing, Tennessee.
Hanes, Samuel L	...do...	18	Oct. 23, 1861	3 yrs.	Transferred to 5th U. S. Cavalry July —, 1862.
Hanes, Wesley	...do...			3 yrs.	Died May 10, 1862, at Pittsburg Landing, Tennessee.
Harvey, John	...do...		Feb. 12, 1862	3 yrs.	Discharged Dec. 11, 1862, at Columbus, O., of disability.
Johnston, John W	...do...	34	Oct. 22, 1861	3 yrs.	
Johnson, Thomas	...do...	25	Nov. 16, 1861	3 yrs.	Mustered out Nov. 15, 1864.
Jones, William J	...do...	25	Nov. 18, 1861	3 yrs.	Transferred to 1st Missouri Light Artillery ——.
Jones, William	...do...	18	Dec. 9, 1861	3 yrs.	Mustered out Nov 15, 1864.
Lloyd, Peter	...do...	44	Oct. 22, 1861	3 yrs.	Transferred to Co. C Jan. 26, 1864; veteran.
Lodwick, Warren	...do...	20	Nov. 22, 1861	3 yrs.	Mustered out Nov. 15, 1864.
Ludgate, Charles	...do...	18	Dec. 1, 1861	3 yrs.	Discharged Feb. 11, 1862, at Portsmouth, O., by civil authority.
McIntire, George W	...do...	24	Oct. 31, 1861	3 yrs.	Transferred to Co. B Jan. 26, 1864; veteran.
McIntire, Joseph	...do...	19	Nov. 23, 1861	3 yrs.	Died Oct. 2, 1862, at St. Louis, Mo.
McKeever, Daniel	...do...	18	Nov. 15, 1861	3 yrs.	Transferred to Co. B Jan. 26, 1864; veteran.
McKnight, James	...do...	18	Nov. 4, 1861	3 yrs.	Transferred to Co. B Jan. 26, 1864; veteran.
McKnight, Calvin	...do...	18	Oct. 31, 1861	3 yrs.	Transferred to Co. B Jan. 26, 1864; veteran.

Names.	Rank.	Age.	Date of Entering the Service.	Period of Service.	Remarks.
Martin, Jefferson	Private	18	Dec. 4, 1862	3 yrs.	Discharged Dec. 15, 1861, by civil authority.
Matheny, James	...do...	45	Oct. 26, 1861	3 yrs.	Died Nov. 12, 1862, at Helena, Ark.
Mault, John	...do...	20	Oct. 25, 1861	3 yrs.	Died Sept. 20, 1862, at Helena, Ark.
Monahan, Hugh	...do...	39	Oct. 19, 1861	3 yrs.	Mustered out Nov. 15, 1864.
Mullen, John	...do...	45	Nov. 13, 1861	3 yrs.	Died July —, 1862, at home in Ohio.
Mullen, Thomas	...do...	18	Nov. 13, 1861	3 yrs.	Died Nov. 9, 1863, at Keokuk, Ia.
Murphy, Wesley	...do...	22	Nov. 4, 1861	3 yrs.	Wounded May 16, 1863, in battle of Champion Hills, Miss.; mustered out Nov. 15, 1864.
Myers, Lewis	...do...	19	Oct. 22, 1861	3 yrs.	Captured May 1, 1863, at battle of Port Gibson, Miss.; mustered out Nov. 15, 1864.
Nicholas, Charles C	...do...	19	Nov. 15, 1861	3 yrs.	Died Aug. 3, 1864, at New Orleans, La.; veteran.
Nicholas, Newman	...do...	45	Nov. 15, 1861	3 yrs.	Discharged ——, of disability.
Newlan, Adam	...do...	33	Oct. 19, 1861	3 yrs.	Transferred to Co. B Jan. 26, 1864; veteran.
Perry, Jacob	...do...	18	Nov. 4, 1861	3 yrs.	Transferred to Co. B Jan. 26, 1864; veteran.
Perry, Abram	...do...	44	Nov. 15, 1861	3 yrs.	Died Sept. —, 1862, at Memphis, Tenn.
Perry, James	...do...	22	Dec. 9, 1861	3 yrs.	Transferred to Co. B Jan. 26, 1864; veteran.
Pershee, Daniel	...do...	19	Nov. 12, 1861	3 yrs.	
Phillips, Amos	...do...	23	Nov. 13, 1861	3 yr-.	Mustered out Nov. 15, 1864.
Phillips, Andrew	...do...	29	Oct. 18, 1861	3 yrs.	Transferred to Co. B Jan. 26, 1864; veteran.
Phillips, Edmond	...do...	18	Nov. 13, 1861	3 yrs.	Mustered out Nov. 15, 1864.
Phillips, Levi	...do...	23	Oct. 8, 1862	9 mos	Drafted; mustered out July 8, 1863.
Roush, John	...do...	18	Oct 19, 1861	3 yrs.	Transferred to Mississippi Marine Brigade, Nov. —, 1862.
Roush, Martin	...do...	21	Oct. 19, 1861	3 yrs.	Mustered out Nov. 15, 1864.
Salliday, George W	...do...	19	Nov. 4, 1861	3 yrs.	Transferred to Co. B, Jan. 26, 1864; veteran.
Sanders, Benjamin	...do...	18	Oct. 22, 1861	3 yrs.	Transferred to Co. B, Jan. 26, 1864; veteran.
Scott, Hamilton	...do...	45	Oct. 29, 1861	3 yrs.	Discharged Oct. 27, 1862, at Cincinnati, O., of disability.
Scott, John	...do...	19	Oct. 30, 1861	1 yrs.	Discharged ——, 1862, at Camp Dennison, O., of disability.
Scott, Adam	...do...			3 yrs.	Discharged ——, 1862, at Camp Dennison, O., of disability.
Selix, Alfred	...do...	38	Oct. 22, 1861	3 yrs.	Discharged April 29, 1862, of disability.
Shiels, William	...do...	45	Oct. 21, 1861	3 yrs.	Discharged April 1, 1862, of disability.
Shipman, John	...do...	35	Oct. 8, 1862	9 mos	Mustered out July 8, 1863.
Sickles, George	...do...	19	Nov. 6, 1861	3 yrs.	Died Sept. 10, 1862, at Helena, Ark.
Sickles, Lafayette	...do...	25	Nov. 29, 1861	3 yrs.	Transferred to Co. B, Jan. 26, 1864; veteran.
Spitznagle, Henry	...do...	18	Dec. 9, 1861	3 yrs.	Transferred to Co. B, Jan. 26, 1864; veteran.
Stevenson, Thomas K	...do...	19	Oct. 29, 1861	3 yrs.	Transferred to Co. B. Jan. 26, 1864; veteran.
Storrer, William	...do...	18	Dec. 22, 1861	3 yrs.	Died Feb. 29, 1862, at Dover, Tenn.
Trailer, Benjamin	...do...	19	Nov. 17, 1861	3 yrs.	Discharged Dec. —, 1862, of disability.
Turner, Ephraim	...do...	44	Nov. 29, 1861	3 yrs.	Transferred to Co. B, Jan. 26, 1864; veteran.
Van Meter, Lewis W	...do...	20	Oct. 29, 1861	3 yrs.	Drowned Aug. 18, 1863, by explosion of steamer.
Wiles, William	...do...	24	Oct. 29, 1861	3 yrs.	Discharged Aug. 30, 1863, of disability.
Wilson, Jacob, Jr	...do...	18	Dec. 4, 1861	3 yrs.	Died June 20, 1862, at Corinth, Miss.

COMPANY I.

Mustered in from Oct. 10, 1861, to Dec. 12, 1861, at Portsmouth, O., and Columbus, O., by John R. Edie, Major 15th Infantry, U. S. A., and A. B. Dodd, Captain 15th Infantry, U. S. A. Mustered out Dec. 11, 1864, at New Orleans, La., by A. H. McDonald, A. C. M.

Names.	Rank.	Age.	Date of Entering the Service.	Period of Service.	Remarks.
Edwin Kinney	Captain	24	Oct. 10, 1861	3 yrs.	Resigned Oct. 3, 1862.
Absalom L. Chenoweth	... do ...	26	Oct. 20, 1861	3 yrs.	Promoted from 2d Lieutenant Oct. 3, 1862; mustered out Nov. 16, 1864, at New Orleans, La.
Thomas Lowery	1st Lieut	42	Oct. 20, 1861	3 yrs.	Resigned Oct. 3, 1862.
John D. Niswonger	... do ...	19	Nov. 23, 1861	3 yrs.	Promoted to 1st Lieutenant Oct. 27, 1862; mustered out Nov. 21, 1864, at New Orleans, La.
Henry Schump	2d Lieut.	21	Oct. 17, 1861	3 yrs.	Promoted from Com. Sergeant, March 17, 1863; mustered out Nov. 11, 1864, at New Orleans, La.
John R. Overman	1st Sergt	33	Oct. 28, 1861	3 yrs.	Discharged Aug. 26, 1863, at Cincinnati, O., of disability.
Abram Hibbins	... do ...	24	Nov. 19, 1861	3 yrs.	Appointed from Sergeant Aug. 29, 1863; transferred as 1st Sergeant to Co. C, Jan. 26, 1864; veteran.
Wilson L. Buchannan	Sergeant	18	Dec. 11, 1861	3 yrs.	Wounded May 16, 1863, in battle of Champion Hills, Miss.; mustered out Nov. 16, 1864.
William Hatfield	... do ...	27	Oct. 31, 1861	3 yrs.	Appointed Jan. 1, 1863; transferred to Co. C, Jan. 26, 1864; veteran.
George Irvine	... do .	20	Nov. 23, 1861	3 yrs.	Died May 17, 1863, of wounds received May 16, 1863, in battle of Champion Hills, Miss.
John Kinney	... do ...	23	Nov. 30, 1861	3 yrs.	Died May 3, 1862, at Pittsburg Landing, Tenn.
William H. McLaughlin	... do ...	23	Dec. 22, 1861	3 yrs.	Appointed Jan. 1, 1863; transferred to Co. C, Jan. 26, 1864; veteran.
Orville G. Pinney	... do ...	26	Oct. 15, 1861	3 yrs.	Discharged Oct. 14, 1862, at St. Louis, Mo., of disability.
James L. Reed	... do ...	18	Nov. 30, 1861	3 yrs.	Appointed Sergeant Jan. 1, 1863; mustered out Nov. 16, 1864.
Joseph Aduddle	... do ...	33	Nov. 6, 1861	3 yrs.	Appointed Corporal Jan. 1, 1863; transferred to Veteran Reserve Corps — —.
Thomas W. Bryant	... do ...	28	Oct. 25, 1861	3 yrs.	Discharged June 23, 1863, at St. Louis, Mo., of disability.
James A. Dolby	... do ...	19	Oct. 26, 1861	3 yrs.	Transferred to Co. C. Jan. 26, 1864; veteran.
William McCarty	... do ...	26	Nov. 30, 1861	3 yrs.	Wounded May 1, 1863, in battle of Port Gibson, Miss.; discharged Oct. 9, 1863, of disability.
John N. Marshall	... do ...	42	Nov. 30, 1861	3 yrs.	Detached as Superintendent of Contrabands Jan. 27, 1863; wounded July 4, 1863, in action at Helena, Ark.; mustered out Nov. 16, 1864.
Evan R. Maxwell	... do ..	28	Nov. 6, 1861	3 yrs.	Discharged ——, at Cincinnati, O., of disability.
Thomas P. Nelson	... do ...	35	Oct. 15, 1861	3 yrs.	Discharged Sept. 21, 1862, at Cincinnati, O., of disability.
John Weter	... do ...	38	Oct. 24, 1861	3 yrs.	Transferred to Veteran Reserve Corps, April 28, 1863; mustered out Oct. 26, 1864.
George Wilson	... do ...	44	Oct. 22, 1861	3 yrs.	Discharged Sept. 1, 1862, at Helena, Ark., of disability.
Thomas Eagon	Musician	25	Dec. 15, 1861	3 yrs.	Discharged Sept. 5, 1862, at Camp Dennison, O., of disability.
Stephen Baird	Wagoner	24	Nov. 30, 1861	3 yrs.	Discharged Sept. 5, 1862, at Columbus, O., of disability.
Alexander, Zachariah T	Private	18	Dec. 11, 1861	3 yrs.	Transferred to Co. C, Jan. 26, 1864; veteran.

ROSTER OF FIFTY-SIXTH REGIMENT.

Names.	Rank.	Age.	Date of Entering the Service.	Period of Service.	Remarks.
Atkinson, Abel W	Private	18	Nov. 30, 1861	3 yrs.	Discharged Dec. 14, 1861, at Portsmouth, O., by civil authority
Atwell, William W	... do ...	24	Nov. 7, 1861	3 yrs.	Transferred to 1st Missouri Light Artillery April 14, 1863.
Bennett, Jacob L	... do ...	18	Oct. 8, 1862	9 mos	Drafted; mustered out July 8, 1863.
Black, Oscar C	... do ...	18	Nov. 30, 1861	3 yrs.	Transferred to Co. C. Jan. 26, 1864; veteran.
Bland, George W	... do ...	19	Oct. 16, 1861	3 yrs.	Wounded July 10, 1863, in battle of Jackson, Miss.; transferred to Co. C, Jan. 26, 1864; veteran.
Brandon, Joseph	... do ...	23	Oct. 8, 1862	9 mos	Drafted; mustered out July 8, 1863.
Brown, William	... do ...		Oct. 8, 1862	9 mos	Drafted; died April 9, 1863, at St. Louis, Mo.
Bollenbaugher, Chris'n	... do ...	24	Oct. 8, 1862	9 mos	Drafted; mustered out July 8, 1863.
Carey, Philip	... do ...	19	Nov. 10, 1861	3 yrs.	Transferred to Co. C, Jan. 26, 1864; veteran.
Clapper, Martin	... do ...	43	Dec. 11, 1861	3 yrs.	Died Sept. 5, 1862, at Waverly, O.
Cluiter, James W	... do ...	19	Oct. 20, 1861	3 yrs.	Died Nov. 9, 1862, in Keokuk, Ia.
Cole, John	... do ...	22	Oct. 19, 1861	3 yrs.	
Conkle, George W	... do ...	32	Oct. 8, 1862	9 mos	Drafted; mustered out July 8, 1863.
Cowan, Wm. G	... do ...		Dec. 7, 1861	3 yrs.	Discharged Jan. 18, 1862, at Portsmouth, O., by civil authority.
Crawmer, Andrew J	... do ...	20	Oct. 8, 1862	9 mos	Drafted; mustered out July 8, 1863.
Cutler, Jacob	... do ...	43	Oct. 19, 1861	3 yrs.	Discharged May 25, 1862, at Cincinnati, O., of disability.
Davidson, Joseph	... do ...	20	Oct. 8, 1862	9 mos	Drafted wounded May 16, 1863, in battle of Champion Hills, Miss.; mustered out July 8, 1863.
Desmond, John	... do ...	41	Oct. 18, 1861	3 yrs.	Transferred to Co. C, Jan. 26, 1864; veteran.
Dolby, Nathaniel	... do ...	28	Oct. 25, 1861	3 yrs.	Mustered out Nov. 16, 1864.
Ellis, Stephen R	... do ...	18	Dec. 11, 1861	3 yrs.	Transferred to Co. C, Jan. 26, 1864; veteran.
Fligor, Andrew J	... do ...	33	Nov. 5, 1861	3 yrs.	Died June 1, 1862, at Cincinnati, O.
Fligor, John E	... do ...	18	Nov. 10, 1861	3 yrs.	Died Oct. 10, 1863, at Omega, Pike county, O.
Frasier, William T	... do ...	29	Oct. 14, 1861	3 yrs.	Killed April 8, 1864, in battle of Sabine Cross Roads, La.; veteran.
Freeman, John	... do ...		Nov. 7, 1861	3 yrs.	
Galbraith, John H	... do ...	39	Oct. 17, 1861	3 yrs.	Died April 8, 1862, at Pittsburg Landing, Tenn.
Gatton, Josephus	... do ...	19	Nov. 20, 1861	3 yrs.	Discharged Dec. 16, 1861, at Portsmouth, O., by civil authority.
Gibbons, Burden	... do ...	38	Nov. 30, 1861	3 yrs.	Discharged June 16, 1863, at St. Louis, Mo., of disability.
Gollum, Ernst	... do ...	43	Nov. 17, 1861	3 yrs.	Discharged July 22, 1862, at Cincinnati, O., of disability.
Gross, Godfrey	... do ...		Oct. 27, 1861	3 yrs.	Discharged Jan. 25, 1862, at Portsmouth, O., by civil authority.
Hahn, Lawrence	... do ...	21	Oct 26, 1861	3 yrs.	Wounded May 16, 1863, in battle of Champion Hills, Miss.; transferred to Co. C, Jan. 26, 1864; veteran.
Harris, Chas. H	... do ...	22	Oct. 28, 1861	3 yrs.	Discharged ——, 1862, of disability.
Hinton, Thomas E	... do ...	43	Oct. 8, 1862	9 mos	Drafted; mustered out July 8, 1863.
Johnson, David	... do ...		Oct. 8, 1862	9 mos	Drafted; died June 2, 1863, at St. Louis, Mo.
Kinnison, George	... do ...	35	Oct. 8, 1862	9 mos	Drafted; mustered out July 8, 1863.
Kuhn, Henry	... do ...	30	Oct. 8, 1862	9 mos	Drafted; mustered out July 8, 1863.
Loney, John	... do ...	31	Oct. 25, 1861	3 yrs.	Died April 12, 1862, at Portsmouth, O.
McCartney, James	... do ...	37	Dec. 18, 1861	3 yrs.	Discharged Aug. 18, 1862, at Cincinhati, O., of disability.
McCormick, Wm. H	... do ...	20	Nov. 30, 1861	3 yrs.	Discharged Feb. 19, 1863, at St. Louis, Mo., of disability.
McDowell, William	... do ...	26	Oct. 8, 1862	9 mos	Drafted; died May 14, 1863, at St. Louis, Mo.
Maury, William	... do ...	21	Oct. 8, 1862	9 mos	Drafted; mustered out July 8, 1863.
Martin, James	... do ...		Dec. 7, 1861	3 yrs.	Died Aug. 8, 1863, at Memphis, Tenn., of wounds received May 16, 1863, in battle of Champion Hills, Miss.

OHIO VOLUNTEER INFANTRY. 187

Names.	Rank.	Age.	Date of Entering the Service.	Period of Service.	Remarks.
Martin, Daniel	Private	35	Nov. 22, 1861	3 yrs.	Discharged Nov. 27, 1862, at Keokuk, Ia., of disability.
Marshall, Wm. J	...do...	18	Nov. 30, 1861	3 yrs	Killed May 16, 1863, in battle of Champion Hills, Miss.
Matthews, Oscar W	...do...	18	Dec. 3, 1861	3 yrs.	
Norris, Henry D	...do...	36	Nov. 7, 1861	3 yrs.	Died May 29, 1862, at Crump's Landing, Tenn.
Nottingham, George M.	...do...	27	Oct. 8, 1862	9 mos	Drafted; died ——, at Vicksburg, Miss., of wounds received May 1, 1863, in battle of Port Gibson, Miss.
O'Reilly, Martin	...do...	21	Oct. 14, 1861	3 yrs.	Transferred to Co. C, Jan. 26, 1864; veteran.
Pauley, James W	...do...	20	Nov. 10, 1861	3 yrs	Discharged Nov. 3, 1863, at St. Louis, Mo., for wounds received May 16, 1863, in battle of Champion Hills, Miss.
Palm, David	...do...	21	Oct. 8, 1862	9 mos	Drafted; mustered out July 8, 1863.
Powers, Martin	...do...	33	Oct. 14, 1861	3 yrs.	Wounded May 16, 1863, in battle of Champion Hills, Miss.; transferred to Veteran Reserve Corps ——.
Ray, James	...do...	24	Oct. 26, 1861	3 yrs.	Died April 8, 1862, at Pittsburg Landing, Tenn.
Rine, Jeremiah L	...do...	23	Oct. 8, 1862	9 mos	Drafted; mustered out July 8, 1863.
Roberts, Edward	...do...	20	Oct. 8, 1862	9 mos	Drafted; mustered out July 8, 1863.
Roll, Samuel V	...do...	27	Oct. 8, 1862	9 mos	Drafted; wounded May 1, 1863, in battle of Port Gibson, Miss.; mustered out July 8, 1863.
Ross, George W	...do...	18	Oct. 30, 1861	3 yrs.	
Shaner, Hiram	...do...	22	Oct. 19, 1861	3 yrs.	
Sherwood, Jacob	...do...	18	Oct. 15, 1861	3 yrs.	Transferred to Co. C, Jan. 26, 1864; veteran.
Sherwood, Levi	...do...	18	Oct. 22, 1861	3 yrs.	Discharged Aug. 9, 1862, at Columbus, O., of disability.
Sherwood, Dennis	...do...	21	Oct. 25, 1861	3 yrs.	Died March 17, 1863, at Helena, Ark.
Siemon, Adam	...do...	18	Oct. 31, 1861	3 yrs.	Wounded May 16, 1863, in battle of Champion Hills, Miss.; transferred to Co. C, Jan. 26, 1864; veteran.
Southerland, David	...do...	18	Nov. 6, 1861	3 yrs.	Transferred to Co. C., Jan. 26, 1864; veteran.
Smith, William	...do...	21	Oct. 18, 1861	3 yrs.	Died March 25, 1862, at Crump's Landing, Tenn.
Smith, John W	...do...	23	Oct. 20, 1861	3 yrs.	
Springer, Henry N	...do...	19	Oct. 26, 1861	3 yrs.	Transferred to Co. C Jan. 26, 1864; veteran.
Steele, Amos	...do...	21	Nov. 30, 1861	3 yrs	
Stetler, Thompson	...do...	26	Oct. 8, 1862	9 mos	Drafted; mustered out July 8, 1863.
Stewart, George M.	...do...	20	Nov. 30, 1861	3 yrs.	Transferred to Co. C Jan. 26, 1864; veteran.
Stockman, Jesse	...do...	18	Oct. 24, 1861	3 yrs.	Captured May 16, 1863, at battle of Champion Hills, Miss.; veteran.
Thacker, Joseph	...do...	26	Oct. 31, 1861	3 yrs.	Mustered out Nov. 10, 1864.
Thacker, Fountain	...do...	24	Nov. 7, 1861	3 yrs.	Transferred to Co. C Jan. 26, 1864; veteran.
Tripp, George	...do...	19	Nov. 6, 1861	3 yrs.	Transferred to Co. C Jan. 26, 1864; veteran.
Tripp, Henry	...do...	18	Nov. 7, 1861	3 yrs.	Discharged ——, on expiration of term
Vancoy, Nelson	...do...	31	Oct. 19, 1861	3 yrs.	
VanFleet, Joseph	...do...	36	Oct. 8, 1862	9 mos	Drafted; wounded May 16, 1863, in battle of Champion Hills, Miss.; mustered out July 8, 1863.
Vanhuff, John	...do...	19	Oct. 31, 1861	3 yrs	Discharged ——, by order of War Department.
Walker, John	...do...	27	Oct. 17, 1861	3 yrs.	Died May 1, 1862, at Cincinnati, O.
Weekley, John	...do...	18	Nov. 28, 1861	3 yrs	Discharged Dec. 1, 1863, at Portsmouth, O., by civil authority.
Whaley, Wm. S.	...do...	18	Oct. 20, 1861	3 yrs.	Discharged Jan. 16, 1862, at Waverly, O., by civil authority.

Names.	Rank.	Age.	Date of Entering the Service	Period of Service.	Remarks.
Wilson, Sylvester.......	Private	18	Oct. 20, 1861	3 yrs	Transferred to Co. C Jan. 26, 1864; veteran.
Wilson, Wm. A..........	...do	23	Oct. 25, 1861	3 yrs.	Transferred to Co. C Jan. 26, 1864; veteran.
Wisener, George W......	...do ..	25	Nov. 30, 1861	3 yrs.	Accidently killed March 17, 1863, on Moon Lake, Miss.
Woolm, James H.......	...do ..	19	Oct. 20, 1861	3 yrs.	Discharged ——, by order of War Department.
Young, Ebenezer........	...do ..	25	Oct. 8, 1861	9 mos	Drafted; mustered out July 8, 1863.

COMPANY K.

Mustered in Jan. 8, 1862, at Columbus, O., by John R. Edie, Major 15th Infantry, U. S. A. Mustered out Dec. 23, 1864, at New Orleans, La., by A. H. McDonald, A. C. M.

Names.	Rank.	Age.	Date of Entering the Service	Period of Service.	Remarks.
John Cook.............	Captain	44	Nov. 19, 1861	3 yrs.	Died May 22. 1863, of wounds received May 16, 1863, in battle of Champion Hills, Miss.
William G. Snyder	...do ...	29	Oct. 29, 1861	3 yrs.	Promoted from 1st Lieutenant Co. A Aug. 10, 1864; transferred to Co. C Nov. —, 1864.
Martin Owens..........	1st Lieut.	44	Oct. 19, 1861	3 yrs.	Wounded May 16, 1863. in battle of Champion Hills, Miss.; resigned July 22, 1863.
Joseph S. Patterson	...do ...	30	Oct. 17, 1861	3 yrs.	Promoted to 2d Lieutenant from Com. Sergeant Aug. 31, 1862; to 1st Lieutenant Feb. 14, 1863; resigned Nov. 26 1863.
William H. Palmer.....	2d Lieut.	40	Oct. 29, 1861	3 yrs.	Resigned July 24, 1862.
Robert M. Steele........	1st Sergt.	44	Dec. 10, 1861	3 yrs.	Discharged July 21, 1862, of disability.
James A. Aleshire......	...do ..	25	Oct. 24, 1861	3 yrs.	Appointed from Sergeant Aug. 26, 1862; wounded May 16, 1863, in battle of Champion Hills, Miss.; promoted to 2d Lieut. May 16. 1863, but not mustered; mustered out Nov. 14, 1864, at New Orleans, La.
Daniel Irwin............	Sergeant	22	Oct. 24, 1861	3 yrs.	Appointed from Corporal Aug. 26, 1862; discharged Nov. 6, 1863, of disability.
Samuel Goheen.........	...do ...	28	Oct. 28, 1861	3 yrs.	Wounded May 16, 1863, in battle of Champion Hills, Miss.; appointed from Corporal Aug. 11, 1863; transferred to Co. C Jan. 26, 1864; veteran.
Lutlius Knowland.......	...do ...	21	Nov. 30, 1861	3 yrs.	Transferred to Co. C Jan. 26, 1864; veteran.
Joseph Lumbeck.........	...do ...	35	Dec. 2, 1861	3 yrs.	
John Morgan............	...do ...	20	Nov. 13, 1861	3 yrs.	Mustered out. Nov. 14, 1864.
George Phillips.........	...do ...	26	Dec. 17, 1861	3 yrs.	Appointed from Corporal July 21, 1862; mustered out Nov. 14, 1864.
David F. Radcliff.......	...do ...	23	Oct. 24, 1861	3 yrs.	Appointed from private Aug 26, 1862; transferred to Co. C Jan. 26, 1864; veteran.
William H. Wait	...do ...	27	Dec. 7, 1861	3 yrs.	Appointed from Corporal Aug. 29, 1862; wounded May 16, 1863, in battle of Champion Hills, Miss.; transferred to Co. C Jan. 26, 1864; veteran.
Hosea B. Bennett.......	Corporal	21	Dec. 12, 1861	3 yrs.	Captured May 18, 1863, at battle of Big Sand Run. Miss., ——; transferred to Co. C Jan. 26, 1864; veteran.
Danial Exline...........	...do ...	23	Oct. 24. 1861	3 yrs.	Mustered out Nov. 14, 1864.

OHIO VOLUNTEER INFANTRY

Names.	Rank.	Age.	Date of Entering the Service.	Period of Service.	Remarks.
James C. Harper	Corporal	18	Nov. 11, 1861	3 yrs.	Appointed Corporal Aug. 26, 1862; transferred to Co. C Jan. 26, 1864; veteran.
Thomas R. Hatton	do	18	Nov. 11, 1861	3 yrs.	Died June 15, 1862, at Crump's Landing, Tenn.
Lafayette Holmes	do		Jan. 14, 1862	3 yrs.	Transferred to Co. C Jan. 26, 1864; veteran.
Leonidas Johnson	do	18	Dec. 8, 1861	3 yrs.	Appointed Corporal Aug. 26, 1862.
George L. Steele	do	21	Dec. 11, 1861	3 yrs.	Transferred to Mississippi Marine Brigade ——.
William Stephenson	do	22	Dec. 11, 1861	3 yrs.	Discharged ——, of disability.
Jacob White	do	18	Oct. 29, 1861	3 yrs.	Appointed Corporal Aug. 26, 1862; transferred to Co. C Jan. 26, 1864; veteran.
Aleshire, Hiram	Private	18	Oct. 19, 1861	3 yrs.	Wounded and captured May 16, 1863, at battle of Champion Hills, Miss.; mustered out Nov. 14, 1864.
Bailey, Girard	do	20	Oct. 8, 1862	9 mos	Drafted; wounded May 16, 1863, in battle of Champion Hills, Miss., mustered out July 8, 1863.
Bates, David R	do	44	Oct. 24, 1861	3 yrs.	Discharged Nov. 11, 1862, of disability.
Bergman, Andrew	do	35	Mch. 19, 1864	3 yrs.	Transferred to Co. C ——.
Boring, David R	do	30	Dec. 10, 1861	3 yrs.	Mustered out Nov. 14, 1864.
Bowen, William	do	35	Dec. 9, 1861	3 yrs.	Wounded and captured May 16, 1863, at battle of Champion Hills, Miss.; transferred to Co. C Jan. 26, 1864; veteran.
Brooks, John J	do		Jan. 14, 1862	3 yrs.	Transferred to Co. C Jan. 26, 1864; veteran.
Brown, John J	do	41	Dec. 23, 1861	3 yrs.	Discharged Aug. 18, 1862, of disability.
Burt, Thomas J	do	36	Dec. 14, 1861	3 yrs.	Transferred to Co. C Jan. 26, 1864; veteran.
Bussey, John	do	18	Dec. 12, 1861	3 yrs.	Captured May 16, 1863, at battle of Champion Hills, Miss.; transferred to Co. C Jan. 26, 1864; veteran.
Byrnes, Patrick	do		Dec. 23, 1861	3 yrs.	Wounded May 1, 1863, in battle of Port Gibson, Miss.; mustered out Nov. 14, 1864.
Clair, George	do	18	Mch. 27, 1864	3 yrs.	Transferred to Co. C ——.
Clark, John S	do	18	Dec. 24, 1861	3 yrs.	Discharged ——, by civil authority.
Clausing, Theodore	do	22	Oct. 8, 1862	9 mos	Drafted; mustered out July 8, 1863.
Claypool, James	do		Dec. 21, 1861	3 yrs.	Transferred to Mississippi Marine brigade ——.
Corriell, Elias	do	22	Dec. 19, 1861	3 yrs.	Transferred to Co. C Jan. 26, 1864; veteran.
Corriell, Thomas J	do	19	Dec. 16, 1861	3 yrs.	Transferred to Co. C Jan. 26, 1864; veteran.
Cummings, John R	do	21	Nov. 15, 1861	3 yrs.	Transferred to Co. C Jan. 26, 1864; veteran.
Daub, John	do	18	Dec. 18, 1861	3 yrs.	Mustered out Nov. 14, 1864.
Davis, Jonathan	do		Jan. 14, 1862	3 yrs.	Captured May 16, 1863, at battle of Champion Hills, Miss.; transferred to Co. C Jan. 26, 1864; veteran.
Davis, Azariah	do		Jan. 14, 1862	3 yrs.	Died June 15, 1862, at Crump's Landing, Tenn.
Davis, Andrew	do		Jan. 14, 1862	3 yrs.	Discharged Sept. 2, 1863, of disability.
Dean, Adam	do		Sept. 7, 1862	3 yrs.	Discharged Jan. 16, 1863, of disability.
Deshler, John	do	42	Dec 18, 1861	3 yrs.	
Downing, William	do	28	Dec. 11, 1861	3 yrs.	Discharged Jan. 4, 1864, of disability.
Erwin, Abram	do	21	Oct. 24, 1861	3 yrs.	Discharged May 9, 1863, of disability.
Ewing, Henry E	do		Jan. 2, 1862	3 yrs.	Discharged Sept. 20, 1862, of disability.
Fells, Adam	do	25	Dec. 11, 1861	3 yrs.	Died July 6, 1862, at St Louis, Mo.
Freleand, Middleton	do	43	Nov 27, 1861	3 yrs.	Transferred to Co. G. Dec. —, 186-.
Gates, David	do	24	Oct 29, 1861	3 yrs.	Transferred to Co. C Jan. 26, 1864; veteran.
Gephart, Daniel	do	42	Dec. 7, 1861	3 yrs.	Transferred to Co. C Dec. —, 1861.

Roster of Fifty-sixth Regiment

Names.	Rank.	Age.	Date of Entering the Service.	Period of Service.	Remarks.
Gilmore, James	Private	44	Nov. 14, 1861	3 yrs.	Died July 13, 1863, at Vicksburg, Miss.
Gordy, George M	...do...	28	Dec. 7, 1861	3 yrs.	Transferred to Co. C Jan. 26, 1864; veteran.
Guynn, William A	...do...	25	Feb. 25, 1864	3 yrs.	Transferred to Co. C ——.
Harshberger, George W	...do...	27	Oct. 8, 1862	9 mos	Drafted: mustered out July 8, 1863.
Hicks, John W	...do...		Feb. 23, 1864	3 yrs	No further record found.
High, Luther C	...do...	25	Dec. 5, 1861	3 yrs.	Transferred to Co. C Jan. 26, 1864; veteran.
Huey, Isaac J	...do...	20	Dec. 4, 1861	3 yrs.	Transferred to 1st Missouri Light Artillery Dec. 17, 1863.
Johnson, James	...do...		Dec. 10, 1861	3 yrs.	
Johnson, James J	...do...	35	Dec. 5, 1861	3 yrs.	Died Dec. 23, 1861, at Portsmouth, O.
Jones, John	...do...	30	Dec. 7, 1861	3 yrs.	
Jones, Elihu	...do...	26	Dec. 26, 1861	3 yrs.	Mustered out Nov. 14, 1864, at New Orleans, La.
Klein, Nicholas	...do...	18	Feb. 27, 1864	3 yrs.	Transferred to Co. C ——.
Lake, Isaac M	...do...	21	Oct. 29, 1861	3 yrs.	Discharged Feb. 23, 1863, of disability.
Leniger, William	...do...	22	Dec. 7, 1861	3 yrs.	Transferred to Co. C Jan. 26, 1864; veteran.
Lenox, Henry C	...do...	24	Oct. 8, 1862	9 mos	Drafted: mustered out July 8, 1863.
Lesser, William	...do...	18	Dec. 7, 1861	3 yrs.	Discharged Nov. 2, 1862, of disability.
Liff, Charles	...do...	18	Dec. 11, 1861	3 yrs.	Died Sept. 1, 1862, at Memphis, Tenn.
Lawery, George	...do...	21	Dec. 12, 1861	3 yrs.	Transferred to Co. C Jan. 26, 1864; veteran.
Lucas, William	...do...	18	Dec. 16, 1861	3 yrs.	Returned to 9th Virginia Volunteers
McCann, Thomas J	...do...	18	Nov. 30, 1861	3 yrs.	Transferred to Co. C Jan. 26, 1864; veteran.
McCann, William	...do...		Jan. 1, 1862	3 yrs.	Drowned April 11, 1863, in Mississippi river at Helena, Ark.
McCartney, Joseph	...do...	44	Oct. 29, 1861	3 yrs.	Discharged Aug. 18, 1862, of disability.
McCartney, Thomas	...do...	22	Oct. 29, 1861	3 yrs.	Died March 11, 1862, at Cincinnati, O.
McCullough, James H	...do...	19	Oct. 8, 1862	9 mos	Drafted; wounded May 16, 1863, at battle of Champion Hills, Miss.; mustered out July 8, 1863, at Vicksburg, Miss.
McManama, William	...do...	40	Nov. 8, 1861	3 yrs.	
May, John	...do...	25	Dec. 10, 1861	3 yrs.	
Mayfield, Watkins	...do...	40	Nov. 17, 1861	3 yrs.	Absent, sick in hospital at Paducah, Ky.
Martin, James	...do...	31	Nov. 29, 1861	3 yrs.	Wounded and captured May 16, 1863, at battle of Champion Hills, Miss.; mustered out Nov. 14, 1864, at New Orleans, La.
Martin, William	...do...	23	Oct. 8, 1862	9 mos	Drafted; mustered out July 8, 1863.
Meeks, Richard A	...do...	23	Dec. 10, 1861	3 yrs.	Discharged Sept. 12, 1863, at New Orleans, La. of disability.
Milner, Isaac	...do...	31	Oct. 29, 1861	3 yrs.	Wounded and captured May 16, 1863, at battle of Champion Hills, Miss.; mustered out Nov. 14, 1864, at New Orleans, La.
Monahon, Michael	...do...	43	Nov. 30, 1861	3 yrs.	Discharged Nov. 27, 1862, of disability.
Monahon, James	...do...	20	Dec. 20, 1861	3 yrs.	
Montgomery, Robert	...do...	18	Oct. 8, 1862	9 mos	Drafted: mustered out July 8, 1863, at Vicksburg, Miss.
Montgomery, Shadrick	...do...	21	Oct. 8, 1862	9 mos	Drafted; wounded May 16, 1863, at battle of Champion Hills, Miss.; mustered out July 8, 1863, at Vicksburg, Miss.
Newcomb, Benjamin F	...do...	25	Dec. 3, 1861	3 yrs.	Wounded June —, 1863, in siege of Vicksburg, Miss.; transferred to Co. C Jan. 26, 1864; veteran.
Noel, Henry	...do...	32	Oct. 21, 1861	3 yrs	Discharged Aug. 21, 1862, of disability.
Oliver, Thomas	...do...	44	Oct. 26, 1861	3 yrs.	
Plummer, Henry C	...do...	18	Feb. 22, 1864	3 yrs.	Transferred to Co. C ——.

OHIO VOLUNTEER INFANTRY.

Names.	Rank.	Age.	Date of Entering the Service.	Period of Service.	Remarks.
Rayburn, W. McNeal	Private	18	Nov. 30, 1861	3 yrs.	Returned to Co. —, 26th O. V. I., April 26, 1862.
Richards, John	...do...	44	Nov. 17, 1861	3 yrs.	
Rife, John	...do...	40	Nov. 10, 1861	3 yrs.	Mustered out Nov. 14, 1864.
Rodgers, Lucius R.	...do...	19	Nov. 30, 1861	3 yrs.	Died Aug. 26, 1862, at New Orleans, La.
Russell, Emanuel	...do...	22	Oct. 26, 1861	3 yrs.	Transferred to Co. C Jan. 26, 1864; veteran.
Russell, Terry	...do...	44	Oct. 26, 1861	3 yrs.	Died Aug. 29, 1862, at Jackson, O.
Salter, Azariah	...do...	31	Nov. 18, 1861	3 yrs.	Discharged Dec. 28, 1861, at Portsmouth, O., of disability.
Scott, Peter	...do...	....	Jan. 2, 1862	3 yrs.	Captured Nov. 18, 1863, at battle of New Iberia, La.; transferred to Co. C Jan. 26, 1864; veteran.
Seibert, John S.	...do...	20	Oct. 8, 1862	9 mos	Drafted; mustered out July 8, 1863.
Sibert, John	...do...	24	Oct. 8, 1862	9 mos	Drafted; mustered out July 8, 1863.
Simer, Andrew J. P.	...do...	28	Dec. 16, 1861	3 yrs.	Transferred to Co. C Jan. 26, 1864; veteran.
Slusser, John B	...do...	21	Oct. 8, 1862	9 mos	Drafted; mustered out July 8, 1863.
Staunn, Christian	...do...	29	Feb. 10, 1864	3 yrs.	Transferred to Co. C
Thompson, John	...do...	24	Dec. 10, 1861	3 yrs.	Transferred to Co. C Jan. 26, 1864; veteran.
Walker, James	...do...	44	Oct. 26, 1861	3 yrs.	Transferred to Co. C Jan. 26, 1864; veteran.
Walker, George	...do...	18	Dec. 20, 1861	3 yrs.	
Walker, Thomas	...do...	....	Feb. 10, 1862	3 yrs.	Discharged June 10, 1862, of disability.
White, Isaac N	...do...	31	Oct. 29, 1861	3 yrs.	Discharged April 6, 1862, of disability.
Williams, Richard	...do...	33	Dec. 4, 1861	3 yrs.	Discharged Dec. 9, 1862, of disability.
Wiseman, Joseph W	...do...	40	Nov. 5, 1861	3 yrs.	Discharged Jan. 10, 1862, of disability.
Yeley, Dennis	...do...	43	Dec. 14, 1861	3 yrs.	Discharged Aug. 11, 1862, of disability.
Yeley, Benjamin	...do...	18	Dec. 7, 1861	3 yrs	Captured Nov. 18, 1863, at battle of New Iberia, La.; transferred to Co. C Jan. 26, 1864; veteran.

www.ingramcontent.com/pod-product-compliance
Lightning Source LLC
Chambersburg PA
CBHW022120290426
44112CB00008B/744